EXPLAINING FOREIGN POLICY

LLOYD JENSEN
Temple University

PRENTICE-HALL, INC., ENGLEWOOD CLIFFS, NEW JERSEY 07632

Library of Congress Cataloging in Publication Data

JENSEN, LLOYD
    Explaining foreign policy.

    Includes bibliographical references and index.
    1. International relations—Research. I. Title.
JX1291.J46   327'.072   81-10535
ISBN 0-13-295600-4   AACR2

Editorial production and interior design by Serena Hoffman
Cover design by Diane Saxe
Manufacturing buyer Edmund W. Leone

PRINTED IN THE UNITED STATES OF AMERICA

10   9   8   7   6   5   4   3   2   1

PRENTICE-HALL INTERNATIONAL, INC., London
PRENTICE-HALL OF AUSTRALIA PTY. LIMITED, Sydney
PRENTICE-HALL OF CANADA, LTD., Toronto
PRENTICE-HALL OF INDIA PRIVATE LIMITED, New Delhi
PRENTICE-HALL OF JAPAN, INC., Tokyo
PRENTICE-HALL OF SOUTHEAST ASIA PTE. LTD., Singapore
WHITEHALL BOOKS LIMITED, Wellington, New Zealand

To my mother and father,

who helped explain

the way of life

CONTENTS

PREFACE

Each night events invade our living rooms via satellite from remote capitals such as Teheran, Kabul, Warsaw, and Moscow—underscoring the importance that foreign policy plays for each of us. Understanding this complex mosaic of events is challenging for even the most expert among us. Yet understanding remains the most important part of placing these events in their proper perspective, whether one is a student, an informed citizen, a scholar, or a decision maker.

The purpose of this volume is to seek to explain why states make the foreign policy choices they do. This will be done by looking at some of the best research on the determinants of foreign policy, as found in both verbal theories and systematic empirical studies, with appropriate illustrations wherever possible. It is believed that understanding can be increased by looking at foreign policy behavior from a comparative and historical perspective. Merely collecting information about events is hardly the key to explaining them. My underlying assumption is that there is pattern in foreign policy behavior, and that decision makers will tend to make similar choices when thrust into similar circumstances.

By focusing upon various determinants in the individual chapters, I hope that student and citizen alike will gain a better understanding of the calculations that have to be made by decision makers as they respond to their respective external environments. Certainly, it is not my contention that *every* determinant—whether it be economic, political, psychological, or systemic—will have an impact upon *every* foreign policy decision, but each will be operative at certain times and under certain circumstances.

This study is the result of many years of teaching and writing about foreign policy issues, and I find these issues just as exciting and perplexing today as when I ventured into my first teaching position almost two decades ago. I hope that the result will prove useful, both as supplementary material in an introductory international relations course or as a core volume in advanced courses on foreign policy. Since the book synthesizes much of what is known about foreign policy, I would hope that practitioner and informed citizen might also benefit equally.

My debts in producing this volume are many. I owe much to my former teachers, Inis L. Claude, Jr., and J. David Singer, who were so helpful in explaining the complexities of international relations to me. Several colleagues have read portions or all of the manuscript, and I have benefited from their advice and encouragement; these include Douglas Bennett, Martin Goldstein, Charles F. Hermann, Bernard Mennis, Lynn Miller, and Sheldon W. Simon.

I am also indebted to the authors of the many studies cited throughout the work. Without them, there would be no basis for a comparative study of foreign policy. In the absence of such materials, it would be impossible to explain how and why foreign policy is made.

Useful research assistance was provided by Bruce Ressner and Anthony Di Santo. I am also grateful to Temple University for a summer research grant, and to Gloria Basmajian and her colleagues in the word processing center at Temple for typing the several drafts of the manuscript.

Finally, I owe the greatest of debts to my wife Jane, a professional political scientist in her own right, who took considerable time out to edit and discuss my ideas, despite her busy and turbulent schedule in law school and the pressures of launching a new career.

Although it might be tempting to explain away whatever errors have crept into the book by blaming them upon the advice and assistance of others, I, of course, accept all responsibility. The help of others has only made it a better and, I trust, more useful product.

LLOYD JENSEN

1 INTRODUCTION

In December 1979 Soviet troops moved into Afghanistan, allegedly at the request of its pro-Marxist government. The incursion came as somewhat of a surprise to American decision makers, leading President Carter to note that he had reassessed his own views of the Soviet Union and the prospects of detente. The frequent occurrence of such events points up the necessity for developing an understanding of why nation–states behave as they do. With such an understanding, one can better anticipate and prepare for various eventualities in the international arena.

Explaining the reasons for a given foreign-policy decision is never an easy task, for many factors enter into any such calculation. Depending on one's assumptions about what motivates Soviet behavior, one might develop a whole range of plausible explanations for the Soviet incursion into Afghanistan. For those who see Soviet objectives largely in terms of the expansion of communism, the incursion into Afghanistan can be interpreted as providing support to a Marxist government in trouble and thus facilitating the spread of Marxist doctrine throughout the state and perhaps the region. Since the decision to replace Hafizullah Amin with Babrak Kamal, an even more Marxist and pro-Soviet leader, was made at about the same time, it merely confirms that ideological motivations might have been the overriding consideration.

Other analysts might assume that in deciding to invade Afghanistan Soviet leaders were motivated by security and power needs, threatened as they were by the rise of a militant Islamic chain of states on their southern borders, with Afghanistan providing the missing link between Iran and Pakistan. From a security perspective, these leaders might also have been concerned that the political instability in Iran after the overthrow of the Shah and the taunting of the United States by the seizure of the United States Embassy in Teheran might lead the United States to invade Iran. An advanced position in Afghanistan might be useful for the Soviets in case of such an eventuality and might well discourage the United States from taking such a step.

Some analysts might suggest that the Soviet move into Afghanistan was merely a continuation of the traditional Russian policy of attempting to gain warm-water ports, which it lacks. From this perspective, Afghanistan is seen primarily as a route to the Persian Gulf. However, it might be noted that troubled Iran would have provided a more direct route if the objective were only to acquire a warm-water port.

Still other analysts might search for economic motivations to help explain Soviet policy. The economic rewards of the incursion into Afghanistan are likely to be limited if one thinks only of the country's resources, which would hardly have been worth the costs of military action. But if one views Afghanistan as the approach to the oil-rich Persian Gulf regions and not as a goal in itself, a more persuasive economic argument might be made. Access to this region could be most helpful in meeting the energy needs not only of the Soviet Union but of Eastern Europe as well. The ability to deny such resources to the West and control the shipping routes through the Persian Gulf might also have been viewed as relevant in the Soviet calculation.

Still others might regard the Soviet move as an effort by a global power to retain and perhaps enhance its international prestige. The overthrow of a Marxist government and its replacement by an anti-Soviet Islamic regime could only damage Soviet prestige abroad, raising concern on the part of other Marxist regimes about Moscow's willingness to support them when their sovereignty is threatened. Questions about the effectiveness of the Soviet Union in world politics in general might be posed. It is probably the case that the Soviet decision makers miscalculated in this regard, for rather than enhancing the Soviet Union's international prestige, their action undermined it.

Their decision to invade Afghanistan led a number of states, including those that generally take a neutral position, to condemn the action publicly in the United Nations and to institute a boycott of the summer 1980 Olympic games, which were held in Moscow.

All of the preceding explanations have one thing in common: They seek to explain Soviet behavior from the perspective of foreign-policy objectives and reactions. A number of analysts would argue that the Soviet decision was influenced as much by internal considerations as by external ones. The most popular of such explanations is the notion that Soviet leaders may have wanted to divert attention from some of their domestic economic and political problems by engaging in foreign adventures. Dictatorial governments have been viewed as particularly prone to such actions. That the Soviet Union was experiencing considerable domestic instability at the time was illustrated by its increased political repression and sluggish economy.

As yet another factor of internal concern, some analysts have suggested that Soviet decision makers might have been motivated by the effect of the growing militancy of Islamic countries on the Muslim population of the Soviet Union. Peoples of Muslim background are among the fastest-growing populations in the Soviet Union today, having increased by some 10 million during the 1970s and totaling 40 million in the 1979 census. Should the militancy of the Muslims in bordering states spill over and affect Muslim populations within the Soviet Union, it would create a considerable domestic threat.

The decision to intervene in Afghanistan might also have been a result of bureaucratic maneuvering in which a more conservative coalition was able to prevail. Indeed, much of the posturing occurring around the time of the incursion was related to the concern about who was likely to succeed the ailing Leonid Brezhnev, who was nearing retirement.

Nor can one rule out various idiosyncratic factors in seeking to explain the Soviet decision. It may be that Brezhnev, who had staked his reputation on detente and looked forward to the culmination of SALT II as an appropriate symbol of his policy, was becoming frustrated by what seemed to be the demise of the SALT II Treaty in ratification debates in the United States Senate. Out of this frustration and the apparently growing militancy of President Carter, Brezhnev and some of those around him may have decided that there was nothing to lose by military action in Afghanistan. Detente seemed to be dead anyway. It may even be that Brezhnev's ego was so involved in SALT that it became psychologically necessary for him to express his disdain for the United States' behavior in a dramatic way.

Whatever the real explanation for the Soviet incursion—and one might expect that several of those described are partially accurate—it is obvious that most efforts to analyze such events involve considerable speculation. One can find pieces of evidence here and there to support one hypothesis against another, but we may never be completely satisfied that the entire truth has been discovered. Indeed, the final decision to invade Afghanistan may have been a combination of most, if not all, of these factors.

In many instances it is difficult to ascertain which factors explain certain foreign-policy decisions simply because the necessary information is lacking. This is particularly true with respect to the more idiosyncratic factors, such as personality traits or personal motivation. Indeed, decision makers themselves often are not certain exactly what motivates them to advocate a given action. Obtaining such information is especially difficult with more authoritarian regimes, in which the dynamics of the decision-making process are not well known. Even in democratic regimes, foreign-policy decision making tends to be conducted by a few individuals behind the closed doors of national security.

The prospects of ascertaining the causal factors in foreign-policy choices may also be hampered by the problem of too much information. It is for this reason that one is able to find pieces of information and select analogies that will support any number of plausible explanations, as can be seen above in our effort to suggest hypotheses concerning the motivation for the 1979 Soviet incursion into Afghanistan. Despite the obvious difficulties, the effort to obtain a clearer notion of why decision makers make the choices they do ought not to be viewed as a fruitless enterprise to be engaged in by bearded intellectuals sitting in ivory towers. The decision makers themselves should also be vitally concerned about what causes other nations to make the choices they do, as well as about their own motivations.

By developing a better understanding of foreign-policy motivation, it will be possible to make more accurate predictions about international events and, in turn, respond more effectively to such events. Yet, on the whole, foreign-policy analysts have not been very accurate in anticipating and predicting international events. A 1965 survey of some 171 experts from the State Department, the Defense Department, academia, and journalism showed an accuracy rate of only 64 percent in making some 25 predictions about the probability of certain international events within a one- to five-year span of time.[1] Since a number of these events involved predicting only the occurrence or nonoccurrence of a hypothesized conflict or treaty, this level of accuracy was hardly better than one might expect from chance.

MODELS OF FOREIGN POLICY MAKING

If one is to be able to explain and predict foreign policy more accurately, it is critical that the right sorts of questions be asked and that appropriate variables be examined. Often the problem of understanding foreign policy is not one of having insufficient information but rather one of being unable to sort through the maze of information that is available about a given situation. To aid in this search, a variety of approaches and models have been developed.

The Strategic or Rational Model

Perhaps the most extensively used model of foreign-policy analysis has been the strategic or rational model. This is the approach often used by diplomatic historians as they describe the foreign-policy interaction of various states or the actions of leaders of those states in response to each other. States or decision makers are viewed as solitary actors searching to maximize their goals in global politics. As such, the decision-making unit is treated as a "black box" and little, if any, effort is made to understand the internal political forces affecting its choices. What one has is an action–reaction model in which the analyst seeks to explain each response as a rational calculation to a move made by the other side. Among contemporary researchers, strategic analysts who study military deterrence or game theorists who construct models or experiments testing rational calculations reflect this approach.

1. Lloyd Jensen, "Predicting International Events," *Peace Research Reviews*, 4 (August 1972), 1–65.

There are certain advantages to utilizing such a research strategy, largely derived from the simplicity of the model itself. It becomes an inexpensive approximation of reality in which analysts can attempt to think about what they would do if they were the other state. This approach has been particularly useful in war game exercises. To the extent that it can actually explain foreign-policy behavior, it has the very real virtue of parsimony, that is, allowing one to understand phenomena with a minimum of complexity.

Its drawbacks, however, are very serious, leading many people to suggest the need for more complex models. If foreign policy is affected by more than just the behavior of the other state and the rational response to that behavior, the rational model will have minimal explanatory value. Certainly both domestic actors and other international actors have a considerable impact on foreign policy.

Perhaps the most serious weakness of this approach is that it assumes rational calculation on the part of decision makers, which is an ideal situation but one that is seldom realized. Moreover, it is often assumed that what is rational for one researcher or actor is rational for another. For example, it was assumed by American decision makers and analysts that increasing the bombing of North Vietnam would soon lead the North Vietnamese leadership to surrender. Instead, such action tended only to increase the resolve of the North Vietnamese, since they were willing to accept far more damage than Americans would have been able to tolerate under similar circumstances. A more accurate model would have been more sensitive to such differences.

Finally, it should be noted that most researchers employing the strategic or rational actor model rely largely on intuition and the observation of sequential events to explain foreign-policy behavior. If State B responds in a hostile fashion, the researcher is likely to look for hostile actions committed by State A, which in turn are used to justify B's response. With such a focus, various conciliatory moves on the part of State A may be completely overlooked, given the researcher's expectations. One must also remember that the researcher is placing his or her own valuation on the transaction, rather than probing the event from the standpoint of the responding state. It may be that the event identified by the analyst as precipitating the hostile behavior was not even perceived and that State B was merely reacting to some real or perceived action or series of actions preceding the event; or perhaps State

B responded in a hostile fashion simply to divert attention from its domestic situation.

The Decision-Making Approach

Recognizing the limitations of the rational-actor model, Richard C. Snyder, H. W. Bruck, and Burton Sapin suggested a more complex procedure for examining foreign-policy decision making.[2] Their scheme went much beyond the "black box" approach of the rational-actor model, postulating numerous internal and external factors that seemed to impinge on foreign-policy choices. Some order was imposed on the model by the fact that, whatever the determinant, it became important to the extent that it was perceived and acted upon by the official governmental decision makers. Only then could the determinant be considered to have affected foreign policy.

The advantage of such a model is that it brings the human dimension into the foreign-policy process more effectively. From the Snyder, Bruck, and Sapin perspective, the most important factors explaining foreign-policy choices are the motivations of the decision makers, the flow of information among them, and the impact of varying foreign policies on their choices. In a subsequent refinement of the model, Robinson and Snyder added the notion of "occasion for decision," which referred to the situational characteristics existing at the time of the decision, such as whether or not a crisis was involved.[3]

The Bureaucratic Politics Model

Rather than focusing solely on the central foreign-policy decision makers of a state, the bureaucratic politics approach emphasizes the role played by the many bureaucrats involved in the foreign-policy process.[4] Since there is considerable turnover in governments and political

2.   Richard C. Snyder, H. W. Bruck, and Burton Sapin, eds., *Foreign Policy Decision Making* (New York: Free Press, 1962).

3.   James A. Robinson and Richard C. Snyder, "Decision-Making in International Politics," in Herbert C. Kelman, ed., *International Behavior: A Social-Psychological Analysis* (New York: Holt, Rinehart and Winston, 1965), pp. 433–63.

4.   The best statement of the bureaucratic politics approach can be found in Graham Allison, *Essence of Decision: Explaining the Cuban Missile Crisis* (Boston: Little, Brown, 1971).

parties in many states, and since politicians often lack foreign-policy expertise, the latter must, of necessity, rely on the more permanent civil servants for information and advice. Bureaucrats, then, have considerable influence in the shaping of foreign policy. At the same time, these bureaucrats are responsible for carrying out that policy and can therefore affect its implementation by moving grudgingly on an issue or perhaps refusing to act at all. In the meantime the central decision makers have moved on to other issues, little aware of the possible subterfuge.

One can, of course, exaggerate the role played by subordinate bureaucrats in the policy process. It might be noted that many of those who take such a view have had experience in government and perhaps may have developed an exaggerated sense of their own roles. Central decision makers, after all, have the opportunity to select the advice and advisers they wish to hear, and often develop competitive centers of information gathering, as well as procedures for monitoring compliance with their decisions. But the role of the bureaucracy as a partial explanation for foreign-policy making should not be overlooked. The evidence concerning the bureaucratic role will be examined in some detail in Chapter 5.

The Adaptive Model

Some of the theorists examining foreign-policy behavior have chosen to focus on how states respond to the constraints and opportunities provided by their respective international environments.[5] Rather than viewing the foreign-policy choices of a state as unlimited, as those who utilize the decision-making approach might, such analysts seek to ascertain those features of the environment that will cause particular outcomes regardless of the action one is talking about. At a minimum, one should be able with such an approach to rule out certain foreign-policy options for a state on the basis of an assessment of that state's limited capabilities, geopolitical position, and so forth. This strategy also allows one to compare the behavior of states in terms of their opportunities and constraints, for these vary from one state to another. Similarly, the adaptive capabilities of states differ depending not only on their capabilities but also on their will.

5. For a discussion of this approach see John P. Lovell, *Foreign Policy in Perspective* (New York: Holt, Rinehart and Winston, 1970), pp.133–56.

Incremental Decision Making

Perhaps the furthest removed from the rational-actor model of decision making is the approach that views decisions as being made incrementally.[6] Because of the great uncertainty and lack of complete information in international affairs, as well as the many public and private actors concerned with foreign-policy issues, decisions cannot be made in terms of comprehensive rational calculation. Instead, they are a product of considerable maneuvering and many false starts over long periods. Given the uncertainty of their environments, decision makers do not even begin to consider a whole range of foreign-policy options but, rather, concentrate on tinkering with existing policies. Choices are often based not on what might best solve the problem rationally but on what the relevant decision makers can agree upon. This particular approach to analyzing decision making thus involves certain aspects of the bureaucratic and adaptive models.

Exactly which model or approach one selects in analyzing foreign policy is dependent largely on individual preferences. It is probably useful at this point, given our limited understanding of exactly what causes states to behave as they do, to utilize several approaches, each of which contains some elements of the truth. As we begin to understand more about what motivates foreign-policy behavior, we can narrow our approach and variables in an effort to better predict and explain such behavior.

EXPLAINING FOREIGN POLICY

The analytical approach used in this book involves an examination of a number of verbal and largely untested theories concerning why states behave as they do in the international system. An effort is also made to summarize studies that test hypotheses concerning the determinants of foreign policy. Since such studies are of recent origin and there are many gaps among them, the supporting evidence for propositions is often anecdotal and illustrative. These illustrations come from a variety of states, for only by comparing many different types of states can one hope to understand foreign-policy choices.

6. Charles E. Lindblom, "The Science of Muddling Through," *Public Administration Review*, 19 (Spring 1959), 79–88.

Since foreign-policy decisions are of necessity made by individuals, we begin in Chapter 2 by exploring how the human dimension affects foreign-policy choices. We ask what factors common to all human beings tend to affect the way they perceive and react to their international environment, and to what extent idiosyncratic factors make a difference in policy choices.

Chapter 3 is concerned with the behavior of individuals in group settings, that is, societies. Here we try to understand the extent to which one's views are shaped by membership in a given society and how different societal conditions affect international behavior.

Chapter 4 examines how societies develop myths about themselves and others that tend to affect their views of reality. The major sources of such myth systems consist of ideologies such as Marxism, fascism, democracy, nationalism, or various religious beliefs. The historical experiences of a nation also contribute to the specific national beliefs that a state develops.

Since societies not only build myths about themselves but also create structures through which policy is formulated and executed, Chapter 5 seeks to ascertain the extent to which different sorts of structures tend to result in different policies. Do authoritarian and democratic regimes pursue different sorts of policies, and what about presidential and parliamentary systems? The impact of bureaucracies, interest groups, and the mass public is also examined.

Also affecting the calculations of decision makers are various economic factors and the power position of the state, which are discussed in Chapters 6 and 7, respectively. The effect of the distribution of economic resources on foreign policy is examined, along with the role various economic interest groups play in the making of foreign policy. Also considered is the impact of growing economic interdependence on foreign policy.

Power, which many students of foreign policy assume to be the core factor in explaining foreign-policy behavior, is examined not only from the perspective of what determines whether or not a state has power but also from that of how power is translated into foreign-policy influence.

If there were no other states in the international system making policies to which a state must react, there would be no foreign policy. Chapter 8 examines the extent to which the behavior of other states influences foreign-policy choices. The approach used by many diplomatic historians and students of military strategy seldom goes beyond this level of analysis because little effort is made to examine what happens within each state. This chapter considers the extent to which systemic factors influence policy choices as we seek to account for the impact of the overall configuration of power and supranational actors on behavior.

The final chapter attempts to tie together the various determinants that help explain foreign policy. Since many such determinants impinge on each and every foreign-policy choice, it is important to think of them as operating in combination, even though for analytical purposes it is necessary to look at them individually. An effort is made to assess the relative influence of these determinants in terms of their explanatory power in affecting foreign-policy choices. In this way we hope at least to sharpen our ability to think about plausible explanations for events like the 1979 Soviet incursion into Afghanistan. Eventually our hope is to be able to predict such events and, perhaps more important, to understand why they occurred. The outcome may be more appropriate foreign-policy responses.

2

THE HUMAN DIMENSION OF FOREIGN POLICY

Assessments of the role of idiosyncratic variables such as psychological predispositions and individual belief systems in the making of foreign policy vary considerably among experts on the topic. They range from the assertion of Michael J. Shapiro and G. Matthew Bonham that "beliefs of foreign policy decision-makers are central to the study of decision outputs and probably account for more of the variance than any other single factor"[1] to the assessment of the social psychologist Herbert C. Kelman, who writes, "In my own view idiosyncratic dispositions are probably of relatively minor importance in affecting foreign policy decision outcomes."[2] Obviously, the characteristics and beliefs of key decision makers do make some difference in foreign-policy output, for the state is nothing more than a legal abstraction. Ultimately human beings must make its decisions. But those who minimize the role of idiosyncratic variables do so by emphasizing the constraints affecting any decision maker. These constraints include those emanating from the role being played by the

1. Michael J. Shapiro and G. Matthew Bonham, "Cognitive Processes and Foreign Policy Decision-Making," *International Studies Quarterly*, 17 (June 1973), 61.

2. Herbert C. Kelman, "The Role of the Individual in International Relations," *Journal of International Affairs*, 24, no. 1 (1970), 7.

individual, ideology and tradition, an obstinate bureaucracy or parliament, plus a variety of international constraints.

THE IMPACT OF IDIOSYNCRATIC FACTORS

After recognizing that there are a number of factors constraining individual choice, one can seek to identify those situations and variables that provide a freer choice to the individual decision maker, allowing his or her idiosyncratic predispositions to have a greater impact on the output. Among the conditions that facilitate a more important role for idiosyncratic variables, one might suggest the following propositions.

1.   The higher the interest of a decision maker in foreign-policy matters, the greater the impact of personality upon foreign policy.

Some leaders have been interested primarily in foreign-policy matters while paying little attention to the domestic arena. Examples of this type of leader are Charles de Gaulle, Richard Nixon, and Jawaharlal Nehru. On the other hand, leaders like Clement Attlee of Britain and Georges Pompidou, who succeeded de Gaulle as President of France, preferred to concentrate on domestic issues. Still others may have been interested primarily in domestic politics but forced by circumstances into concentrating on international affairs, or vice versa. Lyndon Johnson was concerned mainly about domestic politics, but he found it necessary to expend much of his energy on the Vietnam conflict and other international issues. A number of leaders, despite their interest in foreign policy, have been compelled to focus on domestic matters when confronted with serious emergencies such as economic depression. President de Gaulle's failure to pay attention to worsening domestic economic conditions led, in no small measure, to his resignation in 1969.

2.   The greater the decisional latitude permitted the decision maker, the greater the impact of personality variables on foreign policy.

Dictatorial regimes appear to be among the least predictable, for they operate under fewer domestic constraints. As a result, the whims of decision makers are more likely to prevail. Fewer opposition forces can be organized to affect the decision. There tend to be fewer lapses in the implementation of policy, given the greater centralization in such regimes and the fear of challenging their authority.

Another factor contributing to decisional latitude is the charisma of the leader. It is possible for a leader with a charismatic personality to generate considerable popular support for a state's foreign policy, as Nehru of India and Nkrumah of Ghana were able to do. It might also be noted that these two leaders, as well as others like them in the developing states, were better able than decision makers in developed countries to put their personal imprint on the foreign policy of their respective states. This is partly due to the fact that the low level of bureaucratization in most developing states tends to minimize the problems of bureaucratic interference in the formulation and implementation of foreign policy.

3. Personality factors are more important the higher the level of the decision-making structure at which a decision is made.

Studies have found that "when asked if personality plays as great (or greater) a part in behavior as organizational factors such as communication, officials who are at lower echelons tend to say no, while those at high echelons tend to say yes."[3] This difference in response is due largely to the fact that roles tend to be less clearly defined at higher levels. Consequently, there are fewer organizational and role constraints on the occupants of such positions. Personal predispositions are permitted to dominate.

4. Personality variables are more important in nonroutine situations in which standard operating procedures are inadequate.

Among the nonroutine situations in which personality is likely to play an important role are decisions to initiate or terminate major international undertakings like war, alliances, and aid programs. As nonroutine events, crises provide considerable opportunity for leaders to play a more assertive role. Fewer individuals are allowed to participate in crisis decision making, given the time constraints involved. The idiosyncratic input of those who are concerned with making a decision is likely to be highly significant.

3. Richard C. Snyder and James A. Robinson, *National and International Decision-Making* (New York: Institute for International Order, 1961), p. 158.

5.   Situations that are highly ambiguous, unanticipated, remote, or involve contradictory information provide more opportunities for personality variables to influence the outcome.

The preceding situations imply that opposition forces have not coalesced because of the ambiguous, unexpected nature or perceived irrelevance of the issue, thus allowing leaders to make decisions primarily in accordance with their idiosyncratic predispositions. Even if other interested parties have organized to take a stance on the issue, the conflicting information will undermine their ability to provide evidence that will dissuade the central decision makers from taking whatever action they are predisposed to take.

6.   Personality predispositions are more likely to have an impact when information is either overloaded or too sparse to provide appropriate clues for rational choice.

Too much information can be as great an impediment to rational decision making as too little. Wading through a mass of information is a difficult task and is often short-circuited by paying attention only to preferred and expected signals among many contradictory inputs. Lack of information also requires that one rely largely on one's predispositions in reacting to a situation in which choice is required.

7.   Idiosyncratic inputs are more likely to occur in dealing with long-range planning than in dealing with current situations.

Since interested domestic and international constituencies are less likely to be activated on issues dealing with the remote future, more of the personal touches of the individual decision maker are likely to be found in such decisions. Indeed, decision makers who are interested in planning can frequently plan in relative isolation, since few people are interested in analyzing conditions and making recommendations for the long run. There tend to be far greater psychic and professional rewards for those who deal with the large issues confronting a nation in the immediate present.

8.   A leader may purposefully seek to hold in check basic psychological predispositions if he or she perceives an issue to be an important one involving national survival.

It is at such times of emergency that a decision maker, realizing the enormity of the issues involved, seeks to obtain advice from others and to have others share responsibility in any decision that is made. Concern about one's place in history, or perhaps about the survival of the nation, can influence decision makers to constrain their basic impulses, which might lead them to take precipitous action when confronted with a challenge.

While it is clear that personality variables can have varying effects on foreign policy, depending on the circumstances, the critical issue that needs to be examined is how specific psychological predispositions and traits might impinge on foreign policy, assuming that circumstances allow for some impact. In the remaining sections of this chapter, we shall examine whether psychological responses are based on biologically innate characteristics or whether they result from learned behavior. We shall also explore the role that motivational needs, personality traits, and perception play in the making of foreign policy.

BIOLOGICAL EXPLANATIONS

Some authorities believe that human behavior can best be explained by biological traits that predispose human beings to behave in certain ways. Of most relevance to international relations is the assertion that humans are inherently aggressive. Aggression has been identified as an innate drive in much the same way that hunger and sex have been seen as basic drives. Among the most prominent writers holding such a view are Konrad Lorenz, Robert Ardrey, and Desmond Morris, who have utilized the study of the animal world to help them explain human behavior.[4] Konrad Lorenz, in *On Aggression*, developed a number of propositions about the aggressive behavior of humans that might be summarized as follows:

1. Humans, like all animals, have an inherent aggressive drive for which there is no outlet.

---

4. Konrad Lorenz, *On Aggression*, trans. Marjorie Kerr Wilson (New York: Bantam Books, 1967); Robert Ardrey, *The Territorial Imperative* (New York: Atheneum, 1966); Desmond Morris, *The Naked Ape* (New York: McGraw-Hill, 1967).

2.   Animals have built-in mechanisms that prevent them from killing their own kind, for it would mean the destruction of the species. Those with poor defense mechanisms are able to escape easily.

3.   Humans lack the natural weapons to kill big prey, including their own kind and, as a result, have failed to develop through the evolutionary process mechanisms that would prevent destruction of the species.

4.   At the same time, humans have developed instruments that allow them to kill their fellows, as they have been prone to do since the discovery of rocks, tools, and fire.

5.   Although humans can reason and have consequently developed greater moral responsibility than animals, push-button warfare makes killing over long distances easy and tends not to evoke the moral repugnance elicited by face-to-face battle. As a result, the innate aggressiveness of human beings creates a fundamental problem as far as human survival is concerned.

If humans are innately aggressive, as ethologists like Lorenz claim, it becomes difficult if not impossible to reduce the level of aggression through education or by lowering the level of frustration. Lorenz's only solution for controlling violence involves efforts to channel aggressive drives into nonviolent areas such as sports and other forms of competition.

Questions remain about biological theories of aggression, for such theories fail to explain the considerable variation in aggression that one finds among individuals and groups. The differences are too great to be explained away be asserting that there are alternative options for channeling aggression into less violent areas. One might also challenge an approach that tries to infer human behavior from that of animals. Owners of tropical fish, in particular, might question the premise that humans are the only animals that tend to engage extensively in violence against their own kind.

By probing people's unconscious motivations, Sigmund Freud also came to believe that human aggressiveness was inherent. In addition to life forces, Freud saw a set of drives whose primary function was the destruction of the individual as each person seeks to return to an inanimate state.[5] He saw these drives, which he called death instincts, as causing overt aggressiveness against self and others. Freud even went so far as to assert that the atrocities of war are more "natural" than the civilized behavior of peace.

The frustration–aggression hypothesis, first presented in 1939 by Dollard and associates, illustrates yet another instinctual theory. It was premised on the notion that aggression is always a consequence of frustration.[6] Although subsequently there was some effort to modify the assertion that aggression was inevitable, aggression was still viewed as the most likely response to frustration. Whenever an aggressive act occurred, these writers assumed that it had been instigated by frustration.

Later research has suggested that people do not react aggressively to frustration if they believe that interference with their goal attainment is justified by the rules.[7] Nor are they likely to behave violently if they see failure to obtain their goals as related to fate or to their own behavior. The frustration–aggression hypothesis has also been questioned because of the many other possible responses to frustration besides aggression. For example, frustration may lead to such responses as apathy, withdrawal, repression, resignation, self-transcendence, or merely righteous indignation.

Various groups have shown great ingenuity in coping with frustration without resorting to violence. An example is the Indian tribes located in the southeastern part of the United States, who competed with each other in lacrosse but forestalled the development of perpetual schisms by requiring that competitors change opponents after a certain number of losses. Some Eskimo groups worked out their frustrations by singing satirical songs to each other with judges in attendance, and Indian tribes in Colombia were able to settle their disputes by beating a rock or a large tree with a stick while cursing their antagonist. The victor was the one whose stick did not break in the process. But despite such examples and research, which seem to question

5. Sigmund Freud, "Why War," in Robert A. Goldwin et al., eds., *Readings in World Politics* (New York: Oxford University Press, 1959), pp. 31–44.

6. John Dollard et al., *Frustration and Aggression* (New Haven: Yale University Press, 1939).

7. Leonard Berkowitz, "Whatever Happened to the Frustration–Aggression Hypothesis," *American Behavioral Scientist*, 21 (May-June 1978), 696–97.

the validity of the hypothesis, it still might be suggested that the greater the frustration, the more aggressively an individual or group might behave, assuming that the individual or group is predisposed to aggressive responses as a way of coping with frustration.

LEARNED RESPONSES

Rather than seeing human behavior as biologically determined, some authorities believe that such behavior is primarily learned. Indeed, the frustration–aggression hypothesis itself is often viewed from the perspective of learned behavior, since different individuals and societies develop varying ways of responding to frustration. Albert Bandura supports the notion that if people are aggressive when their goal attainment is blocked, this is because their aggressive reactions to frustrations have been reinforced in the past.[8] Aggression in such circumstances was found to have had positive utility for the individual.

Aggression, like other behavior, apparently can be learned by observation. In a careful review of the vast literature on aggression, Dolf Zillman concluded that "there is compelling evidence that shows that *hostile and aggressive behaviors can be acquired, maintained, strengthened, weakened, and eliminated through modeling.*"[9] This is why many authorities are concerned about the extensive violence shown on television.

Further evidence that aggression is a learned response can be found in studies that indicate that more aggressive individuals tend to come from homes where corporal punishment is used, and that criminals often have been abused as children.[10] Research has also shown that individuals who blame and threaten others in everyday conflicts also favor blaming and threatening other nations in international conflicts.[11]

8.   Albert Bandura, *Aggression: A Social Learning Analysis* (Englewood Cliffs, N.J.: Prentice-Hall, 1973).

9.   Dolf Zillmann, *Hostility and Aggression* (Hillsdale, N.J.: Lawrence Erlbaum, 1979), p. 239.

10.   Edwin I. Megargee and Jack E. Hokanson, *The Dynamics of Aggression* (New York: Harper & Row, 1970), p. 43.

11.   Lloyd S. Etheredge, *A World of Men* (Cambridge, Mass.: M.I.T. Press, 1978), p. 11.

Evidence for the assertion that aggressive reactions are based on learned responses can be inferred from Luther Lee Bernard's finding that isolated peoples seem to have been uniformly friendly and hospitable toward strangers, whereas those surrounded by hostile and wandering tribes have always been warlike.[12] Louis S. B. Leakey, whose field research has done so much to help us understand the origins of humanity, has also suggested that humans learned violence only after they developed a rudimentary civilization and began living in communal groups.[13]

Learning theory holds out some hope for humankind in the sense that one can learn nonviolence as well as violence. Children who are not provided with aggressive role models may well be able to develop the habit of not fighting. The purpose of civilization is to reduce the animal-like aggressiveness of humans, whether it is viewed as innate or learned, and indeed considerable progress has been made on this score. But at the same time that humans are generally becoming more civil toward their fellows, the invention of more destructive weapons continues to threaten their existence.

MOTIVATIONAL FACTORS

Determining what motivates individual decision makers to make the choices they do is never an easy task. Indeed, the decision makers themselves often are not certain why they behave as they do. Research on the motivations of decision makers is further complicated by the fact that psychological data about leaders are almost impossible to obtain. Leaders are unlikely to submit to psychological testing and even less likely to be receptive to psychoanalysis. As a result, indirect means have to be utilized to obtain such information. These techniques include content analysis of speeches, making inferences about traits and motivations from behavior, or drawing analogies and comparisons from experimental and interview studies of more accessible subjects. Despite the difficulties of direct observation, the considerable psychological research that has been conducted to date allows one to make some fairly accurate judgments regarding how

12.   Luther Lee Bernard, *War and Its Causes* (New York: Holt, Rinehart and Winston, 1944), p. 119.
13.   Cited in Edward E. Azar, *Probe for Peace* (Minneapolis: Burgess, 1973), p. 7.

leaders with certain needs and personality traits are likely to behave when placed in positions of authority.

A key motivating force for most, if not all, political leaders is a need for power. Social-psychological studies of people who are power oriented suggest that they tend to desire leadership positions, want to dominate others, are argumentative, show little humanitarian concern, tend to be paranoid, and, at the same time, do not like to take risks.

For many leaders, the search for power may be an effort to compensate for deprivations experienced during childhood. As children they may have felt unloved because of a domineering mother or father. In some instances they did not relate well to their peers because of certain physical limitations. Hitler, for example, was "a small, unattractive, somewhat sickly child who was dwarfed by his dignified, uniformed father."[14] Woodrow Wilson also was sickly as a child and had an unhealthy relationship with his exacting father. This may not only have affected his power needs but also have "contributed to Wilson's breakdowns whenever his most intensely held commitments were challenged."[15]

The perceived need for power has been contrasted with two other basic psychological motivations—need for affiliation and need for achievement (often referred to as N affiliation and N achievement). The person who places need achievement at the top of his or her motivational hierarchy tends to take moderate risks. Such a person is unwilling to sacrifice possible achievement of success by taking risks, but at the same time does not want to risk failure by not attempting to achieve a given goal.

The person with a high need for affiliation constantly seeks the approval of significant others. In the political arena such a person has great difficulty firing advisers and may tend to be loyal to them long after such loyalty is useful. It may also be that this predisposition will make a person less of an empire builder because of greater concern for other people as opposed to concern about broader issues. Indecisiveness may also be associated with the need to have the approval of others. A person with a high need for affiliation is hardly likely to fit the description of the inner-directed person who is able to act on his or her own counsel.

14.   James MacGregor Burns, *Leadership* (New York: Harper & Row, 1978), p. 57.
15.   Betty Glad, "Contributions of Psychobiography," in Jeanne N. Knutson, ed., *Handbook of Political Psychology* (San Francisco: Jossey-Bass, 1973), p. 299.

A study of the effects of need for power, affiliation, and achievement on American presidents in the twentieth century found that the power motive was associated with war and failure to reach arms limitation agreements. Presidents with higher affiliation and achievement need scores, on the other hand, were less likely to engage in war and more likely to support arms limitation agreements.[16] Such findings parallel the results found in interpersonal bargaining experiments, which demonstrated that N achievement and, sometimes, N affiliation were related to cooperation, but N power was associated with exploitative and conflict behavior.[17]

In examining power and affiliation needs at the broader societal level, David C. McClelland found that motivational data collected from the popular literature of England and the United States revealed that when the need for power was high, and particularly when it was higher than the need for affiliation, war tended to follow about fifteen years later. His findings also indicated that totalitarian regimes were most likely to show a pattern of high need for power and lower need for affiliation. But such personality patterns have often induced even reformist leaders to support violent acts in the name of progress. Leaders with low need for affiliation may have highly altruistic motivations combined with a propensity to love humanity in general rather than as individuals. They are prone to support zealous actions to right wrongs on behalf of the oppressed. Reformers, intent on extending human rights to others or civilizing other peoples, may become particularly dangerous as they rationalize the use of violence to force others to think and behave as they do.

McClelland also speculates that a high need for achievement may provide a substitute for war and imperialism.[18] Rather than viewing British peacefulness during the nineteenth century as related to the operation of the balance of power, he hypothesizes that Britain was peaceful at home and abroad because it was absorbed in achievement games in the world of commerce and industry. Britain's N achievement

16.   David G. Winter and Abigail J. Stewart, "Content Analysis as a Technique for Assessing Political Leaders," in Margaret G. Hermann, ed., *A Psychological Examination of Political Leaders* (New York: Free Press, 1977), p. 60.

17.   Kenneth Terhune, "Studies of Motives, Cooperation, and Conflict Within Laboratory Microcosms," *Buffalo Studies*, 4 (1968), 29–58.

18.   David C. McClelland, *Power: The Inner Experience* (New York: Halsted Press, 1975), p. 318.

TABLE 2-1. A Typology of Orientations to the International Political System

	Introvert	Extrovert
High Dominance (Reshape)	Bloc (Excluding) Leaders Dulles, Wilson, Hoover, Hughes, Stimson, Acheson, House, Hull, Root	World (Integrating) Leaders Johnson, Theodore Roosevelt, Franklin D. Roosevelt, Byrnes, Hopkins, Kennedy
Low Dominance (Persevere)	Maintainers Herter, Kennan, Marshall, Colby, Knox, Lansing, Coolidge, Day, Sherman, Kellogg, Rusk	Conciliators Bacon, McKinley, Stettinius, Stevenson, Truman, Bryan, Taft, Eisenhower, Hay, Harding

SOURCE: Lloyd S. Etheredge, *A World of Man* (Cambridge, Mass.: M.I.T. Press, 1978), p. 95. By permission of the M.I.T. Press.

scores were the highest of any time since 1500, and its N power stood at its lowest level since 1600.[19]

The need to dominate others, combined with an extroverted personality, was found to affect foreign-policy behavior, as illustrated in a study of thiry-six American decision makers during the present century.[20] The results of this analysis, shown in Table 2–1, suggest that officials scoring higher on dominance in interpersonal relations were more likely to advocate the threat or use of military force and were less sympathetic toward disarmament and arbitration procedures. Such officials also tended to be both bloc and world leaders. Those with low interpersonal dominance became the maintainers and conciliators. Whether or not the same individuals would support exclusionary or status quo policies or would seek to change the world through domination or mediation was related to the degree of extroversion shown, with the more extroverted person more likely to seek change.

PERSONALITY TRAITS

In addition to attempting to make inferences about what motivates people to behave as they do, researchers have sought to identify and classify various personality traits. The schemes developed

19.   Ibid., p. 319.

20.   Lloyd S. Etheredge, "Personality Effects on American Foreign Policy, 1898–1968," *American Political Science Review,* 72 (June 1978), 434–51.

by such researchers are often based on complex personality testing in which respondents react to questionnaires, projective tests, and clinical evaluations. Although such psychological testing is seldom done on foreign-policy decision makers directly, the available research nevertheless allows one to ascertain how given personality types are likely to behave when assuming decision-making roles. A number of personality scales have been developed that often share overlapping characteristics. Among the more interesting ones from the perspective of explaining foreign-policy behavior are Adorno's authoritarian personality, Rokeach's open- and closed-minded personalities, and Maslow's self-actualizer.

The authoritarian personality has been identified in the classic work of Adorno and colleagues, in which the F-scale (fascism scale) was developed.[21] Richard Christie and Marie Jahoda have shown that this personality type is not restricted to the extreme right wing, as suggested by Adorno; people on the extreme left, such as supporters of communism, also demonstrate authoritarian characteristics.[22] Among the traits that have been identified in the authoritarian personality are a tendency to dominate subordinates, deference toward superiors, sensitivity to power relationships, a need to perceive the world in a highly structured fashion, excessive use of stereotypes, and adherence to whatever values are conventional in one's setting.[23] Authoritarians also tend to be highly nationalistic and ethnocentric—characteristics that are closely related to support for war and aggression. Studies indicate that the authoritarian personality also prefers clear-cut choices. An examination of reactions to the Korean War of 1950–53 showed the more authoritarian personality opting either for withdrawal of American forces or escalating the war by bombing China, whereas the less authoritarian personality was more likely to prefer the less emphatic policy of pursuing peaceful settlement.[24]

Given some of the theoretical and measurement problems involved in the F-scale, Milton Rokeach has developed a more general

21. T. W. Adorno et al., *The Authoritarian Personality* (New York: Harper & Row, 1950).

22. Richard Christie and Marie Jahoda, *Studies in the Scope and Method of the Authoritarian Personality* (New York: Free Press, 1954).

23. W. Raymond Duncan, "Development Roles of the Military in Cuba: Modal Personality and Nation Building," in Sheldon W. Simon, ed., *The Military and Security in the Third World* (Boulder, Col.: Westview Press, 1978), p. 82.

24. Robert E. Lane, "Political Personality and Electoral Choice," *American Political Science Review*, 49 (March 1955), 173–90.

instrument for identifying what he calls the closed-minded or dogmatic personality.[25] Closed-minded personalities have been found to have high levels of anxiety; they tend to be concerned more with the source than with the content of new information; and they are unable to synthesize new information that contradicts their belief systems.[26] As a result, they have difficulty making effective and rational foreign-policy choices. Such personalities are unlikely to examine a wide range of alternatives, a trait that precludes the possibility of selecting the best choice. They are also likely to perceive conspiracies and rush to form stereotypic notions of "the enemy" whenever a threat is perceived. Such personalities are less likely to tolerate ambiguity and therefore are less patient in international dealings. The closed-minded person has also been found to be more likely to condone the use of force.[27] It has been suggested that this personality type would be very likely to feel extreme pressure for escalating a long-drawn-out limited war into an all-out war in a "drive for closure."[28] When confronted with the imprisonment of American Embassy personnel in Teheran, the closed-minded person might have found it difficult to refrain from the use of military force for almost six months, as President Carter was able to do prior to the abortive rescue attempt in April 1980. Ultimately even Carter was unable to withstand the ambiguous and threatening situation and was persuaded of the need to risk precipitous military action in an effort to resolve the issue.

The decisional style of the closed-minded person was admirably captured by William Langer in his description of Adolph Hitler, in which he wrote,

> He does not think things out in a logical and consistent fashion. . . . Instead of studying the problem, as an intellectual would do, he avoids it and occupies himself with other things until unconscious processes furnish him with a solution. . . . He then begins to look for facts.[29]

25. Milton Rokeach, *The Open and Closed Mind* (New York: Basic Books, 1960).

26. Jeanne M. Knutson, *The Human Basis of Polity* (Chicago: Aldine, 1972), p. 7.

27. Milton Rokeach, "The Nature and Meaning of Dogmatism," *Psychological Review,* 61 (May 1954), 200.

28. J. David Singer, "Man and World Politics: The Psycho-Cultural Interface," *Journal of Social Issues,* 24 (July 1968), 143.

29. William Langer, *The Mind of Adolph Hitler* (New York: Basic Books, 1972), pp. 74–75.

The relationship between dogmatism and foreign-policy attitudes has been examined in two studies of American foreign-policy officials. The first, based on the responses of 37 State Department officers and 58 Defense Department officials, found a significant (but low) relationship between a composite measure of rigidity and dogmatism and a composite measure of hard-line anticommunism, nonsupport for arms control and disarmament, and verbal derogation of nonaligned states.[30] The other, based on the responses of 274 foreign-service officers, found a significant but low relationship between psychological selectivity and world mindedness.[31] Both studies noted that foreign-service officers scored very low on dogmatism and were psychologically flexible when contrasted with more general populations.

Whereas authoritarianism and closed-mindedness are negative traits and affect foreign policy adversely, Abraham Maslow's self-actualizer has personality traits that are highly desirable for effective decision making.[32] For self-actualization to be achieved, certain basic needs must be met as the individual develops from infancy. These include physiological needs, safety or security, affection and belongingness, and self-esteem. Most decision makers, except possibly those from the developing world, have been able to satisfy their basic physiological needs, which consist largely of sufficient food and shelter. Those like former Prime Minister Golda Meir, who have suffered considerable physiological deprivation as children, may be particularly sensitive to the needs of starving people, especially children. This experience of Meir as well as other Israeli leaders may help explain the considerable Israeli foreign aid directed toward Africa during the late 1960s. It may also be suggestive of why many leaders in the developing world live ostentatiously after achieving positions of power.

The self-actualizer not only has been able to satisfy his or her physiological needs but has also developed a sense of security, belongingness and self-esteem. Satisfaction of such psychic needs is essential to creating trust in one's world. A sense of trust facilitates negotiation with other leaders and the reaching of international agreements. Henry A. Kissinger has suggested that the low level of interpersonal trust

---

30.   Bernard Mennis, *American Foreign Policy Officials: Who They Are and What They Believe Regarding International Politics* (Columbus: Ohio State University Press, 1971).

31.   David C. Garnham, "Attitude and Personality Patterns of United States Foreign Service Officers," *American Journal of Political Science*, 18 (August 1974), 525–47.

32.   Abraham Maslow, *Motivation and Personality* (New York: Harper & Row, 1954).

characteristic of Soviet leaders who lived through the Stalin period made them suspicious of the United States.[33] One could hardly expect them to place more faith in the good will of the United States than they would in that of their own colleagues.

The development of a sense of self-esteem has particularly relevant implications for foreign policy. Some have regarded low self-esteem as a major factor leading to war and conflict. For Harold Lasswell, wars and revolutions served as means for a people and its leaders to discharge their collective insecurities.[34] People with low self-esteem tend to be most predisposed to accept nationalism, for by identifying with the state, the individual is able to raise his or her own self-esteem. If a nation can be successful in its foreign-policy ventures, the self-esteem of the collectivity and its leadership can be raised appreciably.

Lack of self-esteem in the individual decision maker can also lead to problems in the making of foreign policy. Social-psychological research has shown that individuals with a negative self-concept tend to bargain more competitively than those with a positive view of themselves.[35] As a result, compromise and eventual agreement often evade them. Those with low self-esteem have a great need to overcompensate for their feelings of anxiety and are consequently more likely to behave aggressively. Low self-esteem has been found to predispose both isolationists and nonisolationists to hold extreme views on foreign-policy issues, although its influence is much more powerful among isolationists.[36] Inter-state simulation studies indicate that participants with low self-esteem are more likely to attack on warning rather than to delay response.[37] In a world threatened with nuclear annihilation, the predisposition to be quick on the nuclear trigger can be extremely dangerous. Such negative responses underscore the very real dangers

33.   Henry A. Kissinger, "Domestic Structure and Foreign Policy," in James N. Rosenau, ed., *International Politics and Foreign Policy*, rev. ed. (New York: Free Press, 1969), p. 271.

34.   Harold Lasswell, *World Politics and Personal Insecurities* (New York: McGraw-Hill, 1935), p. 25.

35.   Jeffrey Rubin and Bert R. Brown, *The Social Psychology of Bargaining and Negotiation* (New York: Academic Press, 1975), p. 178.

36.   Paul Sniderman and Jack Citrin, "Psychological Sources of Political Belief: Self-Esteem and Isolationist Attitudes," *American Political Science Review*, 65 (June 1971), 401–17.

37.   Charles F. Hermann, Margaret G. Hermann, and Robert A. Cantor, "Counter-Attack on Delay," *Journal of Conflict Resolution*, 18 (March 1974), 75–106.

of recruiting decision makers with low self-esteem, yet positions of authority seem to attract such people, since leadership roles help raise self-esteem.

Often a person with low self-esteem tends to be anxious and paranoid as well as hostile and uncooperative. Such a cluster of characteristics is likely to have a highly negative impact on the making of foreign policy. A person with such traits is likely to misperceive the intentions of others, always believing the latter to be plotting against him or her. It becomes virtually impossible to influence the behavior of such a person; conciliatory moves will have little, if any, impact, and hostile moves will only confirm what that person tends to believe all of the time.

Individuals with high self-esteem, on the other hand, are more likely to trust others, and this may have some positive implications for the making of foreign policy. For example, as Lucian W. Pye points out in his psychological biography of Mao Zedong, the Chinese leader trusted the world enough so that he did not feel it necessary to dominate others in order to have his way.[38] The person who always feels pressure to control others can hardly make conciliatory moves. According to the Georges' biography of Woodrow Wilson, the latter could be particularly effective in handling situations when he did not link success with his need for self-esteem and when he felt a minimum of personal involvement.[39]

Although low self-esteem generally tends to have a negative impact as far as a more peaceful and cooperative foreign policy is concerned, it has also been hypothesized that people with high self-esteem will be less cooperative. The problem lies in the fact that such individuals tend to take advantage of and exploit the situations in which they find themselves. Those with high self-esteem are also more likely to take risks.

Interviews with 126 State Department officials in which the respondents were asked to respond to five scenarios involving international crises confirmed the notion that respondents measuring higher in self-esteem on psychological tests tended more often to oppose the use of force. But when the respondent had both high self-esteem (which

---

38. Lucian W. Pye, *Mao Tse-Tung: The Man in the Leader* (New York: Basic Books, 1976), p. 57.

39. Cited in Michael P. Sullivan, *International Relations: Theories and Evidence* (Englewood Cliffs, N.J.: Prentice-Hall, 1976), p. 33.

alone would tend to make one oppose the use of force) and a strong ambition to feel active and personally influential, the net result was an unusually powerful tendency to advocate the use of force.[40]

Not only are decision makers likely to have some of the personality traits that can affect foreign-policy choices and behavior, but aberrant and even emotionally unstable individuals may occasionally assume positions of leadership, creating even more serious problems for the stability of the international system. According to one estimate, in the last four centuries at least seventy-five chiefs of state have led their states while suffering from emotional disturbances.[41] Although serious emotional illness has not been rampant in democracies, given the opportunity to review the performance of incumbents at regular intervals, incapacitation from illness and age have been fairly prevalent.

In a nuclear age, with its threat of mass annihilation, there is clearly considerable reason to be concerned about the possibility that a leader might suddenly go berserk. Frequently, signs of mental deterioration go unobserved by associates for a long period, as was true with respect to Viscount Castlereagh, who guided British foreign policy during the early nineteenth century, and James Forrestal, who served as the United States' first secretary of defense after that position was created in 1947. The assumption that tends to be made is that such individuals are only showing signs of exhaustion in a very demanding job.

More recently, the behavior of Idi Amin in Uganda and Emperor Bohassa I of the Central African Federation, who indulged in all sorts of personal whims, led many people to raise questions about their sanity. That such behavior will not be tolerated by outside powers was demonstrated by the fact that both were replaced with the aid of outside forces in 1979. The appearance of such aberrant behavior in a leader who might obtain control over nuclear weapons makes such a disposition not only more necessary but at the same time more difficult and dangerous to achieve.

Dealing with aberrant personalities in foreign-policy matters is extremely problematic. For example, it has been said that, given Stalin's extreme paranoia, it was virtually impossible to influence his be-

40. Lloyd S. Etheredge, "Personality and Foreign Policy," *Psychology Today*, March 1975, pp. 37–42.

41. Jerome Frank, *Sanity and Survival* (New York: Vintage Books, 1967), p. 59.

havior.[42] Every move, even a conciliatory one, was viewed by Stalin with extreme suspicion. As a result, there may have been little alternative to the cold war while Stalin was alive, unless it was a hot one.

PERSONALITY AND ENVIRONMENT

Personality is not the same thing as behavior; it merely predisposes the person to move in one direction or another. What sort of reaction will occur is highly dependent upon the broader environment in which the personality finds itself. Two environmental conditions appear to be particularly relevant when it comes to foreign-policy behavior—stress and the impact of other personalities. It has been suggested that "stress cripples some people's ability to consider alternatives, heightens their sense that others have hostile intent, and can reduce the likelihood they will be dissuaded by deterrent threats."[43] Under stress, energetic people behave even more energetically, and anxious people tend to be even more anxious. It is also during periods of stress that the aberrant or potentially aberrant person is likely to become unhinged. When the environment is essentially placid, it is often possible for the psychologically unstable person to maintain self-control, but the same person is highly likely to respond erratically during periods of stress. James Schlesinger, secretary of defense during the Nixon administration, was concerned that President Nixon might take precipitous action, subjected as he was to the increasing pressures of Watergate and demands that he resign. Nixon had, after all, only recently been boasting about his authority to initiate a nuclear strike within a period of twenty minutes. Because of these concerns, Schlesinger ordered the military not to act on nuclear strike orders even if they came from the President himself.

Periods of stress interfere with people's cognitive abilities. During such times they tend to think more simplistically; they lose the ability to examine broader perspectives; they become increasingly intolerant of ambiguity; they tend to focus only on the short-term implications of

42. Morton Schwartz, *The Foreign Policy of the U.S.S.R.: Domestic Factors* (Encino, Calif.: Dickenson, 1975), p. 193.
43. Patrick M. Morgan, *Deterrence* (Beverly Hills, Calif.: Sage Publications, 1977), p. 156.

decisions; and they become more rigid in their cognitions. At the same time, they tend to lose confidence in whatever decisions they make.

During periods of personal stress there is considerable pressure to take precipitous and often unwise action simply to reduce the tension that has developed. Any decision, however unwise it may be, becomes preferable to the burden of sustained tension. Such pressures have been used to explain the Kaiser's desperate responses to the events surrounding World War I despite his recognition of Germany's inferior military position at the time. During particularly stressful times in the Vietnamese conflict, American decision makers were seen to be undertaking actions "just for the sake of 'doing something,' or just to encourage the South Vietnamese, rather than because they were expected to be effective in defeating the Communists."[44] One also has to wonder to what extent the seemingly impossible mission to rescue the hostages in Iran in April 1980 was motivated by the overwhelming stress felt by American decision makers, especially President Carter, who were confronted not only with other international crises but also with severe domestic economic problems and a serious electoral challenge.

Although generally speaking, stress has some exceedingly negative aspects as far as rational foreign policy making is concerned, one should also note that a moderate amount of stress can be exceedingly helpful. As long as stress is not so high that it creates psychological blinders or other interferences with rational thought, it can provide the stimulus for creative solutions. Under conditions of low stress and tension there will be less effort to solve a problem. Studies have shown, for example, that some tension is useful in inducing an environment in which disarmament concessions are made and agreements are reached.[45]

The importance of examining the personality traits of leaders, whether normal or aberrant, is underscored by the fact that such traits affect how leaders relate to each other. In an age of increased interaction among heads of state both at frequent summit meetings and through personal and rapid communications, the meshing of personalities can make a difference in inter-state relations. There was probably some truth in former President Nixon's assertion that he

44. Jeffrey S. Milstein, *Dynamics of the Vietnam War* (Columbus: Ohio State University Press, 1974), p. 175.

45. Lloyd Jensen, "Military Capabilities and Bargaining Behavior, *Journal of Conflict Resolution,* 9 (June 1965), 155–63.

should continue in office, for to change leaders at that critical time would interfere with the positive personal relationships that he had developed with leaders in the Soviet Union and the People's Republic of China. It would take some time before a successor would be able to gain such confidence. Stalin's arrogance and aloofness undoubtedly affected the ability of other leaders to relate to the Soviet Union, just as Khrushchev's insensitivity, erratic style, and bluntness bothered a number of leaders, particularly Mao Zedong and other Chinese leaders. The less bombastic style of Khrushchev's successors has, on the other hand, facilitated high-level diplomacy with the Soviet Union.

Further examples of just how personal attitudes and conflicts between leaders can affect their countries' foreign relations can be seen in President Nixon's tilt toward Pakistan during the 1971 Bangladesh war. There is clear evidence that Nixon and Prime Minister Indira Gandhi had a considerable personality conflict, whereas Nixon liked Pakistan's leader, Yahya Kahn, very much. Rational policy might well have dictated siding with the much more powerful India at the time, but Nixon directed his subordinates to favor Pakistan. During the Kennedy administration, relations between the United States and Canada seemed to sour when John Diefenbaker was prime minister, but they improved with the arrival of Lester Pearson, with whom Kennedy was better able to relate. The success of American–German collaboration during the 1950s seemed in no small measure related to the reciprocal trust and liking between Chancellor Adenauer and Secretary of State Dulles. This contrasted sharply with the strain in relations between President Carter and Chancellor Helmut Schmidt, which resulted in less cordial relations between the two states.

PERCEPTION

Although one can speak of a number of structural and situational factors that influence foreign-policy choices, ultimately those choices are made on the basis of what is perceived by those in positions of authority. It is not the power position of a state, its domestic political and economic conditions, or its national belief systems that determine the choices made in foreign policy; rather, it is the question of how these various factors are perceived by foreign-policy decision makers that becomes critical in foreign-policy choices.

International events are perceived by decision makers on the basis of images they hold about the world. These images, of course, have been shaped over many years and are based not only on the individual experiences of the decision maker but also on the broader myths and traditions that prevail in the society. That such images and goals play an important role in foreign-policy output is suggested by research on Norway's foreign policy, in which a direct connection was found between elite images and foreign policy behavior.[46] It was possible, for example, to predict the failure of the Scandinavian defense negotiations and the subsequent decision of Norway to join NATO simply by analyzing the strategic images held by the elite at the end of the summer of 1948. Potential mediating factors, such as domestic conditions and diplomatic maneuvers, appear not to have made a difference in the outcome.

The role that images and perceptions can play in foreign policy has also been effectively demonstrated in Ole Holsti's studies of John Foster Dulles, who served as secretary of state during the Eisenhower administration.[47] Through a content analysis of all available public pronouncements about the Soviet Union made by Dulles, Holsti found that his subject had an unwavering view of the Soviet Union as an evil actor in the international system. Dulles' belief system led him to perceive that the Soviet Union tended to decrease its hostility toward the United States only when its capabilities relative to those of the United States decreased. Such arguments were used by Dulles to explain Soviet acquiescence to the Austrian State Treaty of 1955, which ended the Allied military occupation and provided a peace settlement with Austria. Given such an image of Soviet behavior, the appropriate response for the United States would always be to exert pressure against the Soviet Union and to retain military superiority over the Soviets.

The extreme lengths to which an individual will go in holding rigid images of the enemy can be seen in former West German Chancellor Konrad Adenauer's perceptions of the Soviet Union. Like Dulles, Adenauer saw communist leaders as masters of deceit and guile, and consequently viewed any nonaggressive move as a trick. Suggestions to the contrary by noncommunist leaders were only viewed as evidence that the person who made the suggestion had been duped.

46. Philip M. Burgess, *Elite Images and Foreign Policy Outcomes* (Columbus: Ohio State University Press, 1968).

47. Ole R. Holsti, "The Belief System and National Images," *Journal of Conflict Resolution*, 6 (September 1962), 608–17.

Although some people may interpret every move of the enemy in a negative way, as Dulles and Adenauer were prone to do, it is also possible that wishful thinking may cause a person to misjudge the intentions of the enemy in a positive way. British Prime Minister Neville Chamberlain, who supported appeasement at the 1938 Munich Conference, was said to have managed to find a ray of hope in everything Hitler and Mussolini said or did.[48]

It is also possible for decision makers to alter their views of reality radically when highly unexpected events occur. President Carter has noted how the Soviet incursion into Afghanistan in December 1979 shocked him into a more cautious stance toward the Soviet Union. He seemed to shift gears completely, asking for significant increases in military spending and shelving the SALT II Treaty. Indeed, it may be that those decision makers who feel the most betrayed by the abrupt change of policies on the part of other leaders whom they had trusted tend to react the most negatively.

Considerable research has been conducted on the question of how decision makers develop their perceptions of foreign policy and, in particular, what factors lead them to misperceive reality on occasion.[49] One's perception of current events and what to do about them is very much influenced by one's perception of the historical record. World War II and the events leading up to it have provided the most important analogies for the decision makers involved in making postwar policy, particularly in the United States. Since most such decision makers were socialized into politics during the 1930s, events such as the Munich Conference have left an indelible impression on their minds. On a number of occasions Presidents Harry Truman and Lyndon B. Johnson called attention to what was perceived to have been the failure of Western appeasement policy toward Hitler as justification for their own tough stance against what they saw as Soviet and Chinese efforts to extend their control in Asia and Europe. Had Hitler behaved somewhat more erratically than he did, with little connection between his

---

48. Glenn H. Snyder and Paul Diesing, *Conflict Among Nations* (Princeton, N.J.: Princeton University Press, 1977), p. 332.

49. Among the best of these studies are two books published by Robert Jervis entitled *The Logic of Images in International Relations* (Princeton, N.J.: Princeton University Press, 1970) and *Perception and Misperception in International Politics* (Princeton, N.J.: Princeton University Press, 1976). Most of the examples in this section are from the latter. Also see John Stoessinger, *Why Nations Go to War*, 2nd ed. (New York: St. Martin's Press, 1978), and Ralph K. White, *Nobody Wanted War: Misperception in Vietnam and Other Wars* (Garden City, N.Y.: Doubleday, 1970).

aggressions, it may well have been that the domino theory would not have been as prominent in the United States' official attitude toward Asia. Instead, American decision makers assumed that communist successes, like Hitler's successes, would only cause communist leaders to continue their aggression; hence the necessity not to concede an inch.

Experience is not always a good teacher because of the problems involved in making the appropriate inferences. To use an example provided by Kenneth Boulding, the Aztecs who offered human sacrifices to obtain good harvests would not necessarily have ceased to do so if one year's harvest was bad.[50] They might have merely increased the number of people they sacrificed, believing that the experience proved only that the previous sacrifice had been insufficient.

A person's expectations also tend to affect his or her perception of new events. Thus, Western decision makers are quicker to see another state as aggressive if a dictator has just gained power than if the new regime assumed control under democratic elections. The fear of another communist regime in the Western Hemisphere led President Johnson and his advisers to conclude, on the flimsiest of evidence, that a 1965 rebellion designed to return Juan Bosch to power in the Dominican Republic was led by communists and thus justified military intervention by the United States. The American decision makers apparently assumed that for the movement to have been so well organized, communists must have been involved. Yet the evidence points to the fact that the revolt involved primarily students who were dissatisfied with the 1963 military overthrow of the democratically elected Bosch by General Wessin y Wessin.

Little evidence is required to lead Western decision makers to conclude that if a new regime is a communist one, it will behave in an aggressive fashion. Yet this is not necessarily the case, as is suggested by the foreign-policy behavior of Tito's Yugoslavia. The problem with such facile assumptions, of course, is that they may become self-fulfilling prophecies as Western decision makers react in a hostile and suspicious fashion to what may very well be inappropriate images. The problem is compounded by the fact that the general expectation of communist regimes is the mirror image of the Western one, namely, that a capitalist state will behave in an imperialist fashion and therefore is not to be trusted.

---

50. Cited in J. D. Armstrong, *Revolutionary Diplomacy: Chinese Foreign Policy and the United Front Doctrine* (Berkeley: University of California Press, 1977), p. 19.

In situations in which there are several plausible explanations for a given event, a person's expectations usually determine which one he or she will choose. It has been suggested that one of the reasons that the German attack on Norway in 1940 took both that country and Britain by surprise, even though they had detected German ships moving toward Norway, was the expectation that the Germans were planning to break out into the Atlantic Ocean.

The particular role that an individual plays in the foreign-policy decision-making process is also likely to affect his or her perceptions of the real world. The oft-repeated notion that what a person sees depends on where that person sits is clearly a truism. One's role affects the flow of information that one is likely to receive. But perhaps even more important, changing roles affects one's perceptions of responsibility and often changes one's reference groups.

Generally, one might anticipate that the higher in the role hierarchy a decision is made, the more likely it is that broader and longer-range interests will be reflected. We are all aware of politicians who make certain commitments when running for office but seem to shift gears upon assuming office. How a new role can affect a person's policy position and sense of responsibility was aptly illustrated by Admiral Darlan of France, who had declared that the French fleet would never fall into German hands. As France began to fall, he declared his intention to order the fleet to sail to Britain or the United States. But when he was appointed minister of marines in the new Vichy government he reversed himself, asserting that he now had a political and governmental duty to keep the fleet intact.[51]

The tendency to change perceptions and attitudes as one moves from one role to another, however, is far from determinative. There are clear differences of perception among individuals as to what a given role requires. Moreover, a strong personality with well-developed notions of foreign policy is less likely to be affected by changing role requirements than one whose world view is less developed.

The range of roles one has played in the past is likely to affect one's world view. Foreign-policy decision makers who have spent most of their professional lives in the military are likely to respond quite differently as to which issues are important and involve the national interest than those who come to the position from a lifetime in an economic ministry.

51. Glen H. Fisher, *Public Diplomacy and the Behavioral Sciences* (Bloomington: Indiana University Press, 1972), p. 66.

Several empirical studies have been conducted in an effort to understand the impact of role on foreign-policy issues. A survey of some sixty-four State Department officers, for example, showed that the precise roles or jobs individuals held within the department explained their attitudes toward multilateral diplomacy better than their social backgrounds or other career attributes.[52] It was found that officers who had served in divisions concerned with multilateral diplomacy held quite different attitudes toward such subjects than those who had served in other sections of the department. That events are perceived quite differently by individuals occupying contrasting roles can also be seen from a 1972 survey of some 214 American military and civilian respondents. The diplomats and domestic-policy specialists included in the study felt that the United States' national security had increased vis-à-vis that of the Soviet Union by a 3-to-2 ratio since 1954, whereas the military, by a 5-to-1 margin, saw a relative decline.[53]

Support for the notion that role makes some difference in terms of an individual's perception and behavior is also provided by a study that examined the impact of party and committee membership on the attitudes of United States senators toward former Secretaries of State Dean Acheson and John Foster Dulles.[54] The findings suggested that Democrats had a more favorable orientation toward Acheson, and Republicans a more positive response to fellow-Republican Dulles. Furthermore, membership on the Senate Foreign Relations Committee led to a more positive attitude toward the secretary of state, regardless of the individual senator's party identification. Glen Stassen reexamined these data by comparing the individual beliefs of the senators with their party and committee roles.[55] By classifying senators in terms of their basic images of East–West relations, he found that such beliefs predicted their attitudes toward the two former secretaries of state better than their specific roles did. Isolationist Democratic senators had difficulty supporting Acheson in accordance with party dictates, and

52.   Andrew K. Semmel, "Some Correlates of Attitudes to Multilateral Diplomacy in the U.S. Department of State," *International Studies Quarterly*, 20 (June 1976), 301–24.

53.   Etheredge, *A World of Men*, p. 25.

54.   James N. Rosenau, "Private Preferences and Political Responsibilities: The Relative Potency of Individual and Role Variables in the Behavior of U.S. Senators," in J. David Singer, ed., *Quantitative International Politics* (New York: Free Press, 1968), pp. 17–50.

55.   Glen H. Stassen, "Individual Preferences vs. Role Constraint in Policy-Making: Senatorial Responses to Secretaries Acheson and Dulles," *World Politics*, 25 (October 1972), 96–119.

more moderate Republicans would support Acheson despite party differences.

The importance of personal images over role was also found in a study concerned with Senate voting on the antiballistic missile system, in which it was discovered that the basic ideological orientations of the senators were more important in explaining their votes on the issue than either party affiliation or potential economic reward from defense contracts destined for a given senator's state.[56] Similarly, in yet another study such role variables as party affiliation, committee membership, and geographic region were found to be less effective in explaining changing congressional attitudes toward aid to India than were the basic images of India held by members of Congress.[57]

Regardless of the sources of one's informational images about reality, there is considerable psychological pressure to keep them consistent. As new information is received, an effort is made to interpret that information so that it will be compatible with existing images and beliefs. Social psychologists have identified a number of ways in which an individual is able to reduce what is called *cognitive dissonance*, which occurs when seemingly conflicting information is received. Perhaps the main psychological mechanism utilized to reduce the amount of dissonant information is selective perception. Individuals tend to focus on information that supports their basic predispositions while overlooking contradictory or conflicting information.

Persuasive evidence of this phenomenon is seen in a study of student responses to a questionnaire in which they were asked to rate themselves and their international relations instructors on a seven-point liberal–conservative scale involving positions on such issues as the United Nations, nuclear disarmament, and foreign aid.[58] The results demonstrated that students tended to rate their instructors very much like themselves, so that a given instructor was seen as basically conservative by the more conservative students and liberal by the liberal students. The respondents apparently were selecting information

56. Robert A. Bernstein and William W. Anthony, "The ABM Issue in the Senate, 1968–1970," *American Political Science Review*, 68 (September 1974), 1198–1206.

57. Joanne Loomba, "The Relationship of Images and Political Affiliations to Orientations Toward Foreign Aid for India," *International Studies Quarterly*, 16 (September 1972), 351–71.

58. Jane S. Jensen, "Attitudinal Selectivity in International Relations Courses," *Teaching Political Science*, 1 (April 1974), 249–52.

from lectures and discussions that tended to bolster their previous opinions, and overlooking information that was contradictory. These findings suggest that the basic political predispositions of students on international issues are fairly rigid by the time a student enters college. Indeed, studies of political socialization suggest that many political attitudes, whether national or international, are formed even before a child goes to school.

Whereas selective perception implies that a person simply fails to perceive a given piece of information, it is also possible to retain cognitive consistency by actively denying the message that is received. Illustrative of this is the reaction of Soviet command headquarters upon the receipt of a message from the Soviet front line on June 22, 1941, indicating that Soviet troops were being fired upon. The response from Soviet headquarters in this instance was that the message senders must be insane, and the latter were reproached for not sending their message in code. An even more blatant example occurred when Hermann Göring, Hitler's second in command, was informed that an Allied fighter had been shot down over Aachen, proving that the Allies had produced a long-range fighter. Göring responded, on the basis of his own experiences as a fighter pilot, that it was impossible. He went on to say, "I officially assert that American fighter planes did not reach Aachen. . . . I herewith give you an official order that they weren't there."[59]

A third coping mechanism with respect to the receipt of contradictory information is the ability to compartmentalize such information. An individual may focus on religious values on the day of worship while concentrating on a scientific approach at school. Atrocities committed by a leader against his or her own population are frequently compartmentalized from an allied leader's thoughts about that person's positive behavior in the area of foreign policy. This phenomenon may help explain why American leaders did not react more indignantly to the atrocities committed by the Shah of Iran. The ability of decision makers to accept and compartmentalize completely contradictory information is shown by the simultaneous acceptance of the notion of "the free world" and the recognition that it is composed of a large number of states led by dictators.

Fourth, efforts may be made to redefine the dissonant information once it has been received. When the secretary of the navy was told

---

59. Robert Jervis, *Perception and Misperception in International Politics* (Princeton, N.J.: Princeton University Press, 1976), p. 144.

about the bombing of Pearl Harbor, his response was that it could not possibly be true and that the message must refer to the Philippines. Considerable redefinition and rationalization is required any time a former ideological enemy becomes a friend, as in the case of the Soviet Union during World War II and the People's Republic of China more recently.

Finally, cognitive consistency can be enhanced by the tendency to bolster one's own choices or viewpoints.[60] Decision makers spend tremendous energy attempting to convince themselves of the correctness of whatever position they take, for the admission of error has a high psychological cost. There seems to be a particular fear of looking weak or foolish. If a response is required, decision makers tend to exaggerate the favorable aspects of the position taken while minimizing its unfavorable consequences. They may also seek to minimize their personal responsibility for the decision by asserting that they had no other choice.

Efforts to retain cognitive consistency often lead to misperception of international events. When information is discarded or reinterpreted simply for the sake of consistency, considerable error is likely to develop. But there are other psychological defense mechanisms that tend to distort a person's image of reality. One of these is the tendency to project one's own feelings on an external object. People who feel a lot of anger, for example, tend to see others as angry and aggressive, while those who are more trusting view others in a similar fashion.

The predisposition to see one's own moves as motivated by magnanimous objectives while viewing the same types of moves by the adversary as being maliciously motivated may also lead to inaccurate interpretations. When the United States intervenes in the affairs of another state, the action is always viewed by Americans as stabilizing, but if the Soviets do the same thing, it is viewed as destabilizing. Regardless of how much one may dislike Soviet intervention in the affairs of other states, a case can be made that in some instances—for example, Hungary in 1956 and Czechoslovakia in 1968—Soviet intervention stabilized a situation that could have drawn the United States into a war not of its choosing.

Misperception about others may also arise from misreading communications that are targeted for another audience but are perceived as

---

60. For a discussion of the use of bolstering in decision making, see Irving Janis, *Decision Making* (New York: Free Press, 1977), pp. 82 ff.

applying to oneself. This is particularly true with respect to messages designed for a state's domestic public that are perceived and reacted to by an external actor. American decision makers, for example, appear to have had considerable difficulty with the highly inflammatory comments about the United States that were made by Prime Minister Gandhi in an effort to divert attention from India's domestic problems by making the United States the scapegoat for some of those problems.

Perceptions about another state may also be distorted by actions and statements made by lower-level officials who act without official sanction and can be countermanded by superiors. Obtaining an accurate reading of Iranian intentions with respect to the American hostages in 1979–80 became a virtual impossibility given the many spokesmen involved, several of whom could not speak for the nation and were often corrected by others, such as the Ayatollah Khomeini.

As if such distortions of perception are not enough, one must also remember that foreign governments often intentionally seek to mislead the decision makers of another state. If a state's intentions and behaviors are not benign, as in the case of efforts to undermine a foreign government, considerable energy will be directed toward covering up such a situation.

But whatever the explanation for the misperception of events and behaviors in the international system, it is clear that such misperception has often led to war and escalation of conflicts. Karl W. Deutsch once estimated that 50–60 percent of decisions to go to war have been due to misperceptions and misjudgments regarding the intentions and capabilities of other nations.[61] A study of deterrent efforts by the People's Republic of China underscored the failure of the United States accurately to perceive Chinese intentions with respect to Korea in 1952, and a similar failure on the part of India in its border conflict with China occurred in 1962.[62] Both the United States and India failed to see their actions as threatening to China and, in any event, believed that the latter was unlikely to respond given its ongoing domestic difficulties. An examination of some eleven wars led yet another analyst to conclude that misperception was the primary explanation of the conflict in each instance.[63]

61. Cited in Etheredge, "Personality and Foreign Policy," p. 38.

62. Allen S. Whiting, *The Chinese Calculus of Deterrence: India and Indochina* (Ann Arbor: University of Michigan Press, 1975), p. 220.

63. Stoessinger, *Why Nations Go to War.*

CONCLUSION

The question raised in this chapter is whether exactly who holds foreign-policy leadership positions makes much difference to foreign-policy output. We began by speculating on the conditions in which idiosyncratic or personality differences might make a difference, concluding that this is likely to be a function of the degree of interest shown in foreign policy, the amount of decisional latitude, and how high one is in the decision-making hierarchy. Personality variables are also more likely to have a greater impact in situations in which considerable uncertainty or lack of interest on the part of other actors exists, as in nonroutine and ambiguous situations or in the case of long-range planning. At the same time, leaders might seek to restrain their own predispositions in critical and dangerous situations by consulting others.

Assuming that psychological differences do affect decisions, the remaining sections of the chapter sought to examine whether human behavior is innate or learned and how specific psychological factors such as perception, motivation, and personality traits affect foreign-policy choices.

The evidence seems to suggest that aggression is more of a learned response than an innate one. Frustration may increase the level of aggressive behavior, but aggression is not the only possible psychological response to frustration; one can withdraw, deny, or redefine a frustrating experience. It was also found that certain personality types tend to be more aggressive than others. Aggressive leaders tend to have a high need for power, have authoritarian personalities, distrust others, have low conceptual complexity, and tend to be nationalistic, closed-minded, and rigid. Sometimes low self-esteem may help explain the aggressive leader, but having a sense of being able to control events may also lead to an aggressive foreign policy. Those with high self-esteem may be less cooperative, since they tend to take advantage of the situations in which they find themselves.

More conciliatory leaders tend to have high need for affiliation, are trusting, can think in more complex terms, tend to be less nationalistic, and are generally open-minded and less dogmatic.

Although personality traits do make a difference in foreign-policy behavior, how the world is perceived in specific situations is also important in explaining foreign policy. A decision maker's perceptions of the real world are affected by a number of circumstances, including memories of past events, expectations, and roles played. Decision makers tend to go to extreme lengths to fit new information however contradictory, into existing belief systems. This not only makes such beliefs extremely rigid and difficult to change, but it also means that there is likely to be considerable misperception regarding the behavior of other states and international events in general. Additional factors leading to misperception include mirror-imaging, which occurs when each side sees itself as virtuous and the enemy as aggressive, and the tendency to misread communications directed toward domestic audiences or statements made by unauthorized personnel. Foreign leaders may also intentionally seek to mislead other leaders, making accurate perception virtually impossible.

To the extent that the individual decision maker can make a difference in foreign-policy decisions, there is some evidence that the rational-actor model discussed in the previous chapter might have some analytical validity. But given the many psychological factors impeding rational choice, the approach has some serious deficiencies. To attempt to predict and explain the behavior of a foreign policy actor on the basis of a comprehensive calculation of the costs and benefits of various alternatives as seen from the perspective of the researcher would seem highly questionable at best. The evidence thus far produced clearly suggests the importance of introducing psychological factors, both rational and irrational, into any analysis of foreign-policy decision making, and models that seek to do so are likely to be more valid and useful than those that do not.

3

SOCIETAL
DETERMINANTS

Although we can partly explain why nations behave as they do by focusing on individual decision makers and their motivations and perceptions, it is also possible to enhance our understanding of international behavior by looking at various attributes of the broader society. Individual decision makers are, after all, products of the societies in which they live. They tend generally to share the values and goals prevailing in the broader societal setting. We might even go a step further and argue that since decision makers are the products of their respective societies, it will make little difference exactly which individuals occupy positions of authority, for the society itself defines acceptable and unacceptable behavior. Although there may be some individual differences in style among specific decision makers, the substance of foreign policy will tend to remain the same, given the many constraints and opportunities imposed by various societal attributes.

In this chapter we shall explore some of the basic societal characteristics that seem to have an impact on foreign-policy choices. Specifically, we want to gain some understanding of whether the national character and cultural attributes of a people make a difference in the conduct and substance of foreign policy, as well as whether nationalism, societal structures, and the political stability of a nation affect its foreign-policy behavior.

NATIONAL CHARACTER

In speaking of a "national character," no one makes the claim that each and every member of a society shares the same characteristics. Instead, writers on national character suggest that there is a *modal personality* type that develops in each state—that is, a type that is representative of the mode or majority of a given population and might be represented in a bell-shaped curve. It may even be that within a given nation there are bimodal or trimodal distributions of traits, but on the whole, one expects that in an integrated and stable society there will be a unimodal distribution, since most citizens share certain traits that distinguish them from people in other societies.

A number of students of national character suggest that a given personality develops within a nation because of the particular child-rearing practices that tend to predominate in that society. The "swaddling theory" of Russian behavior is a case in point. This theory holds that the tight wrapping of babies during most of the day and night for the first nine months leads to extensive frustration, which in turn produces considerable aggressiveness in later years.[1] Rigid toilet training has been blamed for the compulsiveness of the Japanese, although one writer asserts that a better explanation is their experience of hundreds of years of authoritarian rule.[2] The alleged aggressiveness of the German population has been attributed to an authoritarian family structure. Suggestive evidence that child-rearing practices and family structure can make a difference in adult behavior is provided by a study that found that anti-Nazi Germans, as contrasted to the typical German, had escaped the more rigid and conventional family structure generally found in German society.[3] The egalitarian family structure found in

1. Geoffrey Gorer, *The People of Great Russia* (London: Cresset Press, 1950), pp. 97–101.
2. Douglas G. Haring, "Japanese National Character: Cultural Anthropology, Psychoanalysis, and History," *Yale Review*, 42 (March 1953), 382.
3. David M. Levy, "Anti-Nazis: Criteria of Differentiation," in Alfred H. Stanton and Stewart E. Perry, eds., *Personality and Political Crisis* (New York: Free Press, 1951).

American society has also been used to explain Americans' tolerance of different interests and respect for the rights of others.[4]

Some scholars have paid special attention to the educational experiences of a people to help explain the character and culture that evolve within a particular national setting. Educational systems are generally controlled by the state, and considerable effort is expended to produce patriotic and civic-minded subjects. National values permeate textual materials, including even subject matter such as mathematics and science, in which one would not expect social values to be of major concern. Some earlier versions of Egyptian mathematical texts went so far as to include arithmetic problems involving the numbers of Israeli soldiers killed in combat.

Apart from those factors which influence the development of certain characteristics within a national grouping, the critical question is whether we can identify such characteristics and, more important, whether it is possible to explain foreign policy on the basis of certain national traits. Efforts to describe such traits are often controversial, for researchers can readily be influenced by their own biases; if they are favorably predisposed toward a given society, they are likely to see positive traits, and vice-versa. Moreover, much of the research on national characteristics tends to be impressionistic rather than systematic.

Despite these reservations, the best evidence that there are distinguishable national types can be found in cross-national surveys in which respondents from several countries are asked to identify the attributes of a given people. The remarkable finding from such surveys is that these images tend to be similar across national boundaries unless they are colored by extreme amity or enmity for a given nation.

Such a phenomenon was clearly demonstrated in a 1948 poll taken in nine Western nations in which respondents were asked to select from a list of twelve adjectives those that they thought best described the citizens of another nation.[5] The results showed that in assessments of Russian character, "domineering" and "hardworking" were among the top three choices in six of the nine states, and in two others "domineering" was one of the top three and "hardworking" came in fourth or tied for fourth. In the responses from seven states

---

4. Eric Erikson, *Childhood and Society* (New York: Norton, 1950), pp. 244–83.
5. William Buchanan and Hadley Cantril, *How Nations See Each Other* (Urbana: University of Illinois Press, 1953), pp. 51–52.

estimating American character, "progressive" and "practical" were found among the top three selections in five of the countries. Although similar stereotypic adjectives may not be selected today, given recent changes in amity and enmity within the international system, the results do show that people seem to see similar traits in a foreign population.

Assuming that one can identify the national character of a people and that this character is shared by the nation's foreign-policy elite, the critical question becomes that of how differing national traits might affect foreign policy. In the first place, such traits seem to have an impact on how foreign-policy choices are made. The consensus style of decision-making favored by the Japanese is a case in point. Such a process may require considerable time, in contrast to deciding an issue by voting upon it. It has been said that the Japanese decision to go to war with Russia in 1904 and the decision to attack Pearl Harbor in 1941 each took more than six months between the recommendation for war by the middle echelon and the final decision by the government.[6] Such decisions by laborious consensus-making are unlikely to be reopened, for few participants are willing to undertake the time-consuming process again. Although this may contribute to steadiness of purpose, it sacrifices flexibility. Moreover, decisions in which consensus is required are more likely to be vague and unimaginative, given the pressures to arrive at policies that express the lowest common denominator just for the sake of agreement.

American decision makers, on the other hand, are seen as favoring a pragmatic, short-term approach to problem solving. According to Henry A. Kissinger, this is partly due to the fact that the American decision-making structure is heavily dominated by the legal profession, which deals with actual cases rather than hypothetical situations and values quick decisions.[7] Americans are also seen to overstress the self with their emphasis on self-reliance and self-actualization. This results in a strong belief in individual accountability in the making of decisions, which is not directly compatible with consensus decision making.

6.   Chihiro Hosoya, "Character of the Foreign Policy Decision-Making System in Japan," *World Politics*, 26 (October 1973), 364.

7.   Henry A. Kissinger, "Domestic Structure and Foreign Policy," in James N. Rosenau, ed., *International Politics and Foreign Policy*, rev. ed. (New York: Free Press, 1969), p. 268.

Another quite different decisional style is likely to evolve in countries that believe strongly in authoritarian control. In China, for example, the emphasis is on making decisions for the benefit of the collectivity rather than that of the individual. Chinese culture has generated within the individual a great sense of dependency and support for hierarchical structure. Such traits provide considerable latitude for decision makers, who can count on the compliance of subordinates. Tradition and ancestor worship also have important implications as far as the ability to change and adapt are concerned. Richard H. Solomon, in an excellent study of Mao Zedong and Chinese political culture, viewed China's difficulties in responding to the changing world of the past century to be largely due to the cultural and psychological traits noted above, rather than to institutional or economic factors.[8] Studies of Russian character suggest similar traits, with the expectation that those in authority will give detailed orders, demand obedience, and monitor performance.[9] Such traits may impede decisional inputs from lower levels as subordinates wait for orders from above. Individual initiative tends to be at a premium in such societies.

In addition to affecting how decisions are made, national traits may influence the propensity of states to engage in international conflict. This is so for at least two reasons: (1) conflict may be regarded as a value or trait of a particular national group, and (2) the existence of peoples of differing cultures may be a source of conflict because of the fear of alien ideas, which leads to cultural intolerance. The evidence seems to suggest that some societies are more approving of conflict than others. This has been particularly true of African culture, which appears to be more at ease with conflict than either European or American cultures.[10] Africans tend to view conflict as a source of value, particularly insofar as it facilitates integration and conflict resolution. Similarly, the military and samurai classes have enjoyed considerable prestige in Japanese society, at least prior to their defeat in World War II.[11]

8.   Richard H. Solomon, *Mao's Revolution and the Chinese Political Culture* (Berkeley: University of California Press, 1971), p.3.

9.   Alex Inkeles, Eugenia Harfmann, and Helen Beier, "Modal Personality and Adjustment to the Soviet Socio-Political System," *Human Relations*, 11 (February 1958), 9.

10.   Adda B. Bozeman, *Conflict in Africa* (Princeton, N.J.: Princeton University Press, 1976), p. 370.

11.   Ruth Benedict, *The Chrysanthemum and the Sword* (Boston: Houghton, Mifflin, 1946).

Chinese culture, on the other hand, has emphasized the suppression of hostility and aggression. A strong antimilitarist sentiment developed in China at an early date and is reflected in the fact that the warrior ranks somewhat below the scholar and trader in the Chinese hierarchy of importance. There is within Chinese culture considerable meekness and self-effacement. Indeed, a major revolutionary objective of Mao Zedong was to direct the pent-up rage that resulted from this self-effacement against the enemies of the Communist party.[12]

Hans Morgenthau has suggested that antimilitarism, aversion to standing armies, and compulsory military service are permanent traits of American and British character.[13] On the other hand, militarism is seen by Morgenthau as a pervasive characteristic of German and Russian character. Yet it would be difficult to argue that the United States and Britain have employed force outside their territorial boundaries any less often than the Russians have in recent decades.

If militarism is not a pervasive trait of American character, how then does one explain the extensive involvement of the United States in military conflicts throughout the world in recent years? Perhaps the explanation lies in certain other traits that seem to permeate the society. Among these is an optimistic American view of an ability to control events, coupled with a strong sense of mission in the world. Such beliefs can be found among early presidents such as Jefferson, who declared that the United States was "destined to be the primitive and precious model of what is to change the condition of man over the globe," and Lincoln, who asserted that the United States was "the last, best hope on earth."[14]

Differences in national character may contribute to misunderstanding between peoples and therefore affect the level of conflict. For example, a Latin American, used to speaking at a close distance to other Latins, may be insulted when a non-Latin steps back during a conversation. Also the tendency of the Japanese to smile while being reprimanded is likely to be interpreted as the height of impertinence by

12.   Nathan Leites, "On Violence in China," in Elizabeth Wirth Marvick, ed., *Psychopolitical Analysis: Selected Writings of Nathan Leites* (New York: Halsted Press, 1977), pp. 214–46.

13.   Hans Morgenthau, *Politics Among Nations* 5th ed., rev. (New York: Knopf, 1978), p. 138.

14.   Theodore Geiger, *The Fortunes of the West* (Bloomington: Indiana University Press, 1973), p. 73.

those unfamiliar with the practice. Failure to recognize such traits can only lead to negative thoughts about another people; it becomes a particular problem if diplomats themselves are not sensitive to cultural differences.

In general, we often fear people who have different beliefs and ways of behaving from our own. Such differences—whether racial, ethnic, ideological, or religious—often lead to ethnocentric and stereotypic thinking. It becomes easy to blame an outsider for one's problems, rather than to accept the responsibility oneself. The mass public is often encouraged by their leaders and opinion makers to adopt ethnocentric attitudes toward alleged enemies. It may be incorrect, however, to view such stereotypic and ethnocentric attitudes as being the actual cause of inter-state conflict. As Hadley Cantril put it: "people in one nation are hostile to people in other nations not because they have unfavorable stereotypes; rather they have these unfavorable stereotypes because they think these other people are interfering with their own or their nation's goals."[15]

National traits not only affect a people's propensity to engage in international conflict, but they also can make a difference in bargaining styles and efforts to resolve international conflict. There appears to be considerable variation among national groups in such traits as open-mindedness and flexibility, which allow for compromise. A study of Greek interaction with Americans suggested that whereas Americans, given their democratic values, were willing to settle for a position "in between two positions," the Greeks tended to view compromise as a clear defeat. Initial demands were considered justified and immutable by the Greeks.[16] Other studies have found Arabs to be less compromising than Americans, kibbutz children to be more compromising than city children, and Mexican village children to be more cooperative than both their counterparts in the United States and those from Mexican urban centers.[17]

Studies of United States–Soviet disarmament negotiations have

15. Hadley Cantril, *The Human Dimension: Experiences in Policy Research* (New Brunswick, N.J.: Rutgers University Press, 1967), p. 128.

16. E. E. Davis and H. C. Triandis, *An Exploratory Study of Intercultural Negotiations*, Technical Report 26, (Urbana: University of Illinois Group Effectiveness Research Laboratory, 1965).

17. These studies are summarized in Daniel Druckman, "The Person, Role, and Situation in International Negotiations," in Margaret G. Hermann, ed., *A Psychological Examination of Political Leaders* (New York: Free Press, 1977), pp. 409–56.

found that the absolutist and deductive approach inherent in the Russian character constantly clashed with the pragmatic and legalistic logic of Western negotiators.[18] The greater flexibility of American negotiators was illustrated in a detailed examination of seven rounds of postwar disarmament negotiations that showed the Soviet Union making some 75 percent of its concessions during the *last third*, compared with the United States' score of 82 percent during the *first third* of the same talks.[19]

Both the Japanese and the Russians have been identified as extremely conscious of rank in their dealings with each other and also with other nations. This in turn tends to make them more concerned about formality and rank equivalence in diplomatic negotiation than American diplomats coming from a more egalitarian and democratic culture. Concern about such externalities of status, rather than focusing on the immediate issues, can have a highly negative effect on diplomatic negotiations.

The oriental concern for saving face may also impede compromise, as seems apparent in Japanese diplomacy. According to a recent examination of Japanese negotiating behavior based on eighteen case studies covering the period 1895–1941, the Japanese have a "cultural proclivity to oppose rather than propose, to be passive rather than active, defensive rather than offensive, and evasive rather than forthright."[20] Making commitments appears to be particularly difficult, and if compromise is forced upon Japanese negotiators, they are likely to argue that the situation impelled them to act as they did.

Different cultures have devised varying ways of resolving their conflicts. The strongly legalistic approach of the United States, with its emphasis on adjudication, leads it to be supportive of international courts and tribunals. In contrast, Africans are suspicious of adjudication, since their customs and religious practices tend to stress mediation as a device for conflict settlement. Judges in African societies are more concerned with pacifying the contending parties than with determining who is right or who is wrong.[21] Indeed, new states, which

18. Bryant Wedge and Cyril Muromcew, "Psychological Factors in Soviet Disarmament Negotiation," *Journal of Conflict Resolution,* 9 (March 1965), 31.

19. Lloyd Jensen, "Soviet-American Bargaining Behavior in the Postwar Disarmament Negotiations," *Journal of Conflict Resolution,* 7 (September 1963), 529.

20. Michael Blaker, *Japanese International Negotiating Style* (New York: Columbia University Press, 1977), p. 60.

21. Bozeman, *Conflict in Africa,* p. 259.

have not participated in the making of international law and consequently view it as highly biased toward the West, usually prefer mediation and conciliation over adjudication.[22] The same is true for the People's Republic of China, which has been called a nation without lawyers.[23]

What are we to conclude from these illustrations of the impact of national character traits on foreign policy, particularly as they relate to conflict and cooperation? One writer, summarizing the literature on the role of national traits, concluded that there was "no particular reason, at this point, to believe that national character shapes policy any more than that policy shapes national character."[24] Nor should one automatically assume that decision makers share the national traits of the general population. Because of their common experiences in achieving and holding high office and their interaction while in office, decision makers may even begin to share more traits with one another than with their fellow citizens. At a minimum, foreign-policy elites tend to be far more cosmopolitan than their own nationals. Given these arguments, along with the serious difficulties of measuring national character, it is little wonder that the concept of national character as an explanation of foreign-policy behavior has come into considerable disrepute in recent years. Yet it is a factor that cannot be entirely ignored.

NATIONALISM

Generally speaking, we might anticipate that states that have been more successful in building an identifiable national character will also tend to have a higher level of nationalism. Nationalism involves a psychological attachment to the nation–state and has been defined facetiously, although perhaps with considerable accuracy, as a group of people united by a common error about their ancestry and a common dislike of their neighbors. A particularly vocal nationalism has evolved among the developing states, many of which have won independence only since 1960. This nationalism, although quite expressive at times, especially toward the former colonial powers, may at

22. P. J. Boyce, *Foreign Affairs for New States* (New York: St. Martin's Press, 1977), p. 172.

23. Victor H. Li, *A Nation Without Lawyers* (Boulder, Col.: Westview Press, 1978).

24. Bernard C. Hennessy, "Psycho-Cultural Studies of National Character: Relevances for International Relations," *Background*, 6 (Fall 1962), 44.

the same time prove extremely fragile if the governmental elite fails to provide satisfaction of basic societal needs. In a new state a sense of deep commitment has not yet been fully developed, and large segments of the society remain outside the mainstream, with little political involvement. A more profound form of nationalism, and one that is more likely to withstand both internal and external assaults, is found in the more developed countries, such as the United States and those states of Western Europe that have acquired a high level of political participation and enjoy high literacy rates.

Nationalism, as a force in world politics, is of fairly recent origin; some scholars date its rise to the time of the French Revolution. As late as the nineteenth century there was little hesitation about hiring foreign-policy advisers and even military personnel from among nationals of foreign countries. In 1815 Russia's foreign-policy staff consisted of two Germans, a Greek, a Corsican, a Swiss, a Pole, and one Russian; Bismarck, having served as the Prussian ambassador at St. Petersburg, was invited to enter the service of the Czar; and two-thirds of Frederick the Great's army consisted of hired foreigners.[25] Such patterns of recruitment for sensitive foreign- and military-policy positions would be virtually unthinkable in the current nationalistic age.

Nationalism has been viewed both positively and negatively in terms of its effect on national and international politics. It can serve to unify a people. But such unification may result only if the national identity is coterminous with the boundaries of the nation–state, and in many instances this has not been the case. Appeals to one nationality in a multinational state tend to divide rather than unify the polity. Developing states in particular have suffered from serious conflicts between ethnic groups, as can be seen in the recent histories of India, Nigeria, Cyprus, the Congo, and Pakistan. The Soviet government, while often relying on Russian nationalism to build a base of support, finds that in so doing, it frequently alienates non-Russian groups within the Soviet Union. This is particularly true of the fiercely independent Ukrainians and Muslims. The Russians themselves account for less than half of the population of the Soviet Union. Among the multinational states, Switzerland has been perhaps the most successful in generating an overriding sense of nationalism and overcoming the pressure for separatism, whereas in recent years states like Canada and the United Kingdom have had problems with separatist groups.

25. Robert G. Wesson, *State Systems* (New York: Free Press, 1978), pp. 120–23.

Despite efforts by many leaders to develop and exploit the sentiment of nationalism for foreign-policy objectives, there is little agreement as to whether nationalism serves as a positive or a negative force in world politics. Some observers view nationalism as a creative force, for owing to its emphasis on separate national entities, the world is able to benefit from different experimental approaches toward solving its problems. This allows one nation to draw upon the experiences of another to the extent that a given national experiment has proven satisfactory. At the same time, nationalism may be viewed as uncreative because of the unwillingness of a national population to challenge its government's way of doing things. Nationalism might simply induce habit and a general lack of criticism, given the prevailing desire to support the country—right or wrong.

Some theorists believe that nationalism facilitates democracy, whereas others see it largely as a device used by dictatorships. Nationalism encourages participation in the body politic, for it seeks to mobilize formerly submerged elements into social roles, eats away at traditional relationships, and works toward building a new society. At the same time, dictatorships feed on nationalism in an effort to create an undifferentiated mass public that identifies directly with the symbols of the nation–state. A favorite device of authoritarian leaders is to utilize mass plebiscites to emphasize direct connection and loyalty to the leader. A more democratic state, on the other hand, attempts to operate on a pluralistic basis in which interest groups and parties articulate and aggregate their individual interests and struggle to satisfy those interests through the political process.

Finally, there appears to be little consensus on whether nationalism leads to war or to peace. President Wilson saw national self-determination as a way to peace. His reasoning was that if people were given the opportunity to choose their own destiny, they would opt for democracy, and democracies were seen to be more peace loving than authoritarian regimes. Yet there is considerable evidence that nationalism leads to war, for it results in chauvinistic exaggeration, ethnocentrism, and xenophobia. It was French nationalism that aided Napoleon in his effort to create an empire. Competing nationalisms within a state have often led to civil war, and, in an effort to instill a sense of nationalism and national identity, leaders have engaged in external conflict behavior, as will be shown in the final section of this chapter.

As suggested previously, one of the difficulties of developing a sense of national unity is related to the fact that very few states approximate the ideal of a single nationality within a given territorial boundary. Instead, many states have large minority populations, each with its own national consciousness, and some states might be more appropriately labeled multinational states. The prevalence of large minorities that lack a state of their own can be seen in Table 3–1. States like the Soviet Union, India, and China have large minority populations within their borders. But such diversity is also true of many smaller states. In fact, according to one survey, less than 10 percent of some 107 nations analyzed can be viewed as essentially homogeneous from an ethnic viewpoint. In almost one-third of the cases, the largest group fails to account for even half of the state's population.[26]

Detente between East and West has led to some decline in national unity. Ethnic and other minorities within a state begin to press their own selfish demands when it is no longer necessary for such groups to be concerned about national security and the interests of the state as a whole. The successes of small states such as Iceland in its intermittent cold war with Britain also has communicated the notion that it is possible for states to survive and achieve their goals as smaller entities.

In some instances differential economic conditions have inspired pressure for separatism. The French-speaking population of Quebec has been concerned that it is not receiving its fair share of economic goods, and the same concern has been expressed by Ulster Catholics. Scottish nationalists believe that separation might benefit them economically by allowing them a greater return from the North Sea oil fields situated off the coasts of Scotland.

Despite the revival of ethnic nationalism, which inspired a number of separatist movements, such efforts have not been very successful. In fact, the number of successes in this area since 1945 can be counted virtually on one's fingers. One of the most dramatic of these was the separation of East and West Pakistan in 1971, which resulted in the creation of the state of Bangladesh. The Turkish minority in Cyprus gained at least a temporary national territory following the Turkish invasion of 1974, which provided Turkish Cypriots with 40 percent of the total territory of the island. Other successful separatist movements have involved the breakup of short-term federations, as in the case of

---

26. Walker Connor, "Nation-Building or Nation-Destroying," *World Politics*, 24 (April 1972), 320.

TABLE 3-1. Significant People With Self-Determination Potential (In Millions)

Telegu (India)	60	French (Canada)*	6
Bengalis (India)	53	Minangkabau (Indonesia)	6
Marathi (India)	52	Tajik (Afghanistan)	6
Tamil (India, Sri Lanka)*	49.5	Tatars (USSR)	6
Ukrainians (USSR)*	42	Uighur (China)*	5.5
Gujeratis (India)	32	Croats (Yugoslavia)*	5
Kannada (India)	28	Hui (China)	5
Malayalam (India)*	25	Ilocanos (Philippines)	5
Oriyan (India)	25	Nilotics (Sudan)	5
Indians (Bolivia, Brazil,*		Scots (Britain)	5
Ecuador, Guatemala, Mexico,		Yi (Lolo) (China)	4.5
Peru, U.S.*)	23.5	Kanuri (Nigeria)	4
Sundanese (Indonesia)	21	Kashmiris (India)*	4
Bantu (South Africa)	20	Armenians (USSR)*	3.5
Punjabis (India)	18	Baluch (Iran, Pakistan*)	3.5
Yoruba (Nigeria)*	17	Bakongo (Zaire)	3.5
Ibo (Nigeria)*	14	Batak (Indonesia)	3.5
Formosans (Taiwan)	14	Georgians (USSR)*	3.5
Uzbek (USSR,* Afghanistan)	14	Hutu (Burundi)	3.5
Visayans (Philippines)	14	Ibibio (Nigeria)	3.5
Chinese (Indonesia, Malaysia,*		Miao (China)	3.5
Thailand)	13.5	Tibetans (China)*	3.5
Azerbaijanis (Iran, USSR)	13	Edo (Nigeria)	3
Assamese (India)	11	Karens (Burma)*	3
Berbers (Morocco, Algeria)	10	Lithuanians (USSR)*	3
Belorussians (USSR)	10	Luba-Kasai (Zaire)	3
Chuang (China)	10	Moldavians (USSR)	3
Sindhi (Pakistan)	10	Palestinians (Israel, Jordan,	
Tiv (Nigeria)	7.5	Lebanon, Syria)*	3
Pathans (Pakistan)*	7	Tadzhiks (USSR)	3
Kurds (Iran,* Iraq,* Turkey)	7	Tigrinya (Ethiopia)*	3
Kazakh (USSR)	6.5	Oromos (Gallas) (Ethiopia)	2–10
Catalonians (Spain)*	6		

SOURCE: Adapted from Raymond Gastil, "The Comparative Survey of Freedom," *Freedom at Issue* (Jan./Feb. 1981), pp. 14–15.

Indicates groups with medium-high or high subnational consciousness.

Malaysia, which was formed when Singapore separated from the Malayan states after only two years. The federation of Mali and Senegal lasted only two months, and the United Arab Republic, which consisted of Egypt, Syria, and Yemen, proved to be almost as short-lived. But most new nations have remained intact, and even the artificially drawn boundaries of Africa have shown considerable permanence.

One might well wonder why existing national boundaries have been able to persist, since they have, in many cases, little relevance to national groupings. Perhaps the major reason for this state of affairs is related to the fact that outside governments have found it useful to support the status quo, for to do otherwise might only encourage separatist movements within their own countries. Few governments, including even those of states that might be expected to identify with the Ibo because of their common Islamic or tribal identity, supported the efforts of Biafra to separate from Nigeria. The Organization of African Unity has made it a point of official policy not to provide aid to secessionist movements within black African states. President Julius Nyerere of Tanzania recognized the problem when he asserted that "African boundaries are so absurd that they need to be recognized as sacrosanct."[27] One can hardly afford to open the Pandora's box, given the many ethnic forces that might explode out of it. Only decision makers who enjoy considerable national unity are likely to hazard such risks. This may in part help explain de Gaulle's willingness to support Quebec nationalism, whereas leaders of less homogeneous states would hesitate to do so.

As one looks toward the future of nationalism as a force in foreign policy, there is some evidence that supranational cultures may be developing, aided by modern communication and technology. Cities throughout the world are beginning to take on the same shapes, complete with skyscrapers; fast-food chains are penetrating the globe; pop culture, especially rock music, is saturating remote areas. It may even be that certain peoples will find it easier to relate to each other across national boundaries. For example, a "culture of the city" is evolving. This means that people in New York may have more in common with their counterparts in London or Paris than with their own compatriots living in remote hamlets within the United States.

Some analysts attempt to draw cultural boundaries somewhat wider than those of the nation–state. There is the broader tradition of European culture, in which Europeans share certain values and psychological attributes regardless of the specific state they happen to inhabit. Many writers have written about the prospects of a broader African nationalism. The phenomenal growth of Islam and Swahili in Africa are prime examples of cultural growth in that area. As one writer has noted, "Africa's nationalism always had a strong tendency toward continental unity, to a degree not found in Asia."[28]

27. Bozeman, *Conflict in Africa*, p. 24.
28. G. H. Jansen, *Afro-Asia and Non-Alignment* (London: Faber and Faber, 1966), p. 271.

Whereas in the nineteenth and early twentieth centuries nationalism was primarily aggressive and ethnocentric, more recently scholars have called attention to the rise of a "new nationalism" that tends to be defensive and inward looking.[29] The new nationalists, despite their emphasis on domestic welfare, have recognized that states are economically interdependent. As a result, they share a willingness to coordinate their foreign economic policies through economic conferences and organizations. The emphasis is on coordination of policies rather than on economic integration, which was the hope of many Europeans during the 1950s and 1960s. This new nationalism is also reflected in the replacement of earlier heroic leaders such as de Gaulle, Adenauer, and Khrushchev with economic managers such as d'Estaing, Schmidt, and Brezhnev.[30]

SOCIETAL ATTRIBUTES

Considerable quantitative research interest has been shown in the possible linkage between the societal attributes of a state and its foreign-policy behavior. Looking first at studies based on cross-national comparisons of large numbers of states, we find the results not overly promising in terms of helping us understand foreign policy. Michael Haas, for example, correlated some 200 societal characteristics with war and found that very few exceeded a correlation of plus or minus .40.[31] Similar negative results were found when Rudolph J. Rummel related some 230 national characteristics, many of which could be regarded as societal variables, to foreign conflict behavior.[32] Lest one be disillusioned by such results, which seem to explain little, if anything, it should be remembered that societal characteristics might affect the foreign-policy behavior of certain kinds of states but not that of all states. The purpose of social science is to generate a better understanding of when, where, and why certain variables affect foreign-

29. Geiger, *The Fortunes of the West;* Werner Link and Werner J. Feld, eds., *The New Nationalism* (New York: Pergamon Press, 1979).

30. James Caporaso, "What Is the New Nationalism? or Is There a New Nationalism?" in Link and Feld, *The New Nationalism,* p. 9.

31. Michael Haas, *International Conflict* (Indianapolis, Ind.: Bobbs-Merrill, 1974).

32. Rudolph J. Rummel, "The Relationship Between National Attributes and Foreign Conflict," in J. David Singer, ed., *Quantitative International Politics* (New York: Free Press, 1968), pp. 187–214.

policy choices. More detailed analysis is required, rather than simply throwing up one's hands in disgust.

When one relates the societal characteristics of one state to those of another in dyadic fashion, the results show some predictive improvement. Rummel found that cultural similarity was a factor for peace between societies sharing such attributes as type of government, religion, and wealth.[33] Another study found a moderate relationship between the cultural homogeneity of two nations and their mutual relevance. In other words, states that were more similar to each other were more likely to engage in cooperative and integrative behavior.[34] Data for the nineteenth and twentieth centuries, however, showed little relationship between similarity of religion and peace (with the possible exception of Confucianism) and between language and peace.[35] Whereas the overall relationship between shared language and peace was not significant, Chinese correlated positively with peacefulness and Spanish with warlikeness.

Several studies have attempted to determine whether the degree of heterogeneity of the social structure of a state increases its conflict behavior. These researchers assume that such heterogeneity might exacerbate conflict by increasing the opportunity of foreign governments to penetrate a state by appealing to the minority ethnic, cultural, or ideological groups found within that state. This in turn is likely to strain relations between the two states involved. The findings, however, do not entirely support the assumption. One study examining the behavior of eighty-two nations found that the level of ethnic heterogeneity was not associated with either the conflict behavior or the cooperative behavior of the state.[36] Another research effort using data from the classical world (280–150 B.C.), India (1347–1526), Europe (1492–1559), and Latin America (1810–1914) found that inter-state cultural heterogeneity was not related to foreign-linked factionalism except

---

33. Rudolph J. Rummel, *National Attributes and Behavior* (Beverly Hills, Calif.: Sage Publications, 1979), pp. 98–100.

34. Roger W. Cobb and Charles Elder, *International Community* (New York: Holt, Rinehart, and Winston, 1970).

35. Lewis F. Richardson, *Statistics of Deadly Quarrels* (Chicago: Quadrangle, 1960), introduction.

36. Maurice A. East and Phillip M. Gregg, "Factors Influencing Cooperation and Conflict in the International System," *International Studies Quarterly*, 11 (September 1967), 266.

in the classical world.[37] Foreign-linked factionalism was defined in this instance as alliance or cooperation between internal factions and a state's external enemies.

The most extensively researched linkage between societal structure and international behavior involves studies that hold that elites engage in external conflict in order to divert attention from internal societal problems. Geoffrey Blainey found that during the period 1815–1939 at least thirty-one wars, or just over half of the wars occurring in that time, had been immediately preceded by serious disturbances in one of the fighting nations.[38] One writer even went so far as to assert that he doubted whether a totalitarian dictatorship could exist without taunting or attacking a foreign scapegoat.[39] To cite just a few of the instances in which authorities have asserted that the diversion hypotheses was operative, it has been suggested that Louis Napoleon continued the Crimean War partly to deflect French attention from discontent at home, and that Russia supported the Russo-Japanese war in 1904 for similar reasons. On the eve of the clash at Fort Sumter, incoming Secretary of State Seward was reputed to have suggested to Lincoln that the President provoke a war with France or Spain in order to hold the country together. More recently, President Sukarno, who ruled Indonesia from 1949 to 1967, was accused of developing hostility toward Malaysia as Indonesian domestic dissension increased, and Ali Bhutto of Pakistan was alleged to have done the same toward India in 1971 in order to distract the Bengalis from their demands for independence. The list, of course, could go on indefinitely. One point that should be made, however, is that in many instances these allegations have been made by citizens or leaders of unfriendly states in an effort to impugn the motives of foreign leaders.

Beginning in the 1960s, systematic efforts were made to examine the linkage between the domestic conflict situation and external conflict measures on a global basis to determine whether or not there was a positive correlation between the two types of conflict, as the hypothesis would suggest. The first of these were studies conducted by Rudolph J.

---

37.   Alan Dowty, "Foreign-Linked Factionalism as a Historical Pattern," *Journal of Conflict Resolution*, 15 (December 1971), 429–42.

38.   Geoffrey Blainey, *The Causes of War* (New York: Free Press, 1973), p. 71.

39.   Quincy Wright, *A Study of War*, 2nd ed. (Chicago: University of Chicago Press, 1965), p. 272.

Rummel and Raymond Tanter. They found little relationship between domestic and international conflict patterns based on cross-national indicators for about eighty nations during the period 1955–60.[40] In the Rummel–Tanter studies, domestic violence was measured by the frequency of demonstrations, riots, coups, and the like occurring in each state, while foreign conflict behavior was based on such indicators as protests, threats, numbers killed, and so forth. In a study of several polities over the period of 1900–60, Michael Haas found societal problems such as suicide and alcoholism to be generally unrelated to foreign conflict; Louis M. Terrell, using cross-national data from the 1950s, found no significant relationship between political instability and military effort as measured by military expenditures and size of armed forces.[41]

Cross-national studies like those just described, which uncovered a negative correlation between measures of internal and external conflict behavior, may have overlooked some important relationships that are lost because of the aggregation of data concerning the behavior of large numbers of states. Subsequent studies have shown that the predicted relationship does hold for certain kinds of states in specific circumstances, even though it may not hold for the world at large. We have already noted the suggestion that totalitarian regimes are highly prone to engage in foreign conflict to divert attention from domestic problems. Jonathan Wilkenfeld, reanalyzing the cross-national data collected by Rummel and Tanter, found differences among states categorized as personalist, polyarchic, and centrist.[42] Personalist states, located largely in Latin America, showed a statistically significant relationship between internal conflict indicators and diplomatic conflict behavior such as protests and threats, but the same was not true for more violent forms of external conflict. The findings also indicated that centrist (authoritarian) regimes were more likely than polyarchic

40. Rudolph J. Rummel, "Dimensions of Conflict Behavior Within and Between Nations," *General Systems Yearbook*, 8 (1963), 1–50; Raymond Tanter, "Dimensions of Conflict Behavior Within and Between Nations, 1958–1960," *Journal of Conflict Resolution*, 10 (March 1966), 48–64.

41. Michael Haas, "Social Change and National Aggressiveness, 1900–1960," in Singer, *Quantitative International Politics*, pp. 215–46.; Louis M. Terrell, "Societal Stress, Political Instability, and Levels of Military Effort," *Journal of Conflict Resolution*, 15 (September 1971), 329–46.

42. Jonathan Wilkenfeld, "Domestic and Foreign Conflict," in Jonathan Wilkenfeld, ed., *Conflict Behavior and Linkage Politics* (New York: McKay, 1973), pp. 107–23.

(democratic) regimes to engage in external conflict during periods of domestic turmoil and revolution.

Studies also suggest that less developed countries are more likely than developed states to engage in external conflict in order to divert attention from internal problems. A global study similar to those conducted by Rummel and Tanter, using data for eighty-four states during the period 1948–62, discovered that less developed states were more likely than developed ones to show their frustrations in external aggression.[43] A study of African states found a similar relationship between domestic instability and foreign conflict behavior for the period 1964–65, but not for later years.[44] It was suggested that African leaders had begun to discover the limits of power, viewing external conflict as counterproductive to their developmental goals. However, given the general lack of economic resources, skills, and technology, leaders of the developing world may be required to resort to the short-term expedient of finding a scapegoat for their economic and political problems.

Several longitudinal studies, particularly those involving authoritarian and less developed states, appear to support the diversion hypothesis. A study of the People's Republic of China for the period 1950–70 found a moderate relationship between the two conflict measures, with foreign conflict predicting domestic conflict behavior better than the reverse.[45] These findings were confirmed by another case study of Chinese foreign policy that presented evidence that during China's traumatic Great Cultural Revolution Chinese leaders manipulated the level of external hostility expressed in the mass media and the level of anti-foreign protests for their own purposes.[46] Studies of Indo-Pakistani relations covering the period from independence through 1971 also found some support for the linkage between domestic instability and foreign conflict behavior, particularly in the case of Pakis-

43. Ivo K. Feierabend and Rosalind L. Feierabend, "Level of Development and International Behavior," in Richard Butwell, ed., *Foreign Policy and the Developing Nation* (Lexington: University of Kentucky Press, 1969), p. 163.

44. Raymond W. Copson, "Foreign Policy Conflict Among African States, 1964–68," in Patrick J. McGowen, ed., *Sage Foreign Policy Yearbook*, vol. 1 (Beverly Hills, Calif.: Sage Publications, 1973), pp. 189–217.

45. Andres D. Onati, "The Conflict Interactions of the People's Republic of China, 1950–70." *Journal of Conflict Resolution*, 18 (December 1974), 578–94.

46. Kuang-Sheng Liao, "Linkage Politics in China: Internal Mobilization and Articulated External Hostility in the Cultural Revolution," *World Politics*, 28 (July 1976), 590–610.

tan.[47] Longitudinal studies of Middle Eastern countries, on the other hand, have tended to show insignificant results between the two levels of conflict behavior. In case studies of four Middle East countries, only Jordan showed a pronounced correlation between domestic conflict levels and foreign conflict behavior; Egypt exhibited a small positive relationship; but Israel and Syria showed no relationship at all.[48] The negative findings for Syria were confirmed in yet another study utilizing data from the 1960s.[49]

Some evidence suggests that, whereas domestic conflict behavior may not relate significantly to all foreign conflict behavior, it may correlate with certain types of conflict. In one study, for example, domestic conflict was found to be a more effective predictor of less intense foreign conflict (disputes and verbal conflicts) than of more intense foreign conflict (actual hostilities).[50] The same study also found that states with very intense domestic conflict levels tend to reduce their international conflict levels as they become preoccupied with internal difficulties.

Despite the contradictory findings with respect to the diversion hypothesis, it can still be said that developing countries and authoritarian regimes are more likely than developed countries and less authoritarian regimes to utilize the expedient of external conflict for diversionary purposes. Such a tactic is less likely to be used if the domestic problems are viewed as too serious, making internal concentration on solving those problems more imperative. Events in Russia in 1905 and 1917, in Germany in 1918, and perhaps in the United States in 1971, at the time of Vietnam, indicate that serious disunity within a nation inclines leaders to peace rather than war.[51]

To argue that decision makers utilize external conflict in order to unify their populations is not to suggest that such a strategy is always successful. British involvement in World War I helped unify England

47.   Lloyd Jensen, "Levels of Political Development and Interstate Conflict in South Asia," in Butwell, *Foreign Policy and the Developing Nation*, pp. 189–208.

48.   Jonathan Wilkenfeld, "A Time Series Perspective on Conflict Behavior in the Middle East," in McGowan, *Sage Foreign Policy Yearbook*, vol. 3, pp. 177–212.

49.   Robert Burrowes and Bertram Spector, "The Strength and Direction of Relationships Between Domestic and External Conflict and Cooperation: Syria, 1961–67," in Wilkenfeld, *Conflict Behavior and Linkage Politics*, pp. 294–321.

50.   Leo Hazlewood, "Dimension Mechanism and Encapsulated Processes: The Domestic Conflict–Foreign Conflict Hypothesis Reconsidered," in McGowan, *Sage Foreign Policy Yearbook*, vol. 3, pp. 213–43.

51.   Blainey, *The Causes of War*, p. 81.

and Scotland, but it affected English and Irish relations adversely. Similarly, the conflict between India and Pakistan over Kashmir did little to unify East and West Pakistan before they were separated in 1971 as a result of the Bangladesh war. The former simply did not see Kashmir as a particularly salient issue. For an external conflict to provide unification, the various parts of the nation need to view it as impinging on their own interests.

Even if we were to discover a positive statistical correlation between indicators of domestic and international conflict, we should be aware that this may be due to factors other than the attempt to direct attention away from domestic problems. Several alternative explanations might be just as plausible. In the first place, so-called linkage groups might cause domestic conflict to spill over into the international arena. One of the best illustrations of this phenomenon is the Hindu–Muslim conflict in South Asia. Religious riots between Muslims and Hindus, whether they occur in India or in Pakistan, usually affect the treatment of the religious minority of the other state, as well as placing serious strains on official Indo-Pakistani relations.

Second, the positive relationship between domestic difficulties and international conflict patterns might be explained by the incentive for intervention by traditional enemies when a given state is suffering domestic turmoil, as in the case of Indian involvement in the Bangladesh war.

Third, the linkage between the two levels of conflict might simply be related to the legitimation of internal violence in the eyes of the domestic population, given its acceptance on the international level. A study of fifty different cases of nations at war found a dramatic increase in domestic violence as measured by homicides.[52] In the United States, for example, homicide rates approximately doubled during the Vietnam War.

Fourth, the chaos and dislocation generated by international war may lead to civil war and domestic turmoil. One need only reflect on the aftermath of World War I, in which a successful Bolshevik revolution was carried out in Russia. Similarly (though less closely linked in time), G. S. Bhargave suggested that it was "now agreed that the 1965 [Pakistan] misadventure with India contributed considerably to events

---

52. Dave Archer and Rosemary Gartner, "The Myth of the Violent Veteran," *Psychology Today*, 10 (December 1976), 110.

of 1968–69. History is replete with wars having been midwives of revolutions. Regimes defeated in external wars have always been prone to internal revolt."[53]

Fifth, the positive relationship between domestic and international conflict might be due to the tendency of civil wars to escalate into international wars as outsiders support one element against another, as may be seen in the Greek Civil War, the Congo, and Vietnam. In the case of the 1971 Bangladesh war, there has been some suspicion that Pakistan was interested in broadening the civil war to include India in the hope that this might bring international peacemakers into the situation as a last-ditch effort to preserve the territorial integrity of Pakistan.

Finally, the increased levels of inter-state conflict might be due to the difficulty of resolving such conflicts during periods of internal political instability, in which diplomatic negotiations tend to be impeded. Political leaders are hesitant to undertake diplomatic negotiations during periods of domestic turmoil for fear that they would be bargaining from a position of weakness. Their counterparts in another country, capitalizing on the situation, are also likely to be interested in presenting extreme demands, thus making agreement somewhat more problematic. The adversary might even have some doubts regarding the ability of a domestically crippled leader to commit his or her state to an agreement. This apparently was the case with the Soviet elite when it showed reluctance to negotiate any significant agreements with President Nixon during the summit conference held in Moscow in the summer of 1974, despite Nixon's great interest in a foreign-policy success to divert attention from his Watergate problems. After his 1968 decision not to seek reelection, President Johnson had similar difficulties in negotiating seriously on the Vietnam issue, given his increasingly awkward domestic position.

Regardless of whether a significant relationship exists between domestic and international conflict or whether the discovery of such a relationship is related to the diversion hypothesis, it cannot be denied that some decision makers have sought to use foreign conflict behavior to divert attention and to help unify their states. Occasionally such efforts may backfire, as in the case of Ben Bella of Algeria, who was attacked by domestic enemies and forced out of office in 1965 on the

---

53. G. S. Bhargave, *Pakistan in Crisis* (New Delhi: Vikas, 1969), p. 143.

ground that he paid too much attention to foreign-policy issues and too little to domestic economic problems.[54] Still another risk of behaving in a bellicose fashion to divert attention from domestic problems is that another state will reciprocate the hostility and escalate it into an unintended war.

Leaders have found that external conflict is not the only way to divert attention from domestic problems, for success in reaching international agreements or mediating disputes can produce similar results and thereby add to a decision maker's popularity. Nehru's efforts to mediate great-power disputes helped to give the Indian population a sense of identity, something that would have been virtually impossible if he had concentrated on the seemingly intractable domestic problems confronting India. Presidents of the United States have often found that they can gain several percentage points in public-opinion polls by engaging in summit conferences or international travel. At a minimum, such activities capture newspaper headlines and give the appearance of activity and progress. It has even been suggested that former Chancellor Willy Brandt of the Federal Republic of Germany pursued his policy of *Ost-Politik*, or conciliation with Soviet bloc, in the late 1960s primarily for domestic political reasons rather than for foreign-policy or security reasons.[55] A foreign-policy success was necessary if Brandt and his Social Democratic Party (SDP) were to continue in office. Domestic political reform had become impossible because of differences of opinion between the SDP and its coalition partner, the Free Democratic party. Foreign policy became the only area in which to rally public support.

Severe domestic conflict, rather than leading to foreign conflict behavior, may actually induce noninvolvement in foreign policy. This was certainly the case for the People's Republic of China during the Great Cultural Revolution of 1966–69. During that time considerable violence erupted among the population on the mainland; virtually all ambassadors were called home and China became almost totally uninvolved with the external world. Similar domestic turmoil in Mexico during the period 1910–30 retired that state from foreign policy for all

---

54. Robert L. Rothstein, *The Weak in the World of the Strong* (New York: Columbia University Press, 1977), p. 109.

55. Norman A. Graham, "Linkage Politics and Peace Settlements: The Soviet Union and Germany in Search of a Peace Settlement," in David S. Smith, ed., *From War to Peace* (New York: Columbia University Press, 1974), p. 137.

practical purposes, and Argentina's recurring political instability since 1955 has forced it into a less active foreign role than it might otherwise have played.[56]

CONCLUSION

Since decision makers are influenced by the societies in which they live, societal variables can be used to help explain foreign policy. In this chapter we have looked at several such societal factors, including national character, nationalism, and the societal structure and stability of the state. There appears to be considerable evidence that societies develop different national characters, but what is less certain is how this affects foreign-policy behavior. It may even be that foreign policy affects national character as much as national character affects foreign policy. But since national character appears to be more stable than foreign policy, one might assume that national character does make some difference—if not in substance, at least in style.

Nationalism is also a force that has to be reckoned with in foreign policy, but the exact nature of its impact is elusive. It can serve either to unify or to splinter a nation–state; it can be a creative force because it provides many national experiments, or it can dampen creativity by fostering habit. Similarly, the linkage of nationalism with democracy, peace, and war is by no means obvious.

Some observers have called attention to the rise of a "new nationalism" that emphasizes domestic issues over foreign policy concerns, while others predict the splintering of existing nation–states into smaller, subnational components. The replacement of nationalism with a new supranationalism would seem to be the least probable option, as the nation–state is likely to remain the primary actor in world politics for some time to come.

It appears premature to develop any broad generalizations concerning the impact of societal structures on foreign-policy behavior. The statistical studies to date suggest that ethnic heterogeneity between and within states increases the level of conflict. Although the quantitative evidence concerning the impact of domestic instability on

56. G. Pope Atkins, *Latin America in the International Political System* (New York: Free Press, 1977), p. 31.

international conflict behavior is divided, it seems that there is sufficient evidence to argue that certain types of states are likely to use such an expedient to divert attention, particularly more authoritarian regimes and less developed ones. In examining the empirical evidence linking internal and external conflict behavior, one must remember that finding statistical relationships between indicators is not always sufficient. One has to move on to the more difficult exercise of explaining the meaning of such relationships. A number of alternative hypotheses were suggested, each of which might provide a partial explanation for the statistical findings. Despite these uncertainties, it does appear that there is a relationship between internal and external conflict behavior, if not immediately, at least with a brief lag time.

4

IDEOLOGY
AND
HISTORICAL
TRADITION

Foreign policy does not spring spontaneously from the minds of decision makers. Rather, it is a product of the past experiences of a nation and the specific political beliefs and ideologies that have come to be accepted over the years. Collectively, such beliefs might be thought of as forming the "national myth system" of a state. In using the term *myth* we are not suggesting that such beliefs are false, for they are clearly quite real for those who subscribe to them. As Robert M. MacIver has put it, "Every society is held together by a myth-system, a complex of dominating thought-forms that determines and sustains all its activites."[1]

A number of writers have suggested that we are now living in an age of ideology and that among the most important modern ideologies are such belief systems as communism, fascism, democracy, and the world's many religions. Ideologies are distinguished from other parts of the belief system that are derived from the cultural and historical experiences of a people in that they tend to be action oriented and based on a logically coherent set of symbols. Often specific "gospels"

1. Cited in Mostafa Rejai, "Political Ideology: Theoretical and Comparative Perspectives," in Mostafa Reja, ed., *Decline of Ideology* (Chicago: Aldine-Atherton, 1971), p. 5.

can be identified in which some of the beliefs are explicitly stated, as in the writings of Marx and Engels, Hitler and Mussolini, or can be found in the texts of the Bible, the Koran, and the like. Other ideologies, such as democracy, seem less explicit, with support for their viewpoints being found in scattered locations.

Ideologies often extend beyond national boundaries and sometimes are spread from one nation to another with messianic zeal, either by missionaries or, occasionally, by the use of force. As an ideology spreads from one society to another, it tends to be modified so that it becomes more compatible with the society's existing cultural and historical values. For example, communism has been interpreted in many different ways by various states. As a result, ideologies have not always succeeded in uniting people of different nationalities and cultures, and the conflict between nations subscribing to a given ideology can be particularly intense, as in the case of the Soviet Union and the People's Republic of China. Similarly, ideological ties have not been sufficient to foster cordial relations between China and Vietnam, given their history of conflict over many centuries.

The collective experiences of a people generate a historical tradition that forms part of the belief system of a state and can also influence the course of foreign policy. Indeed, one can tell much about the future foreign policy of a state simply by knowing something about its past experiences. Decision makers make judgments about the present on the basis of their images of the past and their perceptions of the consequences of previous decisions. Habit also plays a critical role in providing continuity over time, again suggesting the importance of past experiences.

THE FUNCTIONS OF BELIEF SYSTEMS

Whether a state's belief system is derived from ideology or the tradition of its people, those beliefs influence the formulation and conduct of foreign policy in a variety of ways. First, a state's belief system affects what is seen and viewed as significant in the international system. It provides blinders by which certain international events might be denied or reinterpreted to be made compatible with the prevailing belief system. Some writers have likened the belief system to a prism through which decision makers view reality. As with a prism, any light or information that comes in tends to be refracted and dis-

torted so that it is seen quite differently when it exits. So too are new events colored and refracted as they pass through the prism of ideology and past experiences.

Second, the belief system of a state places certain constraints on the range of foreign-policy options. A group of decision makers, even in the most authoritarian regime, will find it difficult and perhaps politically suicidal to venture far from what is generally conceived as compatible with the belief system of their constituents. A democratic leadership may feel constrained by a population that is likely to disapprove of any action by its government that smacks of undemocratic or unfair manipulation of another state's political system. Similarly, certain alignments generally have to be ruled out as viable options for states with competing ideologies. If a pact is made across ideologies, it often tends to involve weak commitments, as in the nonaggression pact between the Soviet Union and Germany in 1939 or the temporary alliance made by democratic states with the Soviet Union for the purpose of conducting the fight against Hitler during World War II.

Third, a national belief system helps provide continuity in foreign policy. The more comprehensive a state's belief system, the more stable its foreign policy will be. States with long historical traditions tend to have greater continuity in their foreign policy, whereas newer states do not have to overcome a long-established way of thinking or behaving in order to change their foreign policy.

Fourth, national belief systems provide a means for rationalizing foreign-policy choices—choices that are often made on the basis of interpretations of national security interests but are sold to the public on the basis of certain shared values. Soviet decision makers are quick to note that any choice they make in foreign policy is guided by Marxist principles, and the United States tends to rationalize its choices in terms of "protecting the free world," "making the world safe for democracy," or "ensuring representative government."

Fifth, as devices for rationalizing and justifying positions taken, national beliefs are utilized for propaganda purposes. Efforts are made to convince others of the correctness of one's own views as ideologies struggle to gain people's minds through the use of media such as radio, newspapers, and magazines.

Sixth, national belief systems enhance national unity among those who subscribe to a given view. As such, beliefs are important factors in the development of nationalism and a separate national identity. In the developing states, where national identity is not well established because of the lack of a continuous history, leaders have sought to glorify past eras as a way of increasing their national support. Nasser could appeal to the era of the Pharaohs, while Nehru could refer to ancient Hindu empires; Mussolini publicized the success of the Roman Empire, and de Gaulle looked toward the past glory of France in his effort to establish a sense of national pride.

It might be expected that having a common ideology or belief system would help unite nations that subscribe to similar myths. The terms *free world* and *communist world* seem to assume just such a unification among nations with a similar ideological orientation. But ideology frequently has failed to serve as a cohesive force. John D. Sullivan, who coded various nations in terms of their common ideologies over the period 1815–1939, found that such similarity did not predict the stability of alliances.[2] The evidence that ideological values do not cement relations is shown in the deep schisms between communist states such as the Soviet Union and the People's Republic of China. Indeed, China became a thorn in the side of the Soviets, precisely because it espoused a communist belief system and hence threatened the Soviets' leadership of the communist world. There is also suggestive empirical evidence that when a monolithic ideological linkage between two states breaks asunder, it affects all aspects of the relationship, as in the Sino-Soviet split. In contrast, a less hierarchical and ideologically based alliance, such as that which linked the United States and France, will not suffer a complete breakdown. In the case of the alliance between the United States and France, the two states continued to agree on a number of issues following President de Gaulle's noncooperation and the withdrawal of French forces from the North Atlantic Treaty Organization.[3]

Perhaps the impact of the national belief system on foreign policy can be seen more vividly if we examine the role it plays in several of the more prominent states in the international system. For this purpose we will explore the experiences of the Soviet Union, the United States, the People's Republic of China, India, and Iran. Our treatment will reflect the fact that some of these states have very elaborate and systematic

2. John D. Sullivan, "International Alliances," in Michael Haas, ed., *International Systems* (New York: Chandler, 1974), pp. 100–22.

3. See Ole R. Holsti and John D. Sullivan, "National–International Linkages: France and China as Nonconforming Alliance Members," in James N. Rosenau, ed., *Linkage Politics* (New York: Free Press, 1969), pp. 147–95, for empirical evidence supporting this general pattern.

ideological belief systems, while others have a rich historical tradition. Some states lack both, requiring the leadership to try to create a new national belief system. Although we will try to focus on the more enduring beliefs, we will also take note of the newer traditions that seem to be evolving, such as those emanating from the cold war between the United States and Russia.

THE SOVIET BELIEF SYSTEM

In any discussion of the belief system of the Soviet Union, the obvious starting point would be Marxist–Leninist ideology. In contrast to democratic theory, communist theory is readily identifiable, since there are a limited number of writings that have provided the basis for subsequent interpretation. More difficult to determine is the impact of the classics of Marxist literature on Soviet foreign policy.

Opinion varies among students of the subject regarding the role ideology plays in influencing Soviet foreign policy making. Some writers see Soviet behavior as influenced primarily by totalitarianism or by authoritarian values that have existed since czarist days, while others see such behavior as determined by a literal interpretation of Marxist–Leninist thought. Still others view Marxist–Leninist ideology as a vehicle for rationalizing policies arrived at in terms of the national interest of the Soviet Union, or as a system for external and internal propaganda.

Regardless of which of these viewpoints is most accurate—and indeed, the accuracy may depend on the particular issue or time—it seems clear that Marxist–Leninist ideology does have an impact on foreign-policy choices. The ideology affects how Soviet leaders view the world, what things they see as important or unimportant, and what their basic predispositions are in responding to a given issue. Several aspects of Marxist–Leninist doctrine seem to have shaped the way Soviet leaders have perceived the external world and consequently reacted to it. One of the major tenets of Marxist theory is the belief that there are two basic classes in society—the proletariat and the bourgeois. Such a view may partly explain why Soviet leaders were slow to appreciate and to exploit anti-imperialism in the third world. They tended instead to believe that one either had to be for the proletarian revolution or against it. One could not be neutral.

The Marxist belief that the state was an anachronism that would eventually wither away may have influenced Lenin initially to assume that a foreign minister was unnecessary. But the realities of the nation–state system soon became apparent, leading not only to the creation of a foreign ministry but also to the establishment of diplomatic relations with capitalist states.

The historical determinism rooted in Marxist ideology has also influenced the way the Soviet Union has reacted externally. The belief in the historical sequence of feudalism→capitalism→socialism→communism influenced prediction of where socialist revolutions might be expected to arise, and hopes were high that successful revolutions might develop in Western Europe, where the bourgeois revolution had replaced feudalism. Marxist theory hardly prepared Soviet leaders to expect a successful communist revolution in China. Perhaps this partly explains why Stalin supported Chiang Kai-shek in contrast to the Chinese communists, although the more likely explanation is that he was behaving like the traditional nation–state leader fearful of the rise of the Axis powers.

The belief in permanent revolution between classes that is inherent in Marxist–Leninist thought makes it difficult for the Soviet Union to pursue global stability as a goal as long as conflicting classes remain in the international system. Such beliefs probably ensure continued conflict between the United States and the Soviet Union despite efforts to achieve detente. The belief in inevitable conflict between capitalism and communism suggests to the supporters of the latter that it is not only desirable but necessary to destroy capitalism in order to survive.

Although the Soviet Union has become a major supporter of the status quo, particularly in terms of its desire to limit the spread of nuclear weapons and retain its superpower status, its ideological views make it difficult to accept stability as the primary goal of the nuclear deterrent system. This in turn may help explain why the Soviets have been far less preoccupied than the United States with the dangers of nuclear war arising by accident or miscalculation.

Another aspect of Marxism that is likely to affect a decision maker's view of external events is the notion of economic determinism. According to this viewpoint, economics is the basic determinant of social behavior and politics is merely the superstructure. Starting from such a premise leads to a tendency to interpret the external behavior of capitalist states in terms of economic motivation. Much attention is given to the economic role of multinational corporations, economic imperialism, and notions of the military–industrial complex in trying to explain and understand the foreign-policy behavior of the West. Economic factors are used to explain any war in view of the primacy of such factors in Marxist thought.

The effect of the Marxist belief in the inevitable triumph of communism is somewhat more difficult to assess in terms of its impact on foreign policy. Such a belief might make a state take higher risks or possibly even lower risks. The belief in one's own inevitable triumph could induce highly adventuristic policies in the belief that, whatever the risk, one would ultimately prevail. On the other hand, a state might behave cautiously, believing that it can obtain ultimate victory without expending much energy. Perhaps this is what Khrushchev envisioned when he informed Western leaders that "we will bury you." There certainly was little if any evidence that he intended to achieve such a goal through an adventuristic foreign policy.

If Marxist–Leninist ideology ever was a primary determinant of Soviet foreign policy, there appears to be considerable consensus that its importance has declined over the years. A number of moves taken by the Soviet Union that seem incompatible with Marxist doctrine are used to document this trend. Such deviance goes back to Lenin's sacrifice of Russian territory with the Brest–Litovsk agreement, in which the Bolshevik regime accepted a separate peace with Germany in 1918. It is also found in his failure to support Béla Kun's communist regime in Hungary, which was showing signs of collapse in the summer of 1919. Such compromises were viewed as essential to the survival of the fledgling Bolshevik regime, as was Lenin's revival of elements of capitalism in his New Economic Policy, introduced in the early 1920s.

Although such digressions might be explained by Lenin's notion that one can take one step backward in return for two steps forward, the pattern of sacrificing Marxist ideology on the altar of national self-interest continued during Stalin's regime with the latter's attempt to cope with the increasing threat of Hitler and the Axis powers. Among these compromises with ideology were temporary reliance on the League of Nations; the French–Russian alliance of 1935; the Molotov–Ribbentrop agreement of 1939, in which the Soviet Union and Germany agreed on a nonaggression pact; and the support of various noncommunist leaders, such as Chiang Kai-shek rather than Mao Zedong.

Khrushchev continued the trend, utilizing a hard-line ideological interpretation to humble Georgi Malenkov, who had succeeded Stalin in 1953, then turning to a softer line in order to defeat another rival, Vyacheslav Molotov. Basic changes in ideological posture were announced by Khrushchev at the Twentieth Party Congress in 1956, where he declared that capitalist encirclement had officially ended and that a third camp of anti-imperialists had become part of the global picture. With this ideological shift, Khrushchev hoped that the Soviet Union might play a leadership role in the Third World. But perhaps the most profound modification of Marxist–Leninist theory came with the announcement that war between the forces favoring capitalism and those supporting communism was no longer inevitable. It was also at this time that Khrushchev began his de-Stalinization program by attacking the personality cult that Stalin had developed. Marxist–Leninist ideology was thereby threatened because of the need to believe in its infallibility. If Stalin could so blatantly misinterpret Marxism, why could not Khrushchev and his successors?

The Brezhnev period, beginning in 1964, has seen even less reliance on doctrine as the policy of detente with the West has taken precedence. There has also been less concern with clothing foreign-policy moves in ideological trappings. Brezhnev has pushed back the timetable for the rise of a "truly communist society," which he has asserted "will take us quite a long time, since human psychology is remade far slower than material foundations of human life."[4]

Under Brezhnev the Soviet Union has been vitally concerned with protecting its primacy in the international system and has consequently refused to support a number of revolutionary movements, especially those in the Middle East and Latin America, where the United States' interests are greatest. The Soviets went as far as to explicitly condemn Castro's 1966 proposals in support of subversion and violence. Yet despite their divergences from Marxist–Leninist ideology, Soviet leaders continue to view all their foreign policies as Marxist by definition.

Additional empirical evidence of the impact of ideology on foreign policy is found in research conducted by Jan F. Triska and David D. Finley, in which a content analysis of speeches delivered at the Twenty-Second Party Congress in 1961 revealed, among other things, that ideological formulations occurred more often among older elite members and among those who were involved primarily in party work.[5] Such formulations were less apparent among younger elite

4. Morton Schwartz, *The Foreign Policy of the U.S.S.R.: Domestic Factors* (Belmont, Calif.: Dickenson, 1975), p. 199.

5. Jan F. Triska and David D. Finley, *Soviet Foreign Policy* (New York: Macmillan, 1968), pp. 119–27.

members and among those who have pursued government careers— groups that are assuming increased importance in the Soviet decision-making process. With respect to specific individuals, Khrushchev ranked in the middle of thirteen elite members in terms of his score on the doctrinal quotient. His successor, Brezhnev, ranked several points behind, and long-time Soviet Foreign Minister André Gromyko followed at an even greater distance.

The findings of Triska and Finley also suggested that ideological pronouncements were not used extensively in dealing with more immediate problems, which, after all, constitute the bulk of foreign-policy issues. Doctrinal premises were used more frequently in analyzing trends than in dealing with specific events, and were more likely to be employed in long-range planning than in short-term planning. With respect to perceived crises and short-range problem solving, virtually no ideological references were coded, particularly with respect to Khrushchev. The findings also indicated that the use of doctrinal pronouncements tended to be higher with respect to foreign affairs than with respect to domestic affairs, perhaps because the latter are more related to the daily life of the Soviet citizen, who also has less independent information on which to base foreign-policy judgments.

Jerry F. Hough has documented the decline of ideological fervor in the Soviet Union by comparing two editions of an authoritative Soviet textbook. His analysis indicated that the movement away from ideological rigidity that had begun in the 1960s continued in the 1970s on a wide range of topics. He concluded that those "who believe that the Soviet leadership and elite have some master plan on how to take over the world on the basis of rigid ideological prescriptions simply do not understand the contemporary Soviet Union."[6]

Some writers have suggested that the deemphasis of ideology is related to industrialization and have noted an increasing convergence in values among industrialized states—both Marxist and non-Marxist. In rejecting the assertion that industrialization induces a more conservative stance in Soviet foreign policy, it has been suggested that industrialization actually tends to generate a sense of achievement that enhances loyalty to ideology, and that the action commitment involved in industrialization revitalizes ideology. If industrialization does threaten to undermine ideology, Soviet policy is likely to become more aggres-

6. Jerry F. Hough, "The Evolution in the Soviet World View," *World Politics,* 32 (July 1980), 529.

sive in an effort to generate loyalty internally by showing success and expansion abroad.

It is probable that no final answers will be forthcoming regarding the role of Marxist–Leninist ideology in Soviet foreign policy. That there have been changes in the official interpretation of that ideology over time cannot be denied, but the ability of the Soviet Union to adapt to changing conditions may be indicative of the strength of the ideology, not of its weakness. Evidence suggesting the importance of ideology has been provided by David Forte in a study of Soviet responses to developments in the European Common Market. He notes that Soviet ideology has provided more than simply philosophical rationalization, particularly since "shifts in ideological premises nearly always preceded changes in policy; ideological change thus set the stage for a new practical policy."[7] For illustrative purposes he cites several ideological reports that established appropriate doctrinal interpretations, setting the stage for subsequent policy changes. These changes involved initial indifference, based on Marxist predictions that the Common Market would fail anyway, followed by increased hostility when the early predictions were proven wrong and, finally, by acquiescence with an emphasis on containment.

One might also reflect on the implications of increased detente between East and West as far as the future of Marxist ideology is concerned. Detente politics are quite likely to take some of the cutting edge from a messianic ideology. Increased interaction between East and West will also allow increased penetration of Western values, particularly as far as the Eastern European satellites are concerned. As the Soviet Union liberalizes its foreign policy and downgrades its ideological component, the resultant threat to domestic tranquillity and stability will tend to influence the leadership to substitute harsher domestic controls and to punish deviants more severely, as appears to be the case under current detente conditions. Since detente politics are likely to undermine the ability of the Soviet leadership to present the capitalist world as a hostile element ready to destroy the Soviet Union, thus removing a rationale for demanding sacrifice and vigilance on the part of the Soviet citizen, stricter domestic controls may become necessary to counter any possible loss in public support.

The sources of the Soviet belief system go far beyond simple in-

7.   David Forte, "The Response of Soviet Foreign Policy to the Common Market," *Soviet Studies*, 19 (January 1968), 373–87.

terpretations of Marxist–Leninist doctrine; those beliefs are rooted in the very essence of Russian history and tradition. Some writers have seen Soviet behavior largely in terms of its continuity with czarist foreign policy. Expansion into peripheral areas is part of the continuing effort to obtain warm-water ports and buffer areas in order to enhance Russian security. Attempts to control Eastern Europe and Asia were made by various czarist regimes, whose territorial ambitions extended well into Eastern Europe and Asia. Expansionist goals included the desire to acquire the warm-water port of Vladivostok in East Asia and access to the Turkish straits. This interest in gaining access and increased use of the seas is also reflected in the extensive naval buildup of the Soviet Union in recent years.

Soviet leaders are also affected by traditional rivalries, as in the case of Russian animosity toward the Chinese. Border conflicts and armed incursions into territory claimed by the other state are nothing new in Sino-Russian relations. The memories of three invasions of Russian territory from the West within the short period of a century and a half is also likely to influence Soviet security concerns in Europe. The first involved Napolean's penetration to the outskirts of Moscow in 1812. Thanks largely to problems of logistics, the Russian advantage of defense in depth, and the onset of winter, the Napoleonic invasion was unsuccessful. This was followed by the German invasions of World Wars I and II, both of which intruded extensively into the Soviet homeland. During the latter war some 20 million Soviet citizens lost their lives. The issue of security on the western front is an especially sensitive one for the Soviet leadership.

The way in which the Soviet Union goes about making its foreign policy through its highly centralized structure is seen as a continuation of the highly autocratic system employed by the czarist regimes. How different, after all, were the highly personalistic and autocratic foreign policies of Czar Alexander I and those of Stalin in terms of the way decisions were made?

As the Soviet Union gains experience as an actor on the international scene, it is also building its own foreign-policy traditions. Though the rupture between one regime and the next is likely to be greater in an authoritarian system than in a democratic one, Soviet foreign policy has had remarkable continuity over time. Even the break between the Stalinist and post-Stalinist regimes was not as extensive as is sometimes suggested. A reappraisal of Stalin's foreign policy argued that Stalin himself became more conciliatory toward the outside world beginning in 1949 as he adjusted to a changing domestic and international environment.[8]

THE AMERICAN BELIEF SYSTEM

The American belief system has evolved from a myriad of writings and experiences involving democratic and liberal theories and is not to be found in a single set of documents. The nation's founders certainly had a major hand in shaping some of the viewpoints that are now taken for granted. Perhaps the most prominent theme in American foreign policy has been the notion of isolationism. This isolationism has existed on several levels, including geographic separation, spiritual and philosophical separation, fundamental political and ideological distinctions, economic self-sufficiency, and the relative military security and invincibility of the Western Hemisphere.[9] It has never meant noninvolvement in the economic and intellectual affairs of Europe, as President George Washington was to point out. Washington even accepted the notion that temporary alliances with other states might be necessary. What he criticized in his farewell address was the establishment of permanent alliances.

A variety of fortuitous circumstances made it possible for the United States to pursue a policy of isolationism throughout much of its history. Among these was its favorable geographic position, separated from the rest of the world by two oceans. Britain, the dominant sea power of the time, also provided considerable protection by opposing the efforts of any other European power to gain territory at the expense of the United States. The latter's preeminent position in the Western Hemisphere and the fact that it was largely economically self-sufficient also permitted it the luxury of an isolationist foreign policy. Finally, the United States was not forced into world involvement, for as a new, fledgling state it did not threaten other states in the international system.

The policy of isolation provided a variety of benefits for the United States. For one thing, it did not have to devote a large portion of its resources to defense spending. Only about 1 percent of the gross

8. Marshall D. Shulman, *Stalin's Foreign Policy Reappraised* (Cambridge, Mass.: Harvard University Press, 1963).

9. Cecil V. Crabb, Jr., *Policy Makers and Critics* (New York: Praeger, 1976), p. 7.

national product was used for defense during most of the nation's history, compared with 7 percent in recent years. This relative noninvolvement in foreign affairs allowed the United States to concentrate on its domestic needs and expand across the continent. There was also a very practical reason for playing a minimal role in international affairs in that the United States was essentially a nation of immigrants, with some 20 million foreigners settling there during the years 1880–1920. These new immigrants came from a variety of European countries. Whichever way the United States tilted in its involvement in world affairs, it would probably alienate part of its citizenry. It was by no means clear where the nation would turn in terms of support as the war clouds rose over Europe prior to World War I. Not an inconsiderable number of Americans favored support for Germany.

For the century and a half in which isolationism remained the most salient doctrine in American foreign policy, there was also a strong movement toward liberal interventionism. After the American civil war this took the form of strong-missionary movements, particularly in China. Such interventionism was also represented at the turn of the century in the Open Door policy toward China, in which the United States insisted that it should be allowed to share in the exploitation of China along with the European powers.

But the tradition of interventionism had its most prominent expression in Latin America. The Monroe doctrine of 1823 had already communicated to the European world that it was not welcome in the Western Hemisphere. At the behest of various domestic interest groups, the United States government took an increasingly active role in Latin American affairs. A peak was reached toward the end of the nineteenth century with American involvement in the Spanish-American War. That involvement was accelerated during the administration of Theodore Roosevelt with the so-called strategy of dollar diplomacy, in which it was asserted that the United States had a right to intervene in the domestic affairs of Latin American states in order to advance the economic interests of individual American companies. During President Wilson's administration it was argued that the United States was morally obliged to aid in the development of representative government. Armed force might even be used as a last resort. Indeed, American troops were sent to Nicaragua in 1912 and to the Dominican Republic and Haiti in 1915. Subsequent military interventions by the United States occurred in Lebanon in 1958 and in the Dominican Republic in 1965, and the United States has become involved in a large number of civil wars around the world. In fact, American troops have been sent abroad without a declaration of war in over one hundred instances, and in many cases the reason given has been the desire to support representative government. One problem, illustrated by Vietnam, has been that American support has been given to many undemocratic regimes, with the United States propping up such regimes as long as they would support the United States in the cold war.

This liberal interventionist attitude also produced in American foreign policy a tendency to develop legal and moralistic arguments to rationalize foreign-policy choices. President Wilson sought to justify United States involvement in World War I both to himself and to the world by saying that this would be a war to end all wars and would make the world safe for democracy. The legal–moralistic approach was seen by some in the creation of the League of Nations, which President Wilson was instrumental in developing but his own country refused to join.

With that rejection, the United States returned to isolationism with a vengeance during the interwar period, only to have this policy replaced after World War II with an interventionist one as the United States assumed the role of the world's policeman. This led former Senator J. William Fulbright to inquire in 1966 whether a new tradition was being built as the United States moved from isolationism to arrogance, involving itself in issues and problems throughout the world that were of minor concern to itself.[10] Fulbright challenged the United States' efforts to nominate itself as the Lord's agent on earth and saw the United States marching to disaster as the Athenians had against Syracuse and Napoleon and Hitler had against Russia. In his view the solution was not to respond to dogmatism with dogmatism and certainly not to imitate the Soviet Union.

Perhaps part of the tradition of liberal interventionism can be attributed to the fact that the United States has not had the same experiences as most Europeans, who have been confronted with major wars on their territory twice in this century. Europeans are somewhat more pessimistic about their ability to control events, whereas Americans retain a passion for control. The fact that the United States, unlike most European states, has not experienced a social revolution has been cited by Louis Hartz to help explain why the United States has not been adequately sensitive to democratic socialism in Europe and revo-

10.   William J. Fulbright, *The Arrogance of Power* (New York: Random House, 1966).

lutionary movements in Asia, and has sometimes adopted such excessively paranoid views about the threat of communism.[11] Hartz also sees moral absolutism, resulting from past experiences, as inspiring Americans either to withdraw from "alien things" or to seek to transform them. The United States' efforts to shape events by intervening in World War I and in Vietnam, followed immediately by the desire to withdraw from world involvements, are but two examples of this predisposition.

There are those who believe that the United States has not taken an active enough role in its response to the Soviet Union in the postwar period. Instead, they see all the advantages of developing a purposeful foreign policy in the hands of communist leaders, whereas the American value system makes it a reactive state rather than an initiator of policy. Kissinger, for example, has noted that Americans are basically pragmatic and empirically oriented, a trait that dooms the United States "to an essentially reactive policy that improvises a counter to every Soviet move, while the Soviet emphasis on theory gives them the certainty to act, to maneuver, to run risks."[12]

The belief that the United States has simply reacted to events has led to occasional suggestions that it play a more active role in dealing with the Soviet Union. This mood was reflected in 1952, when the Republican party began to press for a policy of liberation in Eastern Europe as a replacement for the policy of containment. Yet when the Eisenhower administration had an opportunity to support liberation during the Hungarian revolution of 1956, it failed to do so. Virtually no one suggested that the United States do anything about the Soviet incursion into Czechoslovakia some dozen years later. A reactive foreign policy based on the concept of containment is what one might expect of a status quo state in world politics.

While there is a common belief system consisting of democratic–liberal myths that is shared by most Americans, as a pluralistic nation the United States contains a wide range of images concerning the nature of the Soviet threat. Many of these images of the enemy have remained remarkably stable despite the fluctuation in cold war politics. This, of course, only confirms the importance of belief systems as filters

11. Louis Hartz, *The Liberal Tradition in America* (New York: Harcourt Brace Jovanovich, 1955), pp. 286, 306.

12. Henry A. Kissinger, *Nuclear Weapons and Foreign Policy* (New York: Harper & Row, 1957), p. 425.

through which reality passes, enabling dissonant information to be disregarded or reinterpreted. These viewpoints range from the more conservative interpretations of an Elliott Goodman, who sees a continuing threat in revolutionary Marxism, to the views of more leftist writers, who blame the cold war on the United States rather than the Soviet Union. In a book entitled *The Soviet Design for a World State,* Goodman dismisses Soviet pronouncements of "peaceful coexistence" as simply an ideological tool designed to mislead the West.[13] To bolster his case regarding the Soviet Union's continuing efforts to communize the world, Goodman engages in extensive quoting from various Marxist and Soviet writings that support his thesis.

Similar conservative views of Soviet foreign policy are provided by writers who see the basic threat arising from the totalitarian nature of the Soviet leadership. The character of this leadership, as opposed to the tenets of Marxist–Leninist thought, is seen as the major determinant of the aggressiveness of Soviet foreign policy.[14]

The theory of protracted conflict as espoused by Robert L. Strasz-Hupé and associates, similarly ascribes highly aggressive motivations to the Soviet Union but does not see ideology as the major determinant.[15] The basic thesis of protracted conflict holds that the United States is being engaged in a global war that the communists, having developed masterful means of conflict management and being favored by the forces of history, are bound to win—unless, and only unless, the West learns to counter the strategy of protracted conflict, in which the Soviets are able to select the theater of conflict. The Soviets are blamed for having instigated or aggravated virtually every conflict in the postwar world. These writers hold that the West will have difficulty winning in conflicts arising in Africa and Asia, and consequently should seek to exert pressure on the Soviet Union in Eastern Europe, which is seen as the Soviets' Achilles heel.

Somewhere in the middle of the more conservative and liberal views of what motivates Soviet foreign policy are writers like Hans Morgenthau, who see the conflict largely as a competition for people's

13.   Elliott Goodman, *The Soviet Design for a World State* (New York: Columbia University Press, 1960).

14.   A prime example of this viewpoint is found in Bertram D. Wolfe, "Communist Ideology and Soviet Foreign Policy," *Foreign Affairs,* 41 (October 1962), 152–170.

15.   Robert L. Strasz-Hupé et al., *Protracted Conflict* (New York: Harper & Row, 1959).

minds.[16] Given the nuclear stalemate, the cold war tends to be diverted to Africa and Asia. Morgenthau, however, is critical of emphasizing military containment and alliance policy as a proper response to the Soviet challenge in these areas, believing instead that the United States should employ less militant instruments of foreign policy, such as propaganda, foreign aid, and trade.

Some students of the subject see the conflict as due to the arms race between the two superpowers, in which threat perception and fear play a major role.[17] For those who hold such a view, the solution is to regulate the arms race. Since there is an action–reaction process at work, this view holds that the United States might even take the initiative by showing restraint in its own armaments program.

Several writers have begun to place increased blame on the United States while exonerating the Soviet Union as the primary cause of the cold war. John Lukacs, though admitting that the Soviet Union initiated the cold war with its drive into Eastern Europe, suggests that the United States, through overreaction and counterexpansion, made a heavy contribution to the continuance of the conflict.[18] Yet others have sought to blame the United States and the West for the origins of the cold war because of the hostility expressed toward the Soviet Union from the very beginning through nonrecognition of the Bolshevik regime and efforts to intervene militarily in the Russian civil war.[19] Soviet distrust of the West was also increased by the Western appeasement policy toward Hitler during the pre-World War II period. Stalin, for example, favored taking strong action against Hitler in the latter's efforts to take over Czechoslovakia. Western leaders, on the other hand, sought to appease Hitler at the Munich Conference in 1938. Thwarted by this affront to its security interests, the Soviet Union signed a nonaggression pact with Hitler in 1939. The pact was short-lived, since Hitler invaded the Soviet Union in 1941. The lesson to be derived from the experience, according to D. F. Fleming, was that the Soviet Union

---

16. Hans Morgenthau, *A New Foreign Policy for the United States* (New York: Praeger, 1969).

17. J. David Singer, "Threat Perception and the Armament-Tension Dilemma," *Journal of Conflict Resolution*, 2 (March 1958), 90–105.

18. John Lukacs, *A History of the Cold War* (Garden City, N.Y.: Doubleday, 1961).

19. F. L. Schuman, *The Cold War: Retrospect and Prospect* (Baton Rouge: Louisiana State University Press, 1962), and D. F. Fleming, *The Cold War and Its Origins, 1917–1960* (Garden City, N.Y.: Doubleday, 1961).

could no longer trust the Western powers with its security, making it all the more necessary for it to establish a buffer area around its territory. Russian advances into Eastern Europe after World War II were seen as motivated primarily by national security interests rather than by ideological concerns.

A final group of writers blame the cold war on the United States, arguing that it has pursued imperialistic and militaristic activities in order to benefit capitalist interests. They see economic interests and multinational corporations wielding all the power in the making of American foreign policy. Since these writers are examined in Chapter 6, which focuses on economic determinants of foreign policy, we will delay our discussion of this viewpoint until then.

THE CHINESE BELIEF SYSTEM

Understanding the foreign policy of the People's Republic of China requires far more than an analysis of Marxist–Leninist theory, which, if anything, has had far less impact on Chinese foreign policy than on Soviet foreign policy. The belief system that shapes Chinese foreign policy is a product not only of communist ideology but also of historical forces and, most important, of the beliefs of Mao Zedong, who served as Chairman of the Chinese Communist party for some 41 years prior to his death in 1976.

The fact that the mainland of China went communist in 1949 certainly was not attributable to the persuasiveness of Marxist–Leninist slogans. The promise of agrarian reform, as well as the ineptness and corruption of the regime of Chiang Kai-shek, contributed to the success of communism. It has also been suggested that Mao actually came to power "by waging a nationalistic struggle. He was a nationalist before he was a communist, and China has always been more important to him than world revolution."[20]

With the death of Stalin in 1953, Mao had some aspirations to succeed Stalin as the authoritative interpreter of Marxist–Leninist doctrine. He was critical of Khrushchev's efforts at revisionism, particularly with regard to de-Stalinization, at the 1956 Communist party conference. If Stalin were to be viewed as having been fallible, perhaps other communist leaders, including Mao himself, might be challenged. But

20.   Robert G. Wesson, *Why Marxism?* (New York: Basic Books, 1976), p. 107.

for Mao to assume the role of global spokesman for Marxism might have been questionable, for his contribution to Marxist–Leninist thought was extremely limited. Robert G. Wesson has even asserted that "Maoism is mostly a mass of homilies and exhortations, hardly a system. As a theoretician he does not stand high; he may never have read Marx and Engels, and his more theoretical statements are likely to be borrowed straight from Soviet sources."[21]

Although Mao's efforts to establish communes during the Great Leap Forward and his emphasis on industrialization were compatible with Marxism, they are hardly sufficient to justify the role of ideological spokesperson. A number of Mao's views conflicted directly with Marxist thought. Whereas Marx argued that the structural qualities and inherent contradictions in feudal and capitalistic systems caused human injustice, Mao tended to emphasize the undesirable moral behavior of individuals within the class structure. Certainly the process by which Mao achieved his successful revolution in China violated Marxist theory, for China had not progressed beyond the feudal period, and considerable reliance had to be placed on the peasants rather than on the workers in order to achieve a successful revolution. Moreover, Mao's belief that it would be possible to move directly from a semifeudal status to socialism without transversing the capitalist stage violated basic notions of Marxist thought.

Mao's interest in Marxism, which he apparently never really understood, lay in his concern with changing Chinese society, with its emphasis on love of peace and interpersonal harmony, into a force capable of meeting the challenges of modernization. As a revolutionary ideology, Marxism provided a vehicle that could be used to explain current injustices as well as give hope to a people that had endured decades of war and hunger. Marxism became primarily a means to other ends. Other revolutionary ideologies might have served Mao's purposes just as well.

China has supported communist movements throughout the world with more revolutionary zeal than the Soviet Union has, and in this sense it has shown itself to be more supportive of Marxist-Leninist revolutionary goals. With the increase in China's interest in improving its relations with the United States, these external ambitions may be modified. It should also be remembered that many of China's efforts on the external revolutionary front have been made at the verbal rather

21. Ibid., p. 112.

than the action level, and that China in general has not taken many risks in foreign policy. Peking's general advice to its revolutionary clients abroad has usually been for the latter to do the job themselves and to remain self-reliant.

One authority, after reviewing a number of Chinese foreign-policy decisions, concluded that these decisions can all be explained on nondoctrinal grounds and that, consequently, ideology must be viewed as at most a supplementary factor.[22] He argued further that Chinese communist ideology was not much of a guide for action, since he knew of no key foreign-policy decisions since 1949 on which the small cadre of Chinese decision makers was not divided. The fact of the matter is that Marxist–Chinese doctrine, like any doctrine, is compatible with alternative courses of action.

A study of the Chinese application of its United Front doctrine vis-à-vis Indonesia, Pakistan, Cambodia, and Tanzania revealed that this ideological doctrine had more relevance in shaping policy toward states of less strategic importance, those at a greater geographic distance, and those about which one has less complete information.[23] If one lacks information about another state, it is quite natural to resort to stereotypic ideological thinking, but if the state is important strategically, one may be more careful about relying on ideological impulsiveness.

As time has progressed, even less lip service has been given to Marxist ideology. For example, in the 1973 Chinese Communist Party Congress China portrayed itself as the defender of the interests of the small and medium-sized countries and the leader of the Third World, to which it claimed to belong rather than to the communist world. A content analysis of ideological themes in the *People's Daily* has shown a particularly sharp reduction in the use of ideological themes. Thus, references to communism, which scored 115 and 109, respectively, in 1972 and 1973, dropped to a mere 16 in the following year.[24] Similarly, references to imperialism, racism, and colonialism were reduced by almost half between 1972 and 1974.

During the 1960s, the chairman's closest comrades began to speak

---

22. Donald S. Zagoria, "Ideology and Chinese Foreign Policy," in George Schwab, ed., *Ideology and Foreign Policy* (New York: Cyrco Press, 1978), p. 116.

23. J. D. Armstrong, *Revolutionary Diplomacy: Chinese Foreign Policy and the United Front Doctrine* (Berkeley: University of California Press, 1977), p. 238.

24. Davis B. Bobrow, Steve Chan, and John A. Kringen, *Understanding Foreign Policy Decisions* (New York: Free Press, 1979), pp. 168–69.

more of the thought of Mao Zedong and less of Marxism. The primary source for determining proper action was no longer the gospels of Marx, Engels, and Lenin but, rather, the "little red book" of Chairman Mao. The Soviet Union, given these trends, asserted that the People's Republic of China was actually anti-Marxist.

Traditional Confucian values appear to be as important as, if not more important than, Marxism in affecting Chinese behavior. There is some compatibility between the two in that both tend to emphasize contradictions. Marxism, with its concept of thesis and antithesis, appears quite compatible with the predisposition of the Chinese to accept opposites as they support the pacifism of Confucianism while at the same time holding great respect for the violent Warring States period of ancient China, which lasted from 403 to 221 B.C.

A central part of Confucian thought is its emphasis on authority. The traditional Chinese respect for authority helped place Mao Zedong in the eminent position he held during most of his lifetime, and Mao was not beyond exploiting such traditions. In fact, he explained that Khrushchev's problem, which led to the latter's downfall, was his failure to develop a cult of personality.

Chinese foreign policy is also a function of a rich historical and cultural tradition. Several centuries prior to the rise of the Greek city–state system, a highly developed civilization was evolving in China under the Chou dynasty. At the center was a king who was viewed as the "son of heaven" and treated surrounding feudal lords as vassals. China was the Middle Kingdom, to which others were to pay tribute. The last sovereign, Empress Tzu-hsi, who ruled until China was made a republic in 1911, retained the myth of "governing the whole world" in her decrees. Her imperial edicts spoke of the duties of the French and English as if they were part of the structure of the Middle Kingdom.[25]

Juxtaposed against centuries of dominance and status as the Middle Kingdom came a century of humiliation, which began in 1839 with the First Opium War, and continued with foreign occupation and the imposition of unequal treaties on China. These treaties established extraterritoriality, allowing foreign courts to have jurisdiction over their citizens if they committed a crime on Chinese territory—an activity that clearly interfered with the sovereign rights of the Chinese people.

The century of humiliation has remained in the minds of Chinese leaders, who have sought to restore China's position in the interna-

---

25.   Alain Preyrefitte, *The Chinese* (Indianapolis, Ind.: Bobbs-Merrill, 1977), p. 246.

tional system. Given this feeling, it is small wonder that Zhou En-lai reacted so sensitively to Secretary of State John Foster Dulles' refusal to shake his hand at the 1954 Geneva Conference, and every effort was made not to repeat any similar affront in 1972, when President Nixon visited China. The humiliation imposed on China by foreigners also helps explain why China has stressed self-reliance in its efforts to build its economy. Until recently the Chinese have been particularly reluctant to receive technological and economic aid from the outside, even though it would help them exploit important resources like oil. The People's Republic has also been unwilling to accept anything less than full recognition as the government of China, with the concomitant requirement that recognition be withdrawn from Taiwan. In 1971 the People's Republic established its position as a major actor in the international system by assuming China's permanent seat at the United Nations. But it took eight more years for the United States to extend full diplomatic recognition to the People's Republic.

Historical relationships also help explain policies toward specific states, as in the case of the long tradition of conflict with the Soviet Union over boundary issues. The long-harbored suspicions between China and Vietnam also make the recent conflict between the two states more understandable. Historical claims to territory continue to affect relationships between China and neighboring states, since official Chinese maps based on 1840 claims include all of Southeast Asia except the Philippines and Indonesia, along with parts of the Soviet Union. Despite these claims, Chinese irredentism (concern about regaining lost territories) has been extremely limited. A number of territorial claims have been compromised in border agreements with Mongolia, Afghanistan, Nepal, and Burma. In fact, the Chinese government unilaterally withdrew from the disputed eastern Himalayan region, which its troops had occupied during the 1962 war with India.

China is likely to remain sensitive to invasions from the outside, as it has suffered from its own "yellow perils" over the centuries. The first was the invasion by the Huns, which led to the building of the Great Wall in an effort to increase security. The Mongols later invaded and ruled China for about one hundred years, and the Manchus controlled the country for three hundred years. The fourth incursion was by the Japanese, who occupied major parts of China from 1931 to 1945.

It remains to be seen whether Marxist, Maoist, or more traditional Chinese values will shape Chinese foreign policy in the years to come. Efforts to diminish the role of Mao have begun with the forced removal of Hua Guofeng, Mao's choice for successor as party chairman, the trial of Mao's wife, Jiang Qing and her associates, and the development of a publicity campaign against Mao himself. In the interest of modernization, China has softened its foreign policy toward the West. Since its relations with the Soviet Union appear to be beyond repair, China has little choice but to obtain technical assistance and trade from the industrialized West and Japan if it hopes to modernize its economy.

THE INDIAN BELIEF SYSTEM

As another example of how belief systems affect foreign policy, let us turn to a developing country and examine the ideological values and traditions of India. For the most part, developing countries have less entrenched ideologies and traditions than their longer-established, more developed counterparts. This is partly due to the disruption brought about by the period of colonial rule during which the imperial rulers sought to change values and even impose their own languages upon many of these states. But it is also a result of the condition of underdevelopment itself, which undermines the growth of national belief systems. In countries in which illiteracy is high and participation in politics is minimal, the attention of the people tends to be limited to the village or the immediate region rather than the nation. Also, the condition of underdevelopment, with its limited mass communication capabilities and its low levels of literacy, makes it difficult for a national leadership to instill a sense of national unity and identification by utilizing the myths and beliefs of the state.

Despite India's experience as a colonial dependent of Britain, Indian leaders have been able to gain inspiration from a rich heritage dating back some five thousand years. As the birthplace of both Buddhism and Hinduism, India's values and philosophies spread into many parts of Asia, and India itself served as a focal point for religious pilgrimages. The pride in a past in which the Indian subcontinent, under various Hindu rulers, may well have been the richest area in the world for over a millenium and a half provides an important source of unity and inspiration for an impoverished modern India. It may have been partly this pride of tradition that led Jawaharlal Nehru to play a more important role in world politics than would have seemed justified, given the power of India.

India was subjected to a number of invasions by various Islamic rulers beginning in the eleventh or twelfth century. These invasions eventually resulted in the establishment of the Mogul empire in the sixteenth century. Two centuries later the European colonial invasions began, leading to the ultimate triumph of Britain. British rule lasted until 1947, when independence was granted and the subcontinent was partitioned into the states of India and Pakistan.

Despite its rich historical tradition, India, like other developing states, has been forced to comply with the Western-dominated international system in its postindependence foreign policy. Instead of operating in accordance with the well-established rules developed by diplomats like Kautilya as early as the fourth century B.C., the Indians have had to accept Western ways of diplomacy. Kautilya had established complex rules as to how states with various degrees of power should behave in the international system. These even show considerable similarity to the writings of Niccolo Machiavelli, the adviser of Italian princes, but predate the latter by some two thousand years.

The colonial experience affected states like India in a number of ways. In the first instance, it established English as the basic language of communication between peoples of different linguistic and cultural backgrounds. Despite efforts to make Hindi the national language, English has continued to dominate as the language of government and the educated elites. The sections of India where Hindi is not spoken have been particularly opposed to efforts to make Hindi the national language.

The close connection to the former colonial power has also resulted in the borrowing of political institutions as well as continued political and economic ties to the West. India is a member of the Commonwealth of Nations and cooperates with Britain in a number of economic and cultural activites. Other former British colonies have followed the same pattern, and most former French colonies retain close economic and political ties with France.

Another aspect of colonial rule that has helped shape Indian attitudes was the explicit racism of the colonial period during which Europeans and British subjects were provided with segregated facilities such as rail cars, park benches, and social clubs. Indians were also systematically excluded from certain elite positions in their own country. These experiences, needless to say, have been a major factor affecting India's view of racial discrimination in other countries as well as its attitude toward international conflict between peoples of different races. The bitterness with which Indians attacked United States action in Vietnam may well have been due to the memory of their own treatment as inferiors.

A tradition that has been strongly associated with India over the centuries is nonviolence. Some Indian writers date this tradition from the time of Emporer Ashoka, who ruled an extensive portion of the Indian subcontinent during the third century B.C. Ashoka's acceptance of nonviolence, however, came only after he had conquered everything in Aryan India. Following his experience with the horrors of war, he turned to Buddhism, with its strong proscription against killing, and began preaching nonviolence. Others see the origins of nonviolence in Indian thought in the example and teachings of Mahatma Gandhi. Gandhi championed nonviolent civil disobedience as a device for pressuring government to change discriminatory laws and ultimately as a means for getting Britain to "quit India"—a goal that was finally achieved in 1947.

One writer, Nirad C. Chaudhuri, has expressed skepticism about India's nonviolent tradition, finding instead considerable martial boasting among both Hindu and Buddhist rulers.[26] The whole of Sanskrit literature is seen as a series of epics exulting war. Nor can the Islamic influence on India during the Mogul empire explain a nonviolent tradition, for Islam is one of the most militant of religions.

India's first prime minister, Jawaharlal Nehru, although clearly influenced by Gandhi, found himself at odds with his mentor on a number of occasions. Nehru, unlike Gandhi, favored higher military spending, greater control over Kashmir, and the establishment of the separate states of India and Pakistan. The intellectual source of Nehru's pacifism, imperfect as it was, may have been derived largely from the writings of Western leftists after World War I, rather than from Indian tradition or the teachings of Gandhi.

Nehru, despite his tendency to moralize to other nations, was not totally averse to the use of the military, as can be seen in the 1961 Indian invasion of Goa. This action enabled India to regain control of territory on the western coast of India that had been ruled by the Portuguese for some four hundred years. But Nehru's predominant commitment to nonviolence may partly explain the unprepared state in which the Indian military found itself during its border war with China in 1962.

With its underground explosion of a nuclear device in 1974, India

---

26. Nirad C. Chauduri, *The Continent of Circe* (Bombay: Jaico, 1965).

has perhaps removed itself from the tradition of nonviolence, although it can be argued that nonviolence has always been more a myth than a reality for Hindu India.

A closely related tradition in Indian foreign policy has been that of nonalignment, which Nehru strongly advocated. His concept of nonalignment was not one of noninvolvement in world affairs, for he played an active role. Nor was it based on neutralism, for Nehru had decided opinions about the behavior of other states that he was not timid about stating publicly. As a result, he often antagonized other states with his moralizing. For Nehru, nonalignment meant abstention from the cold-war alliance systems. He could even accept the notion that alliances were appropriate for some states but not for India. The strategy of nonalignment had some utility for India, as it was able to obtain economic and military assistance from both superpowers and, at the same time, reduce the likelihood of being pulled into cold-war conflicts and military actions.

As a reflection of its nonalignment policy, India has been active in several conferences involving nonaligned states, beginning with the Bandung Conference in 1955. The course set by Nehru has largely been followed by his successors, although some eyebrows were raised when his daughter, Prime Minister Indira Gandhi, signed a Treaty of Peace, Friendship, and Cooperation with the Soviet Union on August 9, 1971. The public commitment to nonalignment, however, was reaffirmed in February 1981, when New Delhi hosted the Nonaligned Foreign Ministers Conference.

THE IRANIAN BELIEF SYSTEM

Both nationalism and religion appear to have had their impact on recent Iranian foreign policy. Nationalistic symbols and images of a great past were particularly emphasized during the tenure of Mohammad Reza Shah Pahlavi, who assumed the title of Shah of Iran after his father abdicated in 1941. Although the Pahlavi dynasty included only the father and the son, it laid claim to the world's oldest continuous monarchy, which had existed for some 2,500 years. In speeches and writings the Shah referred frequently to the founder of the Persian Empire, Cyrus II, who was able to establish Persian rule over a vast region in a single generation. Like his father before him, the Shah assumed ancient titles such as Shahanshah (king of kings), Shadow of the Almighty, Vice-Regent of God, and Center of the Universe. The Shah's personal guard was even called the Ten Thousand Immortals, after the guard of Cyrus.

The Shah's efforts to modernize Iran and to reestablish a "Great Civilization" were modeled on earlier experiences in Persian history. His White Revolution reform movement, which he announced in 1963, was equated with Cyrus' efforts to establish a benevolent monarchy with minimal bloodshed. Inspired by a great past, the Shah hoped to make Iran one of the "five biggest powers" in the world before the turn of the century.[27] To aid in building his new civilization, he began to divert more and more resources to military spending, aided somewhat by Iran's increasing oil revenues and the willingness of the Nixon administration to sell arms to the Shah in significant amounts. Such shipments totaled $6.7 billion during the years 1974–78, making Iran by far the largest recipient of American arms during the period. Iranian military spending more than doubled in terms of constant dollars between the years 1973 and 1976.[28]

The impact of Islam on the foreign policy of the Pahlavis was limited. One authority has suggested that its effect on foreign policy during Reza Shah's tenure (1925 to 1941) was "almost nil."[29] As modernizers, both Pahlavis frequently came into conflict with the mullahs, or Islamic religious leaders. The latter were particularly disturbed by the Shah's assertion in 1976 that "we, the Pahlavi dynasty, nurse no love but that for Iran, no zeal but that for the dignity of Iranians, and recognize no duty but that of serving our state and our nation."[30] Such a viewpoint clearly conflicted with the Muslim concept of *umma* (community of the faithful), which is recognized as taking precedence over national loyalties.

Despite behavior and statements that would seem to be in contradiction with Islamic thought, the Shah attempted on numerous occasions to utilize Islam for his own purposes. He claimed to have had religious visions on at least three occasions, and often asserted that he

---

27. R. K. Karanjia, *The Mind of a Monarch* (London: George Allen and Unwin, 1977), p. 243.

28. U.S. Arms Control and Disarmament Agency, *World Military Expenditures and Arms Transfers, 1969–1978* (Washington: A.C.D.A., 1980), pp. 52 and 160.

29. Rouhallah K. Ramazani, *The Foreign Policy of Iran, 1500–1941* (Charlottsville: University of Virginia Press, 1966), p. 305.

30. William H. Forbis, *Fall of the Peacock Throne* (New York: Harper & Row, 1980).

was guided in his actions by a supreme being. To help shore up his shaky regime in the early years of his rule, the Shah vigorously sought the support of the mullahs. He also used the Islamic connection in his dealings with other states, as in his appeals for Islamic unity to prevent the rupture of relations between Iran and the Arab states.[31] During the period 1969-75, the Shah was accused of using religion to stir up the Shiite majority in Iraq against their leaders, most of whom belonged to the minority Sunni sect.[32]

With the assumption of power by the Ayatollah Ruholla Khomeini in 1979, the powerful role that religious beliefs can play in the making of foreign policy became apparent. Americans were made aware of the impact of religion on political life as they viewed nightly televised scenes of obedient Muslims chanting anti-American and religious slogans outside the American Embassy in Teheran, which had become a prison for about fifty American hostages beginning in November 1979. Subsequent attacks on American facilities by Islamic groups in other countries reminded the world that the political role of Islam was not limited to Iran. With some 750–900 million Muslims in various parts of the world, Islam is likely to remain a potent force in world politics. Its growth is particularly striking in regions like Africa, where some twenty-five years ago only one in four, or perhaps one in three, people were Muslim, whereas by the early 1980s over half are expected to be Muslim.

When political power is assumed by the religious leadership itself, as in the case of Iran under the Ayatollah Khomeini and his Revolutionary Council, it is likely that religion will have its greatest impact on foreign policy. Various other secular leaders have sought to establish their own Islamic republics based on the teachings of the Koran, which is viewed as a complete guide to living. This has been especially true of General Mohammad Zia al-Haq of Pakistan and Libyan leader Muamm el-Qaddafi. The latter has used considerable amounts of Libyan oil revenues to support Islamic causes throughout the world. He claims to have been the first to have helped the Ayatollah Khomeini in his efforts to gain power in Iran and has been reported to have aided Pakistan in its quest for an "Islamic" nuclear bomb.

31.   Shahran Chubin and Sepehr Zabih, *The Foreign Relations of Iran* (Berkeley: University of California Press, 1974), p. 299.

32.   A. I. Dawisha, "The Middle East," in Christopher Clapham, ed., *Foreign Policy in Developing States* (Westmead, England: Saxon House, 1977), p. 55.

There are certain aspects of Islamic thought that may influence the way Iran and other Islamic states behave in terms of foreign policy. The first thing to note about Islam is that it is an activist religion, not passive like Buddhism or Hinduism. As such, it has served to rationalize the use of force in order to spread the faith, beginning with the Prophet Mohammad. Closely related to the notion of using the sword to obtain converts is the concept of holy war, which has been particularly salient in the thinking of the dominant Islamic sect in Iran—the Shiites. Iranian leaders spoke of a holy war in their defense against the Iraqian invasion of 1980, and the concept has been promoted over the years by various leaders of Arab states with respect to the conflict with Israel.

The Islamic belief in martyrdom can also serve the purposes of a leader who is intent on a holy war and having others sacrifice for the cause. This in itself provides an important power base, since morale is so important in determining who is to prevail. Being willing to sacrifice more lives than your adversary can often compensate for a deficiency in number of troops.

When the willingness to sacrifice and even to welcome martyrdom is combined with yet another characteristic of Islamic thought, respect for authority, the power of the leadership is strengthened even more. A particularly strong form of militant Islamism can develop when the religious and political power of the state is concentrated in one man, as in the case of the Ayatollah Khomeini. This is reflected in the constitution drawn up for Iran in late 1979, in which ultimate power is given to the clergy, led by the ayatollah, who is to "safeguard against any deviations by various government organizations from their true Islamic functions and obligations." The ayatollah and his successors can dismiss the president at will, declare war, and select both military and judicial leaders.

Politico-religious leaders like the ayatollah often believe that God is with them and that they have complete understanding and knowledge of the truth. With a highly emotional view of right and wrong, they are hardly likely to bargain in the usual sense of the term. The 444-day standoff over the issue of the American hostages in Iran illustrates the difficulties the true believer often has in making concessions. It might be noted, however, that the rigidity shown by Khomeini not only was a function of his religious beliefs but also may have been explained by his years in exile and isolation, which engendered a deep feeling of resentment against the Shah.

Although the hope of the devout Muslim is for unity among all
Islamic peoples, Islam, like communism, has been subjected to many
schisms and has had to compete with nationalism. The major split
within the Islamic world, as noted earlier, is that between Sunni and
Shiite. The failure of some Islamic states to support the Ayatollah
Khomeini is partially attributable to the fact that Iran is primarily
Shiite, whereas most of the other Moslem states are Sunni. Anwar
Sadat of Egypt, in particular, was so disturbed by the impact of Kho-
meini on the image of Islam that he referred to the Iranian leader
as a lunatic.[33]

In attempting to gain the hearts and minds of the population,
Islam has had stiff competition from nationalism. In states with large
religious minorities, there is likely to be greater emphasis on secular
nationalism, as in the case of Syria, but where religious and national
identities share the same boundaries, efforts toward religious patrio-
tism may be encouraged, as in Saudi Arabia. The devout believer in
Islam, however, is more likely to reject nationalism in favor of Pan
Islam. This is particularly true of those of the Shiite faith, such as
Khomeini, who believe that a descendent of Mohammad will return to
bring justice to the world and unite it under Islam.

Since 1970 a permanent Islamic secretariat has been located in
Jiddah, Saudi Arabia, and there have been periodic meetings of Islamic
foreign ministers. One such meeting was held at Islamabad, Pakistan,
in January 1980 in response to the Soviet incursion into Afghanistan. In
an unprecedented show of unity some thirty-six Islamic states voted to
condemn the Soviet Union for its action in what was among the
strongest, if not the strongest, anti-Soviet statement adopted to date by
any group of third world countries. The divisions among the Islamic
countries at the conference were more demonstrable with respect to
Iran's efforts to condemn the United States for instituting economic
sanctions against Iran. Some felt Iran itself had gone too far in its
insistence upon detaining the hostages.

Despite the attempts at Islamic unity, splits and even wars have
been a recurrent phenomenon among Islamic states, as in the 1980 war
between Iraq and Iran, Libya's border war with Egypt in 1973, and Syria
and Egypt's attack on Jordan in 1970. On one occasion, Syria even inter-

---

33.   Christopher S. Wren, "Cairo Said to Worry About Islam's Image," *New York Times*,
November 12, 1979.

vened in the Lebanese civil war on the side of Christian forces rather than in support of its Islamic brethren.

Whether or not Islamic thought will continue to play an important role on the world stage remains to be seen. Recent events may well be an aberration, and one might anticipate a reemphasis on nationalism from time to time. After all, even in the more militant Islamic states of Iran and Pakistan a more secular approach has been emphasized, as was the case during the Shah's reign and prior to the assumption of power by President Zia. Ayub Kahn, who was president of Pakistan during most of the 1960s, went so far as to declare in a visit to the Middle East that Islam was no longer a solid tie between peoples and that nationalism was the force that triumphed in the world.[34]

THE IMPACT OF NATIONAL BELIEFS

Having identified some of the general functions of national belief systems and examined the role they have played in several states, let us now attempt to evaluate the general impact of these beliefs on foreign-policy behavior. Werner Levi has cited two conditions under which he feels the ideological determinant will be instrumental in shaping foreign-policy choices.[35] The first involves situations in which established values are being challenged, as they are, for example, during revolutionary times, for throughout history people have shown themselves willing to die for an idea. Second, Levi suggests that ideological influences are likely to have a greater impact in political systems that concentrate decision making in a very few individuals. As long as those individuals share a revolutionary ideology, they will be less constrained by other factors in the pursuit of their objectives. Katarina Brodin has suggested that the restraint of ideological doctrine is higher in more developed bureaucratic states than in less bureaucratically developed states.[36] In other words, the ideological system serves as a guide for action for a small and cohesive elite but as a constraint on

34. Arif Hussain, *Pakistan: Its Ideology and Foreign Policy* (London: Frank Cass, 1966), pp. 149–50.

35. Werner Levi, "Ideology, Interests, and Foreign Policy," *International Studies Quarterly*, 14 (March 1970), 1.

36. Katarina Brodin, "Belief Systems, Doctrine, and Foreign Policy," *Cooperation and Conflict*, 7, no. 2 (1972), 109.

the actions of decision makers in highly bureaucraticratized states which tend to have more entrenched myth systems.

In studying negotiating behavior during the Kennedy Round of trade negotiations (1963–67), Gilbert R. Winham has noted yet another situation in which ideology becomes a more salient determinant of foreign policy, namely, when there is high complexity and uncertainty regarding the issues involved.[37] It is at such times that decision makers rely more on their basic belief systems and "gut" reactions to an issue. Complexity increases the probablity that governments will adopt simplified, overriding goals. Had it not been for the predominant ideology favoring trade liberalism, which predisposed the participants to lower trade barriers regardless of whether an identifiable *quid pro quo* was obtained, the Kennedy Round would have been much less successful.

The role ideology plays in foreign policy depends on the specific beliefs inherent in the ideology itself. A democratic ideology will stress the notion of a people determining its own future. Such an emphasis does not preclude the possibility that democratic decision makers will use force in foreign policy, but by and large, more peaceful options allowing democratic choice for others will be selected.

Advocates of messianic ideologies, such as communism, and some religions, such as Islam, are more likely to utilize aggressive means to extend their belief systems. Certain ideologies are even used to rationalize killing and violence as the price a people must pay in order to enjoy a brighter future. The aggressiveness of fascist leaders can be explained in part by fascism's organistic view of the state, which holds that a nation must expand or it will decline. Mussolini declared, in invading Ethiopia, that "fascism sees in the imperialistic spirit a manifestation of its vitality."[38] Similarly, Hitler was concerned with *lebensraum*, or living space.

Different ideologies may also lead to conflict because of the fear that is generated by people who think differently than oneself. The mere existence of another group with a different viewpoint can be threatening because it implies that one's own views may be wrong. The contemporary world has often been described in terms of a struggle between communism and democracy. Although this view is far too

37. Gilbert A. Winham, "Complexity in International Negotiations," in Daniel Druckman, ed., *Negotiation: Social-Psychological Perspectives* (Beverly Hills, Calif.: Sage Publications, 1977), p. 364.

38. Robert W. Tucker, *The Inequality of Nations* (New York: Basic Books, 1977), p. 24.

simplistic, the labels are quickly applied to rally support for one belief system over the other.

Several studies have concluded that ideology is a more important determinant of foreign-policy choices than economic variables, particularly when it comes to issues related to the Soviet threat. In an analysis of Senate voting on the antiballistic missile decision, Bernstein and Anthony found that the individual ideological values held by each senator was a better predictor of that individual's vote on the issue than either party affiliation or whether the senator's state would benefit from increased military spending.[39] Moyer also discovered that ideological orientations were more important than a congressional district's economic dependence on military contracts in explaining congressional voting on military spending,[40] and in surveys of business executives Russett and Hanson found that ideological considerations appeared to take precedence over economic concerns.[41]

Richard Cottam, on the other hand, has suggested that power and security interests are more critical than ideological interests.[42] The United States is far more tolerant of human-rights violations in states that are important to its security interests. In 1977 the Carter administration despite its strong verbal support for human rights and the congressional requirement that aid be denied to violators of such rights, could find only three states to which it would deny aid. These were Argentina, Ethiopia, and Uruguay. Overlooked in the selection process were repressive regimes like those of the Shah in Iran, Park in Korea, and Marcos in the Philippines. The latter states were simply viewed as more important to American security interests. This unequal treatment based on perceived security interests is vividly illustrated by the reaction of the *New York Times* to two successive regimes in Iran. In the mid-1950s, when Mossadegh desperately attempted to stage a plebiscite in an effort to retain power in opposition to pressures from the United States and the United Kingdom, a *Times* editorial labeled it as a totalitarian action; but when his successor, the Shah, did the same

39. Robert A. Bernstein and William W. Anthony, "The ABM Issue in the Senate, 1968–70," *American Political Science Review*, 68 (September 1974), 1198–1206.

40. Wayne Moyer, "House Voting on Defense: An Ideological Explanation," in Bruce M. Russett and Alfred Stepan, eds., *Military Force and American Society* (New York: Harper & Row, 1973), pp. 106– 41.

41. Bruce M. Russett and Elizabeth C. Hanson, *Interest and Ideology: The Foreign Policy Beliefs of American Business* (San Francisco: Freeman, 1975).

42. Richard W. Cottam, *Foreign Policy Motivation* (Pittsburgh, Pa.: University of Pittsburgh Press, 1977), p. 87.

thing some ten years later, gaining over 98 percent of the vote, he was congratulated on his well-deserved popularity.[43] Similarly, during the 1978 riots against the Shah, the United States government maintained its steadfast support of his regime for fear of what the fall of the Shah might mean in terms of possible Soviet influence in the area.

What is perhaps most remarkable about national beliefs is the extreme length to which decision makers will go to retain a given belief when the evidence contradicting it is overwhelming. As suggested, the United States has been guilty of this tendency when it classifies the vilest of dictatorships as part of the "free world"; Hitler's apologists even went so far as to define the Japanese as part of the Aryan race after the Berlin–Tokyo axis was forged; and Soviet leaders have engaged in a considerable amount of ideological gymnastics in order to keep their Marxist beliefs compatible with their real-world needs as they have sought to redefine class enemies whenever temporary alliances were desirable.

CONCLUSION

The national belief system of a state, based on varying ideological beliefs and historical traditions, clearly affects its foreign policy. This impact comes largely from the role beliefs play in influencing perceptions about the world, defining the range of choices, fostering continuity of policy, enabling decision makers to rationalize choices, serving propagandistic purposes, and even enhancing national unity. Ideological beliefs that transcend the nation–state have been less successful, because they compete with nationalistic belief systems (as discussed in the previous chapter).

Our review of the belief systems of specific states has revealed that some states, such as those that subscribe to Marxism, have a more identifiable ideology than others. Yet the evidence is overwhelming that national beliefs and experiences have affected the interpretation of Marxism, and that on the whole Marxism probably has been used more for rationalizing foreign policy decisions than for determining them. Both China and the Soviet Union have become less doctrinaire in their references to Marxist–Leninist thought, and the foreign policies of both

43. Ibid., p. 88.

states should be viewed as much from the perspective of their respective historical experiences as from that of ideology.

A distinctive American belief system seems to have taken shape over the years. It is a product not only of democratic values but also of historical experiences. Two noteworthy trends have evolved: isolationism and liberal interventionism. The extensive overseas involvement of the United States since World War II has led some observers to suggest that a new foreign-policy tradition has been developing based on concern about the communist threat.

The problem of creating a coherent belief system is a serious one for the developing countries. India and Iran have sought to achieve a cohesive belief system on the basis of references to a period of greater glory and also, in the case of India, by attempting to create a new, but not always successful, tradition of nonalignment. The case of Iran illustrates how religion as ideology can affect foreign policy. As a messianic religion, Islam seeks to go beyond the nation–state with its hope of uniting all people. In practice, however, national differences have impeded such a development, and national leaders have more often exploited Islam for their own ends.

Despite the fact that national beliefs anchored in ideology and tradition can be manipulated by decision makers and used to rationalize decisions, such beliefs also influence choice. National beliefs are likely to play a more deterministic role in situations of greater complexity, when information is limited, or where the national interest is not as clearly defined. Several studies undertaken in the United States have suggested that ideological orientations toward the perceived communist threat have taken precedence over the economic interests of various groups, whereas broader ideological values concerned with global human rights have not preempted national security interests.

5

THE
DECISION-MAKING
PROCESS

Foreign policy is affected by much more than simply societal conditions and beliefs, since such policy has to be made within the context of a political structure, which in turn affects the outcome. National myths and societal conditions obviously shape the foreign-policy goals and general view of the world held by the foreign-policy elites of each state, but for goals to be obtained, decisions need to be made on foreign-policy choices. The way decisions are made and which actors participate in the making of those decisions have an important impact on the content of the choices made. In this chapter our focus will be on the domestic political determinants of foreign policy, as we concentrate on the effects of various institutional arrangements and domestic actors on the conduct and content of foreign policy. We shall begin by contrasting the impact of democratic and authoritarian structures on foreign policy.

DEMOCRATIC VERSUS AUTHORITARIAN STRUCTURES

A number of writers have been critical of the more democratic processes in foreign policy, feeling that they are simply not as effective as the more authoritarian or aristocratic forms. For example, the French chronicler of American democracy, Alexis de Tocqueville, argued that the management of foreign affairs requires knowledge, secrecy, judgment, planning and perseverence, qualities in which autocratic systems are superior to democratic ones.[1] In a similar vein, Walter Lippmann criticized democratic foreign policy making on the ground that the mass public is generally uninformed about foreign policy and will always opt for taking the easy way out of situations that demand more assertive action.[2] Raymond Aron has also criticized democratic decision making because of the danger of "conservative paralysis" and a corresponding inability to deal with pressing problems.[3]

If one is looking simply at the effectiveness and efficiency of foreign policy, there are several reasons why one might expect the more authoritarian structure to perform in a superior fashion. In the first place, the more authoritarian structure ought to be able to make more rapid decisions, since by definition it is not as responsive to a mass public and usually involves a smaller number of elites who need to be consulted or at least considered in the decision-making process. Moreover, less intraorganizational bargaining is required, since opposition from within the bureaucracy can be bypassed or crushed.

Second, the effectiveness and efficiency of the authoritarian regime is enhanced by the fact that it can better ensure compliance with its foreign-policy decisions, for there is a clear hierarchy of command, and the punishment for noncompliance may be harsh. The failure of subordinates to carry out President Kennedy's order to remove the intermediate-range ballistic missiles from Turkey some months prior to the Cuban missile crisis in October 1962 would have been less likely in a state like the Soviet Union. This failure in implementation had an adverse impact on American foreign policy, for it provided the Soviet Union with an apparent justification for stationing missiles in Cuba in retaliation for the United States' placement of similar missiles near the borders of the Soviet Union.

Third, the centralization of foreign-policy decision-making power enables the more authoritarian regime to present a united front in its

---

1. Alexis de Tocqueville, *Democracy in America*, vol. 1 (New York: Knopf, 1945), pp. 234–35.

2. Walter Lippmann, *The Public Philosophy* (New York: Mentor, 1955), pp. 23–24.

3. Raymond Aron, *Peace and War: A Theory of International Relations*, trans. Richard Howard and Annette Baker Fox (Garden City, N.Y.: Doubleday, 1966), p. 67.

foreign policy, as all spokesmen are expected to follow the party line. On the other hand, owing to their pluralism democracies often speak with several voices. This lack of unity might be particularly disadvantageous when a state is attempting to present a credible deterrent or even a promise of reward, only to find its position undercut by others in the foreign-policy establishment.

At the same time that an authoritarian regime can guarantee a more consistent external presentation of its foreign-policy views and thereby enhance the credibility of the message it desires to present, such a regime would seem to enjoy a fourth advantage in that it can pursue a more adaptable foreign policy that is responsive to changing conditions. Since, by definition, the authoritarian regime is less constrained by the mass public and the number of different groups it has to satisfy, it need not wait until the mood of either the elite or the public changes to make a shift in policy. President Franklin D. Roosevelt felt quite constrained in his desire to involve the United States in the Allied cause prior to World War II. Various Democratic Presidents who wanted to open up relations with the People's Republic of China prior to President Nixon's initiative in 1972 felt impeded by what they perceived as public opposition to such a move. The Soviet Union has been able to make some radical departures from its foreign-policy course with minimal internal repercussions, as in the case of Khrushchev's announcement of peaceful coexistence with capitalism presented at the Twentieth Party Congress in 1956.

A fifth advantage for the authoritarian regime is the ability to pursue contradictory policies at the same time, if such a strategy is desirable for obtaining a given foreign-policy goal. During his tenure as secretary of defense, James Schlesinger complained that, in contrast to the United States, a "closed society like the Soviet Union has no difficulty in pursuing detente and simultaneously strengthening its defense efforts."[4] Publicizing detente in a more democratic regime, on the other hand, is likely to make it more difficult for the decision makers to convince the public that increased military spending is necessary.

Most of these advantages of authoritarian regimes derive from the alleged freedom of action that such a regime enjoys, given its minimal need to be responsive to the public and other interested groups. But one can perhaps exaggerate the amount of decisional latitude that dictators

---

4. Cited in P. Williams and M. H. Smith, "The Conduct of Foreign Policy in Democratic and Authoritarian States," *Yearbook of World Affairs*, (London: Stevens, 1976), p. 205.

enjoy in the making of foreign policy. Although the foreign-policy elite is smaller in authoritarian regimes like the Soviet Union than in democratic regimes, experts on the subject have increasingly noted that struggles similar to those involved in the political process of a democratic polity are now occurring within the Politburo of the Communist party and among bureaucratic agencies and interest groups.

Perhaps the most serious deficiency for the authoritarian regime lies in the fact that it may be severely hampered when it comes to policy innovation. Since its command and control structure is so centralized and there is a tendency toward paranoia in such structures, authoritarian regimes often generate "yes men" who tend to accept whatever the dictator desires (or whatever the subordinates think the dictator desires). Initiative is lost in such a system, and there is no opportunity to explore a range of options. Reliance on heavily centralized structures with their emphasis on secrecy and isolation from external criticism also destroys the opportunity to tap fresh viewpoints and obtain new information. As a result, there is a tendency for the foreign policy of an authoritarian system to rely extensively on precedent, particularly with respect to minor issues, which the higher-level bureaucracy is too busy to determine and the lower levels of the bureaucracy have no authority to decide. A rigid, rather than flexible, foreign policy tends to be the outcome of such structural arrangements.

Kenneth Waltz has suggested yet other reasons why an authoritarian government does not have a natural advantage over a democratic government in the making of foreign policy. Among these is the argument that authoritarian regimes blind themselves and stultify their successors' development. Moreover, such regimes are not immune to the politics of interest groups and have to worry about the relationship of the policies they espouse to their own political fortunes. Waltz concludes that "democracies less often enjoy the brilliant success that bold acts secretly prepared and ruthlessly executed may bring. With the ground of action more thoroughly prepared and the content of policy more widely debated, they may suffer fewer resounding failures."[5]

The relative efficiency and effectiveness of the two polar types of government have been examined in several empirical studies, but the results are far from conclusive. Frederick S. Butler and Scott Taylor

---

5. Kenneth Waltz, *Foreign Policy and Democratic Politics* (Boston: Little, Brown, 1967), p. 311.

were particularly interested in the effect of various types of decision-making structures on the consistency of foreign policy as well as the ability to adapt to changing conditions.[6] On the basis of data collected by the CREON Project at Ohio State University, which covered some thirty-two nations during the period 1959–68, they found that governments that were categorized as more accountable or democratic showed more consistency in their foreign policy and were better able to adapt to changes in the international system than authoritarian regimes. These patterns persisted when the researchers controlled for the size and level of development of the state, which were also believed to affect consistency and adaptability. It should be noted, however, that although virtually all of the specific indicators were in the predicted direction, only a minority of the relationships were significant at the .05 level.

Similar results were found in yet another CREON study, which discovered that, among several indicators of regime constraints, accountability and constraints arising from legislative and tenure considerations explained the most variation in foreign-policy behavior. The more accountable regimes in the study were found to pursue a more cautious, less expansive, and less dramatic foreign policy than regimes that were less constrained.[7]

In addition to questions of consistency, adaptability, and general efficiency in the making of foreign policy, it has been asserted that authoritarian regimes, which are generally able to keep their negotiating positions secret, can be more effective in international negotiations. In the first place, democratic pressure to publicize positions taken in negotiations may create constraints to making further concessions or force rejection of an agreement in which the public feels that too much was compromised. For example, United States bargaining over the Test Ban Treaty in the early 1960s was adversely affected as domestic enemies of the treaty argued that the United States' movement from asking for twenty on-site inspections to as few as six, in contrast to the Soviet proposals, which ranged between zero and three, represented a

6.   Frederick I. Butler and Scott Taylor, "Toward an Explanation of Consistency and Adaptability in Foreign Policy Behavior: The Role of Political Accountability," paper delivered at the Annual Meeting of the Midwest Political Science Association, Chicago, 1975.

7.   Barbara G. Salmore and Stephen A. Salmore, "Regime Constraints and Foreign Policy Behavior," paper delivered at the Annual Meeting of the American Political Science Association, San Francisco, 1975.

giveaway by the United States. Soviet negotiators might be expected to enjoy greater flexibility in the negotiating process, because they are able to keep their concessionary behavior secret and can be less responsive to public, parliamentary, and interest-group opinion. The same latitude in making conciliatory moves, of course, also enables the Soviet Union to be inflexible and intractable should it decide that such a strategy is in its interest.

A more serious impediment for a democratic state in the pursuit of its negotiating goals lies in the greater possibility that such a state's bargaining strategy will be communicated to the adversary in advance owing to informational leakages. Henry A. Kissinger was particularly disturbed by the 1970 publication by a *Los Angeles Times* reporter of the United States' fallback position in the SALT negotiations.[8] In fact, this incident was largely responsible for Kissinger's support for the wiretapping of some of his colleagues as well as certain reporters.

There is considerable difference of opinion as to whether democracies have been less belligerent than authoritarian regimes in their conduct of foreign policy. Totalitarian states have been viewed as quite willing and able to initiate war for several reasons: they can mobilize great military power; they are predisposed to unlimited action; they are predisposed to engage in war for economic reasons; and they are better able to exploit situations, for they can decide to go to war without the approval of the people.[9] But one can also cite examples that seem to suggest that liberal and democratic governments have frequently been less than peaceloving. Democratic Athens was said to have engaged in more foreign conquests than its authoritarian rival, Sparta, while the Japanese, despite the prevalence of militarism within their society, lived in isolation for many centuries. Similarly, Tito's Yugoslavia and Franco's Spain have been quite peaceful in their external relations, whereas the liberal regimes of Britain and France pursued vigorous imperialist policies, particularly during the nineteenth century. But as Evan Luard reminds us, Britain and France may not have been expansionist because they were democratic. Rising prosperity, commerce, and a sense of adventure may have induced both the development of democracy and the desire for expansion.[10]

8. John Newhouse, *Cold Dawn: The Story of SALT* (New York: Holt, Rinehart and Winston, 1973), p. 6.

9. Alastair Buchan, *War in Modern Society* (New York: Harper and Row, 1968), pp. 21–24.

10. Evan Luard, *Types of International Society* (New York: Free Press, 1976), p. 122.

Empirical studies relating democratic and authoritarian regimes to foreign conflict behavior are divided in their findings. Quincy Wright, in his monumental study of war covering the past six centuries, concluded that democracies are generally slower to move into war, yet once they have done so they fight as vigorously as or more vigorously than authoritarian regimes.[11] Perhaps a major factor in the hesitancy with which a democratic regime goes to war is related to concern that an opposition party will rally the public against the war, particularly if the war threatens to be a long, inconclusive one. Russett and Monsen suggested that a similar pattern exists in business firms, where decision makers in an openly held corporation perceive the shareholders as more ready to punish them for costly failures than to reward them for successful risk taking.[12] They hypothesized, therefore, that more accountable regimes would be less likely to engage in war, particularly since their tenure is likely to be threatened if the war turns into a lengthy one, as in the cases of Korea and Vietnam. Their findings failed to confirm the hypothesis, although the relationship was in the predicted direction.

Several other quantitative studies find that democratic governments are slightly less likely than authoritarian regimes to engage in foreign conflict behavior, as was suggested in the last chapter. These include Haas' analysis of data for a number of states covering the period 1900–1960, two studies by Salmore and Salmore that found that accountable regimes are significantly more cooperative and generally less active in the external arena than less accountable regimes, and Wilkenfeld's reanalysis of dimensionality of nations data, which showed that the decision makers of democratic regimes were less likely to utilize external conflict behavior to divert public attention from domestic problems.[13]

On the other hand, a study of seventy-seven nations for the period 1955–57 found that there was no relationship between degree of to-

11.   Quincy Wright, *A Study of War*, 2nd ed. (Chicago: University of Chicago Press, 1965), p. 842.

12.   Bruce M. Russett and R. Joseph Monsen, "Bureaucracy and Polyarchy as Predictors of Performance: A Cross National Examination," *Comparative Political Studies*, 8 (April 1975), 5–31.

13.   Michael Haas, "Societal Approaches to the Study of War," *Journal of Peace Research* 2, no. 4 (1965), 307–23; Barbara G. Salmore and Stephen R. Salmore, "Political Regimes and Foreign Policy," in Maurice A. East, Stephen A. Salmore, and Charles F. Hermann, eds., *Why Nations Act* (Beverly Hills, Calif.: Sage Publications, 1978), p. 122; Jonathan Wilkenfeld, "Domestic and Foreign Conflict," in Jonathan Wilkenfeld, ed., *Conflict Behavior and Linkage Politics* (New York: David McKay, 1973), pp. 107–23.

talitarianism and foreign conflict behavior.[14] Rosenau and Hoggard, utilizing event data collected from the *New York Times* for the period 1966–69, found a positive relationship between the more democratic governments and their conflict behavior, although the relationship was less potent in predicting conflict behavior than the size of the state and its level of development.[15] Two earlier studies utilizing data from both the nineteenth and twentieth centuries also found that democracies have been neither more peaceful nor more warlike than autocratic states.[16]

The extent to which a democratic polity shows a more peaceful orientation in foreign policy may be due to the fact that democratic values instill a belief in the importance of compromise, which is then applied internationally. The more conciliatory orientation taken by a democracy can be illustrated by a study that found that the more open or democratic political systems tended to utilize international courts or general international organizations more frequently than the more closed systems.[17] Also increasingly removed from the repertoire of the democratic regimes are actions that are perceived as inhumane or immoral by the public. Zbigniew Brzezinski, President Carter's national security adviser, observed that a discrepancy between the external conduct of a democratic society and its internal norms is no longer possible, for mass communication would quickly expose the gulf and undercut the support needed for it to be effective.[18] One need only reflect on the public outcry in the United States in response to the exposure of the Central Intelligence Agency's role in assassination plots against foreign leaders. Similarly, a democratic and liberal orientation is likely to lead one to reject food boycotts and economic block-

14.   Rudolph J. Rummel, "The Relationship Between National Attributes and Foreign Conflict Behavior," in James N. Rosenau, ed., *Quantitative International Politics* (New York: Free Press, 1968), p. 207.

15.   James N. Rosenau and Gary Hoggard, "Foreign Policy Behavior in Dyadic Relationships," in James N. Rosenau, ed., *Comparing Foreign Policies* (Beverly Hills, Calif.: Sage Publications, 1974), pp. 122–23.

16.   Ivor Thomas, "War and its Causes, 1815–1914," in E. F. M. Durbin and George Catlin, eds., *War and Democracy* (London: Routledge and Kegan Paul, 1938); Lewis F. Richardson, *Statistics of Deadly Quarrels* (New York: Quadrangle/The N.Y. Times, 1960), p. 176.

17.   William J. Coplin and J. Martin Rochester, "The Permanent Court of International Justice, the International Court of Justice, the League of Nations, and the United Nations," *American Political Science Review*, 66 (June 1972), 529–50.

18.   Zbigniew Brzezinski, *Between Two Ages* (New York: Viking Press, 1970), p. 255.

ades as a means of foreign policy except in the direst national emergency.

Labels like "authoritarian" and "democratic" are extremely broad terms, which may account for some of the divergences among the empirical findings just cited. To understand the impact of domestic political structures on foreign policy, it becomes necessary to examine those structures in more detail. This we will do by first looking at federal–unitary arrangements and then proceeding to a discussion of the relative contribution to decision making of various executive, legislative, and bureaucratic groups. The role of the military, political parties, interest groups, and public opinion will also be examined.

FEDERAL AND UNITARY STRUCTURES

Decision-making structures have varying degrees of centralization. A basic distinction, for example, has been made between unitary political structures, such as those established in most European states (with the exception of Switzerland), and federal systems, such as those found in Canada, the United States, Nigeria, and Australia. Although the Soviet Union is nominally a federal system, and in 1945 Stalin went so far as to modify the Soviet constitution by giving the sixteen individual republics control over their own foreign policy in the hope that the Soviet Union might obtain sixteen seats in the United Nations, it is clear that the making of Soviet foreign policy is heavily centralized. Stalin's ruse did have some positive reward for the Soviet Union, since it helped produce a compromise at Yalta in which the Soviets were awarded seats for the Ukraine and Byelorussia in addition to their own. Little more could have been expected, for President Franklin D. Roosevelt countered with a request for forty-eight seats for the United States.

In the area of national security policy, the unitary–federal distinction probably does not make much difference, since in both cases defense policy tends to be highly centralized, with the national government enjoying a monopoly on the use of force. Although the national government in the United States provides some recognition of the power of the states by allowing separate national guards for each, these units may be called up at the request of the national government at any time.

It is in the area of commercial and trade policy that the federal structure makes a real difference, as can be seen in Australia and Canada, where the provinces send their own representatives abroad to look after provincial economic interests. Individual American states and even cities have also begun to send trade missions abroad in recent years.

Pressures for provincial participation in foreign affairs will perhaps be greatest in federal systems in which ethnicity makes a critical difference. This is the case in Canada, with its French- and English-speaking provinces. Similarly, in the late 1960s the Ibo tribe of Nigeria attempted unsuccessfully to establish a separate state, Biafra. The federal divisions within Nigeria were so pervasive that the regional governments often made foreign-policy statements that contradicted the position of the central government. For example, in 1965 the northern regional premier declared that "the state of Israel does not exist," despite the fact that Israel had an embassy in Lagos, and in 1961 the eastern regional premier visited New Delhi and expressed support for an Afro-Asian bloc that was opposed by the central government.[19]

Federalism increases opportunities for manipulation of the internal affairs of the federal state. When President Charles de Gaulle visited the French-speaking province of Quebec in 1967 he made strong public statements favoring Quebecian separatism. The United States government also tried to take advantage of the federal system in Brazil while the leftist regime of João Goulart was in power by offering foreign aid directly to the governors of the states whose leaders happened to be political opponents of Goulart.[20]

THE EXECUTIVE

Whether the governmental decision-making process is authoritarian or democratic, federal or unitary, the executive branch of the government and, within it, the top decision maker—the president, prime minister, or chancellor—has assumed the primary role in the making of foreign policy. The superior position of the executive is particularly apparent in more authoritarian regimes, where the par-

19. Olajide Aluko, "Nigeria and Foreign Policy," in Olajide Aluko, ed., *The Foreign Policy of African States* (London: Hodder and Stoughton, 1977), p. 181.

20. Annette Baker Fox, *The Politics of Attraction* (New York: Columbia University Press, 1977), p. 186.

liamentary body, if it exists at all, is reduced to the position of rubber-stamping decisions emanating from the executive rulers, as in the case of the Supreme Soviet in the Soviet Union, which meets for only a few days once a year. But even in more democratic polities a number of factors have intruded to provide the executive and within it its chief executive officer with increased power in the development and execution of foreign policy. Among these factors are:

1. The increased salience of international affairs and the atmosphere of almost perpetual crisis have increased the need for a more centralized foreign-policy process.

2. Improved communications and modern technology have allowed the highest-level decision makers to participate directly in the foreign-policy process through the use of summit meetings and direct communication links via telephone and satellite communication systems. Foreign diplomats have been reduced largely to serving as message carriers as basic policies are developed at higher levels.

3. The executive is able to assert a more prominent role in the conduct of foreign policy because of its superior informational channels. Political, military, and economic officers stationed around the globe report directly to their departmental chiefs in the executive branch. The ability of the legislative branch and other possible claimants to power to obtain independent information is highly circumscribed owing to the much smaller size of their staffs and resources.

4. It is easier for a unitary actor like the chief executive officer to initiate policy than it is for a collective body like a parliament to do so.

5. International problems affect many bureaucratic units, which are often of equal status. Since, in many cases, they cannot overrule each other, decisions tend to be pushed upward to be resolved at the highest executive levels.

6. Tradition has favored a strong executive in the conduct of foreign policy, since national populations habitually have not been very interested or knowledgeable about foreign-policy issues. As a result, parliamentary bodies, which represent those populations, have not been very assertive on foreign-policy issues. This situation may be changing, however, as it becomes more obvious how

much foreign-policy decisions affect the economic well-being of a nation.

Among the various executives in the world, there is considerable variability in the way foreign-policy decisions are made. To a certain extent this might be a function of the particular person occupying the position of chief executive, since some leaders are more interested in foreign affairs than others. But it is also a function of the structure of the decision-making process, as can be seen by contrasting the presidential system of decision making with the parliamentary system.

There appears to be some difference of opinion as to whether the parliamentary system or the presidential system has the advantage in terms of providing a more consistent and coherent foreign policy. Some writers suggest that the presidential system, with its regularly scheduled elections, facilitates continuity of policy. The chief executive of a presidential system like the United States is guaranteed at least four years in office and need not worry about the whims of a parliament, which can vote the executive out of power at any time through a vote of no confidence. Nevertheless, several factors combine to aid the continuity of policy in the parliamentary system. The first of these is the existence of highly disciplined political parties. As long as the prime minister enjoys a parliamentary majority, he or she can count on continued support for executive policies and need not adjust them for want of funding or the refusal of the parliament to ratify and support those policies. Second, parliamentary systems tend to have greater bureaucratic continuity. In a parliamentary system only the cabinet minister tends to be replaced, while the civil servant, who basically runs the department, continues to play that role under a new cabinet head. In a presidential system like the United States, when the administration changes, several layers of each department tend to be replaced with political appointees, a fact that dictates against continuity of policy. It is also common for all ambassadors to submit their resignations when a new president takes office, and many are accommodated. Third, continuity of foreign policy is facilitated in a parliamentary system by the fact that prime ministers are selected only after long service within the major party. For the most part, only those who are capable and willing to reflect the consensus of the ruling party will be able to rise to the top. It would be highly improbable in a parliamentary system for a person to become prime minister by pursuing a campaign like the one conducted by Jimmy Carter in 1976, in which he ran against the Washington establishment. The only exception might be during periods of extreme national emergency, as in the case of party renegade Winston Churchill's assumption of the office following the utter failure of Neville Chamberlain's appeasement policy toward Hitler.

Despite these arguments in favor of parliamentary systems in terms of the continuity of foreign policy, the only empirical study that sheds some light on the subject concluded that during the period 1959–68 the least change in foreign policy between administrations occurred in presidential systems, followed by parliamentary systems, with the most change in policy arising when governments were changed by extralegal means.[21] It may be that the lower continuity score recorded for parliamentary systems is due to the fact that some of the parliamentary governments included in the analysis have been subject to frequent turnover, as in the case of postwar Italy, where the average life of a government has been less than a year.

In comparing Britain with the United States, Kenneth N. Waltz has concluded that the latter, with its presidential system, has certain advantages in developing a creative and adaptable foreign policy.[22] In the British system power is fused in the office of the prime minister and the prime minister's cabinet and party. Given this concentration of power, British governments have tended to avoid problems while seeking broad accommodation. The prime minister tends to be blamed for any failure of foreign policy, which could lead to loss of power through a vote of no confidence, whereas in the American system it is difficult to assess fault, since the American voter does not know which party to blame. The competitive structure between power centers in the American system has, according to Waltz, actually encouraged innovative zeal, vigorous leadership, and willingness to take risks. In contrast, British foreign policy has suffered from painfully slow adjustments to changing conditions, as well as a tendency to react only when a crisis has become severe. Whereas the British style in foreign policy has been one of obscuring issues rather than confronting them, as can be seen by British ambivalence toward the decline of empire and their attitudes toward Europe, the American response has been one of dramatizing differences and confronting problems directly in order to solve them.

21. David J. Rosen, "Leadership Change and Foreign Policy," paper delivered at the American Political Science Association Convention, Chicago, 1974.

22. Waltz, *Foreign Policy and Democratic Politics*, p. 304.

Whether speaking of a presidential or a parliamentary system, the consensus is that the legislative body plays a limited role in the making of foreign policy. Although there is some variation between nations, legislative bodies, at least in democratic societies, often share in the treaty-making process and approve foreign-policy appointments. They usually play an important role in the budgetary process and share in the ultimate decision to engage in war. The trend in most states, as noted earlier, is one of ever-increasing power to the executive at the expense of legislative and other groups.

The preeminent position of the executive branch over the legislative body can be seen most clearly in the United States, where most foreign policy initiatives have arisen within the executive. In an analysis of twenty-two major foreign policy decisions taken between 1930 and 1961, only three were found to have been initiated by Congress, and congressional influence was dominant relative to the executive in only six cases.[23]

The efforts by the United States Senate to help redress that imbalance with the passage of the War Powers Act in 1973 hardly change the situation, for the President still retains the power to use force without congressional approval, as he has done historically in more than one hundred instances. Should Congress disapprove of such use, it may exercise its power over the purse, but once troops are committed, this becomes less feasible.

To suggest that Congress has been systematically excluded by the executive from all foreign-policy arenas is not supported by the data. An examination of all nonclassified American foreign-policy commitments revealed that from 1946 to 1972 there were over six thousand international agreements; of these, 87 percent were statutory and another 6 percent involved treaties, which require senatorial approval. Only 7 percent of the total were in the form of executive agreements, which do not require congressional approval.[24]

Legislative bodies in parliamentary systems would seem to have less impact on foreign policy making than Congress, for in parliamentary systems power tends to be centralized in the hands of the cabinet. Parliamentary sessions in France and Britain, for example, have been little concerned with foreign-policy issues, which were

23. James A. Robinson, *Congress and Foreign Policy-Making*, rev. ed. (Homewood, Ill.: Dorsey Press, 1967), p. 65.

24. Lock Johnson and James M. McCormick, "The Making of International Agreements," *Journal of Politics*, 40 (May 1978), 468–78.

found to constitute less than 5 percent of the debates in the French National Assembly and only about 5 percent of the parliamentary questions posed in the House of Commons.[25] Although in most instances the parliament enjoys the power to demand that the prime minister and his or her foreign-policy cabinet submit to question-and-answer periods, the effect of such activities is limited, particularly if the prime minister enjoys a firm majority. The leverage parliament does have over the executive lies largely in its power to issue a vote of no confidence, but this may result in the dissolution of parliament, forcing its members to run again for office, which they often are not eager to do. Foreign-policy crises have brought down governments in the past, but such changes have often been limited to members of the cabinet while the party alignment remained the same, as in the case of Churchill's replacement of Chamberlain after Munich, and Macmillan's assumption of power from Eden following the Suez crisis in 1956.

THE BUREAUCRACY

Apart from the chief executive and his or her immediate advisers, the executive branch of government is made up of a large number of bureaucrats, many of whom are involved in the making and implementation of foreign policy. Recently there has been great interest in the role such bureaucrats play in the foreign-policy process, as some experts see them as the major architects of foreign policy. Chief executives and their immediate advisers are usually transitory and, as a consequence, must rely heavily on the permanent bureaucracy for advice and cooperation in developing and implementing foreign policy. The bureaucracy has achieved the essential skills for dealing with foreign governments and must of necessity be deferred to in the conduct of such policy. Moreover, the bureaucracy collects the relevant information and makes decisions at each level as to what information and which issues will rise to the next level of decision making.

If expertise, experience, and control of information are not enough to give the bureaucracy a very important role in decision making, bureaucracies also become critical at yet another stage in the process—that of policy implementation. Policies do not implement

25. Simon Serfaty, *France, de Gaulle, and Europe* (Baltimore: Johns Hopkins University Press, 1968), p. 80.

themselves; they must be executed by subordinates. Through strategies of procrastination, not listening to instructions, or even intentional sabotage, many policies remain dormant. The chief decision maker often becomes preoccupied with other issues and as a result fails to monitor adequately the activities of the subordinates charged with executing a given decision. The frustration of President Kennedy upon learning that the presidential order to withdraw missiles from Turkey had not been carried out is merely one example of a fairly common phenomenon. It is not enough simply to issue orders, as President Harry S. Truman noted with regard to his successor, Dwight D. Eisenhower. Truman was speculating on the problems the latter would probably have as President, given Eisenhower's previous experience as chief of staff of the Army, in which compliance with official orders is taken for granted.

Before evaluating the role of the bureaucracy in the making of foreign policy, it might be useful to examine some current trends with respect to that bureaucracy. The most obvious of these is the extensive increase in the size of the bureaucracy concerned with foreign-policy matters. This can be seen in the overwhelming increase in the number of advisers and analysts within the foreign office itself. In the 1870s Bismarck's foreign office had only four permanent officials, roughly the scale at which all foreign offices operated about the turn of the century.[26] As late as 1939 the entire State Department had a smaller staff than is found in a single large American embassy today. Foreign-policy personnel now number in the thousands and are located not only in the State Department but also in the Departments of Defense, Agriculture, Treasury, Labor, and so forth. Even small, developing states have established fairly large foreign-policy bureaucracies. Kwame Nkrumah, for example, celebrated Ghana's independence by opening some seventy embassies, which required extensive staffing both at home and abroad.

A second major trend among foreign-policy bureaucracies has been the substantial increase in the size and significance of non-foreign-office bureaucracies which deal with foreign-policy issues. In some systems defense and economic ministries are challenging the preeminent position of the foreign minister in the making of foreign policy. With increased global economic interaction, economic well-being is no longer determined by activities within the nation, but is

26. Henry A. Kissinger, "Bureaucracy and Policymaking: The Effects of Insiders and Outsiders on the Policy Process," in Morton H. Halperin and Arnold Kanter, eds., *Readings in American Foreign Policy* (Boston: Little, Brown, 1973), p. 88.

very much affected by external economic activities. The power OPEC has to affect national economies throughout the world by manipulating the price of oil is but one illustration of the impact of external economic decisions. One can add governmental policies establishing tariffs, manipulating currency values, dumping products at cheaper prices abroad, and the like, all of which have serious repercussions for economic interests throughout the world. Consequently, in many countries experts on international issues are being added in large numbers in such departments as agriculture, treasury, commerce, and labor in an effort to look after their country's special interests. These experts also become involved in continuing negotiations abroad concerning a whole range of economic concerns. Many such experts are being assigned to overseas embassies on a permanent basis. It has been reported that some twenty-three American agencies are represented in the Tokyo Embassy alone.[27]

The growth in the foreign-policy role of defense ministries has been even more impressive. Traditionally, defense ministries have assumed critical roles in foreign policy during wars and international crises, but continuing national security concerns in the postwar world have increased both the power and size of defense establishments. Never before have military alliances such as NATO and the Warsaw Pact persisted during peacetime to the extent that they have in the post-World War II period. Nor have standing armies been as pervasive as they are today. Given the continuing concern about national security issues and the tremendous resources available to defense departments, they are able to make themselves heard by decision makers on many foreign-policy matters.

A third general trend in bureaucratic decision making is that of increasing specialization. Contemporary foreign policies have become extremely complex, involving political, economic, technological, and cultural factors and hence requiring individuals with specialized skills. Although one still sees some generalists in foreign offices, the vast expansion of the foreign-policy bureaucracy has brought with it experts in issues involving much more than political and diplomatic affairs.

There are those who argue that the trend toward bureaucratization in foreign policy making has some positive aspects and can facilitate a more rational foreign policy. Some of these arguments have been summarized recently by Charles W. Kegley, Jr., and Eugene R. Wittkopf,

27. Eric Clark, *Corps Diplomatique* (London: Allen Lane, 1973), p. 63.

who make the following points in favor of bureaucratic decision making:

1. Administrative efficiency increases because of specialization, which facilitates the division of labor and provides expertise.

2. Bureaucracies are efficient because they are hierarchically structured.

3. Decision-making procedures are established for getting things done. Such procedures reduce the danger of capricious decision-making and facilitate consistency.

4. Bureaucracies keep records and provide a collective memory of past actions, making current problem-solving simpler and hopefully more rational.

5. Bureaucracies emphasize achievement rather than ascriptive criteria in selecting personnel.

6. Similarly, promotions usually are made on the basis of merit and performance.

7. The existence of many agencies in a bureaucratic structure encourages consideration of a wide range of alternatives.[28]

Certain negative aspects of bureaucratic decision making have also been noted by a number of writers, who argue that the existence of large bureaucracies tends to fragment foreign policy. With many different agencies involved, each with its standard ways of doing things as well as its jealousy and suspicion of outsiders, a coherent policy becomes difficult to achieve. Since foreign-policy issues affect many agencies, decision making is likely to proceed at a snail's pace if all relevant agencies are provided with the opportunity to "sign off" on a given report or decision. Failure to consult all the appropriate agencies, on the other hand, can sometimes lead to disastrous results, particularly if such an agency has critical information or can make a difference in the implementation of policy.

The existence of several layers of decision making also means that information relevant to rational decision making can be scattered among many agencies, making a reconstruction of the broader picture almost impossible. Had the various pieces of information relevant to

28. Charles W. Kegley, Jr., and Eugene R. Wittkopf, *American Foreign Policy: Pattern and Process* (New York: St. Martin's Press, 1979), pp. 339–40.

the surprise attack at Pearl Harbor in 1941 been available and coordinated in a single place, that intelligence failure might well have been averted.

Fragmented bureaucratic decision-making structures may also affect how other states relate to a given nation. There often seems to be a preference for dealing with governments that are more centralized, for it adds to the predictability and the speed with which a given transaction can be executed. At the same time, fragmentation can enable external actors to gain bureaucratic allies to influence a given nation's policy or perhaps even to counter a decision that has already been made. Lobbying across national borders often involves bureaucratic-to-bureaucratic interaction in an effort to influence one's own foreign policy as well as that of the other state. For example, American bureaucrats within the Department of Agriculture regularly negotiate levels of grain exports with their counterparts in other countries rather than going through diplomatic channels.[29]

Another problem of bureaucratic decision making that concerns some observers is the fact that the narrow interests of an agency may be substituted for the broader national interest. Agencies are more concerned with their own special interests and tend to view problems only from that narrow perspective. Policies that will contribute to the budgetary prowess and role of the bureau are likely to be favored. Indeed, there will often be considerable mutual back-scratching, as in military budgetary requests, when each service agrees either tacitly or formally not to challenge the pet weapons systems of the other in the expectation that its own projects will not be questioned. Obtaining unbiased recommendations becomes difficult for the central decision maker who is forced to rely on such advice in making foreign-policy choices.

Concern about individual career interests is a problem in any bureaucracy. Such concerns place pressure on the individual not to rock the boat or object to the position of a superior if he or she wants to advance within the bureaucratic structures. Bureaucrats frequently move slowly in uncharted territory until they are able to see which way the wind is blowing. In a much-cited study of the State Department, Chris Argyis has found the department afflicted by too much bureaucratic self-protection, which causes its members to avoid

---

29. Raymond F. Hopkins, "Global Management Networks: The Internationalization of Domestic Bureaucracy," *International Social Science Journal*, 30 (1978), 37.

creative initiatives that might provoke opposition and controversy.[30]

While he was a professor at Harvard University, Henry A. Kissinger wrote articles that were extremely critical of the role of the bureaucracy in the making of foreign policy. He argued that because of the pervasive bureaucratization of American society, leaders have been socialized in the direction of insecurity and orthodoxy, precluding creative responses to the demands of foreign policy.[31] Moreover, he suggested that, owing to the tremendous energy required to prevail in bureaucratic politics, once a decision has been made, flexibility in international affairs is diminished because of the reluctance to hazard a hard-won domestic consensus.

Kissinger's disillusionment with the bureaucracy was shared by his boss, President Nixon, who hired Kissinger first as his national security adviser and then as secretary of state. In the former role Kissinger effectively neutralized the bureaucracy by requiring that all decisions ultimately go through an enlarged National Security Council, which he directed. In turn, Kissinger presented the options directly to Nixon in daily morning meetings, allowing the latter to choose between carefully structured alternatives.

Similar efforts to make the executive less dependent on career bureaucrats can be found in Britain, where the foreign-policy staff of the prime minister's office has been increased substantially as both Labor and Conservative party officials have criticized the imperviousness of the Foreign Office to political direction. Efforts to minimize the role of the foreign-policy bureaucracy can also be seen in developing countries, as is shown in Kwame Nkrumah's efforts during the 1960s to assume the role of sole initiator of foreign policy because of his overwhelming distrust of the bureaucracy.[32] Concern about the role of the bureaucracy in policy making is not limited to the modern age. An eighteenth-century czar suggested that not he but, rather, ten thousand clerks ruled Russia.

Some of the criticism leveled at bureaucratic decision making is really directed at the issue of decision making by committee. Rational and strategic choice becomes particularly difficult when decisions are

---

30. Chris Argyis, *Some Causes of Organizational Ineffectiveness Within the Department of State,* Department of State Publication 8180 (Washington, D.C., January 1967).

31. Henry A. Kissinger, "Domestic Structure and Foreign Policy," in Henry A. Kissinger, ed., *American Foreign Policy* (New York: W. W. Norton, 1969), pp. 11–43.

32. P. J. Boyce, *Foreign Affairs for New States* (New York: St. Martin's Press, 1977), p.

subjected to endless rounds of discussion by committees both within and between various agencies concerned with the making of foreign policy. William Wallace noted the problem with respect to decision making in Britain when he wrote that "extensive use of inter-departmental committees in which civil servants must arrive at a compromise position means that proposals too often lose their bite long before they reach their final form."[33]

Others have objected to committee decision making on the grounds that it reduces individual responsibility and stifles imagination owing to the unending need to compromise. Irving L. Janis has criticized small-group decision making at the highest policy levels for what he views as the tendency to develop "groupthink."[34] After surveying what he considered to be policy failures in such cases as the Bay of Pigs, Korea, and Pearl Harbor, Janis suggested that within each small group making the relevant decisions were "a number of socio-psychological factors which impeded independent critical thinking, resulting in irrational and dehumanizing actions directed against outgroups." Among the symptoms of "groupthink" noted by Janis are the following:

1. An illusion of group invulnerability, which creates excessive optimism and encourages the taking of extreme risks.

2. Collective rationalization to discount warnings that might lead the group to reconsider its assumptions.

3. An unquestioned belief in the group's inherent morality, causing its members to neglect the moral consequences of their acts.

4. Stereotyping of the enemy as evil, weak, or stupid.

5. Pressure against any member who challenges the stereotypes or assumptions of the group.

6. Self-censorship of deviations from apparent group consensus.

7. A shared illusion of unanimity among group members (silence is often viewed as approval).

8. The emergence of self-appointed "mindguards," who seek to make certain that others in the group do not deviate from the established norms and consensus.

---

33. William Wallace, *The Foreign Policy Process in Britain* (London: Royal Institute of International Affairs, 1975), p. 77.

34. Irving L. Janis, *Victims of Groupthink* (Boston: Houghton, Mifflin, 1972).

Janis goes on to argue that these processes are at work not only in authoritarian regimes but in democratic ones as well. Indeed, the greatest risk is seen as arising when the members of a small decision-making group are highly amicable and enjoy high esprit de corps, as each reassures the others that a given course of action is desirable and that no further questions need be asked.

Although there are plausible arguments both supporting and detracting from the utility of bureaucracy in the making of effective and rational foreign policy, the critical issue from the standpoint of foreign-policy determinants remains that of the explanatory accuracy of the bureaucratic model. Several authorities have argued that bureaucracies are not the major architects of foreign policy in most nation-states, and the mere increase in the size and activities of bureaucracies is hardly proof of their impact on final choices. It might be noted that a number of those who subscribe to the bureaucratic model have been involved in governmental politics and as a result follow the natural inclination to view their own role as perhaps more significant than in fact it was. It is somewhat reminiscent of Francis Bacon's fly, which sat on the axletree of the chariot wheel and declared, "What a dust do I raise."

The case studies that have been developed to indicate bureaucratic politics at work tend to focus on issues that have the bureaucracy exercised, neglecting those that enjoy broader consensus or those that are decided at higher levels without much bureaucratic input. By selecting such cases one can document a great deal of bureaucratic bargaining and maneuvering. Whether such activities influenced or determined the final foreign-policy output cannot be ascertained from an analysis of bureaucratic infighting.

The chief decision maker usually has the power to select his or her immediate advisers and to determine which advice will be accepted. The natural tendency is to listen to that advice which will confirm the decision maker's own predispositions. Advisers themselves have a vested interest in providing the kind of information and advice that they believe their boss desires.

The latitude of the chief executive tends to be somewhat less constrained by domestic actors when it comes to foreign policy than in the case of domestic policy. Foreign policy has a less interested public, fewer interest groups, and some decided advantages for the executive in terms of access to and control of the flow of information. The interest of the chief executive in foreign-policy matters will, of course, have a critical impact on the role bureaucratic politics is able to play in foreign policy, being somewhat less important when executive interest is high.

Just as bureaucratic politics may not be the most accurate model for policy planning and decision making, it may not be that critical at the implementation stage, as is sometimes argued. At least one should not assume that any failure in implementation of foreign policy is in itself indicative of bureaucratic politics at work. Bureaucratic inertia or failure to act may be related only to confusion over values that divide the broader society as well as its top leadership. It may be that the chief executive is not interested in seeing a given decision fully implemented, but for either domestic or international reasons may desire to give the impression that something is being done about a given problem.

Since the bureaucratic model is of necessity based largely on anecdotal case studies, there is little systematic empirical research available to help one assess the relative role of the bureaucracy in the making of foreign policy. One of the few such studies that correlates bureaucratic characteristics with foreign-policy behavior as measured by the activities of some thirty-two states during the period 1966–69 concluded that attributes of bureaucracies exert only a modest impact on external conduct.[35] In this study the size of the bureaucracy failed to account for the variation in foreign-policy output, although its age and degree of institutionalization did make some difference in terms of continuity and inertia as younger and less institutionalized bureaucracies tended to demonstrate greater discontinuity and innovation in their foreign policies.

In the empirical study by Russett and Monsen cited in our discussion of open and closed polities, the size of the bureaucracy was found to make some difference in foreign-policy output.[36] In fact, the finding that larger bureaucratic regimes appeared more willing to engage in war than less bureaucratized ones proved to be the only statistically significant finding in the study. Even here one must ask whether this is due to the size of the bureaucracy or to the size of the state, since larger states tend to have larger bureaucracies than smaller ones.

35.   Linda P. Brady and Charles W. Kegley, Jr., "Bureaucratic Determinants of Foreign Policy Behavior: An Events Data Test of the Bureaucratic Politics Paradigm," paper delivered at the Annual Meeting of the International Studies Association, Washington, D.C., 1975.

36.   Russett and Monsen, "Bureaucracy and Polyarchy as Predictors of Performance."

THE MILITARY

Among bureaucratic groups, special attention needs to be paid to the role of the military in the making of foreign policy. As international conflict becomes more ubiquitous and national security is seen as a more critical issue, one might expect to see the military assuming a more prominent role in such policy. Since the military controls the primary means of coercion in a society, it is able in many instances to determine who will rule. One study, focusing on the less developed countries, counted some 128 successful military coups during the period 1945–75. Of the 78 nations surveyed, only 22 had not experienced a coup.[37] Moreover, four countries accounted for 21 percent of the total: Syria had experienced 11 coups; Bolivia, 7; Dahomey, 6; and Haiti, 5. The military coup, however, is not limited to the postwar period; some 115 successful military changes of government occurred in Latin America alone during the nineteenth century.[38]

The role of the military in the making of foreign policy depends on the state's form of government. To illustrate this point, let us examine the patterns of civil–military relations as they occur in a military oligarchy, a totalitarian state, and a democratic society. Illustrations of the military oligarchy are most prevalent among third world nations, as one might guess by the large number of military coups occurring in such nations. But even when the military is in control, it frequently has to rely on civilian expertise; the military leadership often turns to political parties and bureaucrats to fill roles in which it lacks expertise.[39]

One factor that has enhanced the role of the military in many developing countries has been military training and assistance by the United States. Important organizational skills are derived from such training, along with military resources that increase the prospects of political control. It has even been suggested that Mexico has remained more aloof from the United States than many other Latin American

---

37. Morris Janowitz, *Military Institutions and Coercion in the Developing Nations* (Chicago: University of Chicago Press, 1977), p. 51.

38. Claude E. Welch, Jr., "Civilian Control of the Military: Myth and Reality," in Claude E. Welch, Jr., ed., *Civilian Control of the Military: Theory and Cases from Developing Countries* (Albany: State University of New York Press, 1976), p. 17.

39. Henry Bienen and David Morell, "Transition from Military Rule: Thailand's Experience," in Catherine M. Kelleher, ed., *Political-Military Systems* (Beverly Hills, Calif.: Sage Publications, 1974), p. 19.

states for fear that alliance or cooperation with the United States would threaten civilian rule in that country.[40]

The existence of military oligarchies may affect relations with other countries, as one might expect military oligarchies to relate better to each other than to civilian regimes. However, the United States, for one, has often had more cordial relations with military regimes in the third world than with civilian governments. Official American relations with Brazil have tended to improve when the military was in the ascendance rather than when leftist regimes like those of Quadros and Goulart were in power.[41] Business interests in the United States have also preferred to deal with centralized military regimes, for they are more predictable and stable.

Civil–military relations are perhaps most sensitive in totalitarian regimes. Since the governments of such states rely heavily on force and terror to control their populations, such governments need to be concerned that this force not be used against themselves. Whenever a national emergency requires that the military assume a preeminent position, considerable effort will be made to place the military under civilian control or, at a minimum, to reduce its power once the crisis has passed. In the Soviet Union, political commissars have on occasion been appointed to oversee military units, most often to the detriment of an effective fighting unit. In the People's Republic of China, Mao Zedong found it necessary to bring in the military to check the excesses of the Red Guard during the Great Cultural Revolution of 1966–69. This provided the People's Liberation Army (PLA) with increased power, which was subsequently diminished after a suspicious air crash resulted in the death of PLA leader Lin Biao in 1971. By 1974 the Chinese Communist party had regained its pre-Cultural Revolution primacy. Despite the bureaucratic ascendancy of the military during and immediately after the Great Cultural Revolution, there was no major change in Chinese foreign policy "that correlated in any discernible way with changes in the bureaucratic balance of power."[42]

Some observers have assumed that the rapid military progress made by the Soviet Union in recent years, to the point where it now

40. Fox, The Politics of Attraction, p. 71.

41. Ibid.

42. Allen S. Whiting, The Chinese Calculation of Deterrence (Ann Arbor: University of Michigan Press, 1975), p. 226.

equals (or, it is sometimes claimed, surpasses) American strategic capability, is indicative of the vast increase in the influence of the Soviet military. Analysts also have noted the promotion of Marshal Andrei Grechko to full Politburo membership in 1973 as further evidence of the increasing power of the military. Although Marshal Georgi Zhukov held a similar position briefly in 1957, his appointment seemed designed to exploit the popularity of a retired military officer rather than to give any real power to the military. As a pressure group, however, the military may be in a less advantageous position in a totalitarian state than in a democracy in terms of ability to influence governmental policy. This is so because of the lack of opportunity in the former to develop outside constituencies composed of economic interest groups or the public.

To assert that the recent militancy of the Soviet Union is a result of the increased political power of the military may not be entirely accurate. Such policies would, at a minimum, require the acquiescence of the top party leadership. It may be that there is little difference of opinion between the military and party hierarchies on national security issues. The military leadership, after all, is coopted by the party leadership and serves at its pleasure. It is therefore likely to mirror the policy preferences of the latter. Extensive investigations using content analysis have shown that "there are no essential differences between the political comments of the military and civilian politicians."[43]

After reviewing a number of foreign-policy decisions, Malcom Mackintosh concluded that when a foreign policy adopted by the leadership coincided with the views of the military, it was difficult to distinguish whether the policy was initiated by the party or the military, and that when their views differed, there was nothing to suggest any diminution of the party's primacy in foreign policy.[44] It has also been noted that to the extent that there is division between the military and civilian viewpoints, it is largely intrainstitutional, with the lower levels of the bureaucracy opposing the higher levels.[45]

43.   Egbert Jahn, "Four Approaches to the Analysis of Soviet Foreign Policy," in Egbert Jahn, ed., *Soviet Foreign Policy: Its Social and Economic Conditions* (New York: St. Martin's Press, 1978), p. 21.

44.   Malcom MacKintosh, "The Soviet Military: Influence on Foreign Policy," *Problems of Communism*, 22 (September-October 1973), 10–11.

45.   William E. Odom, "The Party–Military Connection: A Critique." in Dale R. Herspring and Ivan Volgyes, eds., *Civil–Military Relations in Communist Systems* (Boulder, Col.: Westview Press, 1978), pp. 35–36.

The democratic regime is concerned primarily with retaining civilian control over the military. In the United States the President is the commander-in-chief. President Lincoln was very much within his constitutional authority when he dismissed General McClellan during the Civil War, just as Truman was in firing MacArthur almost a century later. Other democratic governments have had military challenges on occasion, as in the case of a 1944 crisis in Canada during which members of the High Command came close to resigning rather than accept the policy of the government.

In Germany and Japan the military appears to be limited in its ability to influence foreign policy, despite its previous high standing in those societies. Part of this is due to the disillusionment produced by defeat and destruction during World War II. As these experiences become more remote, public opinion appears to be less condemnatory. Nevertheless, both states are still restricted in terms of their military policy, as Germany may not produce nuclear or chemical and biological weapons and Japan is limited from developing an offensive military capability by Article 9 of its American-dictated constitution.

Civilian control of the military in democratic societies is guaranteed largely by tradition. Structural lines of authority generally place military leaders under civilian defense ministries. The fact that there are several services, often competing with each other for resources and with conflicting views of the world, also provides security for the civilian regime, which would be most vulnerable to a unified military command that was vehemently opposed to its policies.

It appears that when intense conflict arises between civilian and military decision makers, the latter tend to prevail. An analysis of sixty-two such cases involving France, Germany, Japan, and the United States from the late nineteenth century to the mid-twentieth century revealed that the outcome tended to favor the military.[46] Moreover, control by the military was greater in situations in which mass public participation was restricted.

Although civilian rule has predominated in democratic polities and is likely to continue to do so, some observers, such as Harold Lasswell, have been concerned about the threat of the rise of a garrison

---

46. Richard W. Benjamin and Lewis J. Edinger, "Conditions for Military Control over Foreign Policy Decisions in Major States," *Journal of Conflict Resolution*, 15 (March 1971), 5–31.

state.[47] The danger is that as appeals to national security are made in an age of world insecurity, which has certainly been characteristic of the post-1945 era, major nations will become less democratic and more militaristic in their value orientation. The United States suffered through the communist witch hunts of the McCarthy period in the 1950s, and the Soviet Union's incursion into Afghanistan may lead to similar paranoid thinking in the 1980s.

Regimes in which the military is prominent tend to be fairly conservative and unwilling to take risks in foreign-policy matters. The military is very aware of what death and destruction mean. It also is hesitant to use its most sophisticated weaponry, recognizing that such use will lead to the destruction of extremely high-priced weapons. The expensive dreadnoughts built in the early 1900s became largely showpieces of the state of the art in shipbuilding—few politicians or military officers wanted to risk their destruction.

It may be inappropriate to regard the military as any more militant than any other group in a given society, for its personnel usually reflect the broader society from which they are drawn. In the modern military, large numbers of recruits are involved in jobs that are not strictly military and have civilian counterparts, such as engineer, clerk, and cook. In the mid-nineteenth century only about 10 percent of the specialties within the military had civilian equivalents, but today this figure may well be approaching 80 percent.[48] In China the People's Liberation Army actually performs a number of civilian tasks involving agricultural production, mass mobilization efforts, and various administrative responsibilities.

Support for high defense spending is not limited to military interests; economic interests and the public have also pressed for higher military budgets, as will be shown in Chapter 6 when we discuss the role played by the military–industrial complex. Nevertheless, the evidence suggests that military regimes tend to spend more for defense than civilian regimes. A quantitative study of Latin American regimes covering the period 1950–67 found that civilian regimes generally spent less for defense and more on welfare than military regimes.[49] The

---

47.   Harold Lasswell, "The Garrison State," *American Journal of Sociology*, 46 (January 1941), 455–68.

48.   Odom, "The Party–Military Connection: A Critique," p. 35.

49.   Phil C. Schmitter, "Military Intervention, Political Competitiveness and Public Policy in Latin America, 1950–67," in Morris Janowitz and Jacques Van Doorn, eds., *On Military Intervention*, (Rotterdam: Rotterdam University Press, 1971), p. 454.

tendency for military regimes to spend more on defense was also confirmed in a global examination of some 150 countries conducted by Tong-Whan Park and Faris Abolfathi circa 1970.[50] Health and education budgets were found to have decreased as military influence increased.

Although military regimes may budget more for military efforts, they have not engaged in extensive international conflict, at least in Latin America. One authority noted that during the present century, apart from the Salvador–Honduras football war, the Chaco War, and the Leticia border dispute between Peru and Colombia, there have not been any serious military confrontations between states within the region.[51] It has even been suggested that the large number of Latin American military coups may have been due to the existence of a fairly benign international environment in which the military is confined to dull, repetitive garrison duty. Involvement in external wars might have kept the armed forces out of the domestic arena, whereas enforced idleness led them to engage in domestic plotting.[52]

POLITICAL PARTIES AND INTEREST GROUPS

Nongovernmental groups may also affect foreign-policy choices, although their distance from the central decision makers tends to mute their impact. Perhaps the most important of these are political parties and interest groups, which are formed to aggregate and articulate the interests of the broader society. In the area of foreign policy, their impact is likely to be less than that of the executive and its bureaucracy. Looking first at political parties, we find that their structures and functions vary widely from one polity to another. The party plays a particularly significant role in authoritarian regimes, which usually are organized around a one-party system. In the Soviet Union and the People's Republic of China, one's position in the Communist party is more important than one's governmental role. At various times in Soviet history, the person occupying the highest position in the

50.   Cited in Sam Sarkesian, "A Political Perspective on Military Power in Developing Areas," in Sheldon W. Simon, ed., *The Military and Security in the Third World*, (Boulder, Col.: Westview Press, 1978), p. 9.

51.   Edy Kaufman, "Latin America," in Christopher Clapham, ed., *Foreign Policy Making in Developing States* (Westmead, England: Saxon House, 1977), p. 135.

52.   Welch, "Civilian Control of the Military: Myth and Reality," p. 26.

party's presidium has not held the chief governmental position, that of prime minister. Instead, these roles have been separated, as they were between Khrushchev and Bulganin and Brezhnev and Kosygin, with the latter member of each pair serving as prime minister.

A number of less developed states are also structured around a one-party system. Abdul Nasser, the former president of Egypt, objected to the creation of a multiparty system out of fear that it would involve a continual struggle between parties supported by outside nations.[53] But parties in less developed states, even states dominated by a single-party system, tend to be weak and ineffectual. Charismatic leaders or military oligarchies are more likely to provide what ever stability is obtainable. A smoothly functioning competitive political party system is a rarity among third world states and, as a result, can hardly be viewed as a major factor in foreign policy.

Among democratic polities, one might suggest that the larger the legislative majority enjoyed by a political party, the more likely it is to have an impact on foreign policy. Since 1951 foreign policy in Japan has been dominated for the most part by the Liberal-Democratic party (LDP), which was able to force ratification of the renewal of the security treaty with the United States in 1960 while the opposition parties were absent from the Diet. Japan does suffer from considerable factionalism within the LDP, and the majority position of the Liberal Democrats in the Diet is no longer taken for granted.

Parties within a multiparty system, which by definition consists of a number of small parties, tend to have less of an impact on foreign policy. Because of ever-changing coalitions, both governments and parties often have some difficulty ruling, and the bureaucracy is more likely to assume an important role in such a system. Nevertheless, during the Fourth Republic of France, despite rotating governments some semblance of stability in foreign policy was achieved because Robert Schuman was able to retain the position of foreign minister during several successive governments.

In the United States the leverage of political parties in the foreign policy area has been limited by their extreme decentralization. The leadership seems incapable of controlling its membership. Even with large majorities of his own party members in Congress, President Carter found it difficult to generate support for a number of foreign-policy

53. Miles Copeland, *The Game of Nations* (New York: Simon and Schuster, 1969), p. 127.

programs. Liberals and conservatives on foreign-policy issues are found in both political parties in the United States.

The lack of polarization on foreign-policy issues among American political parties helps explain why there are few dramatic shifts in foreign policy when one party replaces another in Congress. American foreign policy has been remarkably consistent over the entire postwar period, despite party platforms that threaten change. Although the Republican party pressed for liberation of Eastern Europe in the early 1950s, in 1956, when the opportunity arose to support the rebellious, anti-Soviet Nagy government in Hungary, the Eisenhower administration failed to act.

Even in polities with more differentiated political parties, changes often are not as drastic as predicted. Britain's Labor party campaigned vigorously on an anti-Common Market platform, but its position changed after its leaders gained office. Failure to deliver on promises is related to the fact that there are a number of international constraints that limit foreign-policy choices, as will be shown in Chapter 8.

Another nongovernmental group that can influence foreign policy, but seems to have even less of an impact than political parties, is the interest group. Although an interest group may sometimes take on the characteristics of a political party by running its own candidates, as various agricultural and business groups have done, especially in multiparty states, more often their activities are limited to attempting to influence the foreign-policy process by lobbying before executive and legislative groups and engaging in information campaigns among the mass public.

Various types of interest groups are involved in lobbying activities on foreign-policy issues. Economic interest groups, such as those representing labor, business, and agriculture, are especially concerned about trade and tariffs; ethnic groups may become concerned about relations with countries whose people share the same ethnic background; and some groups may even be organized explicitly to affect foreign-policy choices—examples are World Federalists, Associations for the United Nations, and human rights organizations.

The impact of interest groups on foreign-policy decision making is extremely limited, since such groups have no authoritative position in the foreign-policy process. They must be able to persuade government officials of the appropriateness of their viewpoints. This is often difficult to do, particularly with respect to general political and military policy, for interest groups cannot demonstrate that they as a group have an overriding interest in an issue apart from that of the nation as a whole. Even where an overriding interest can be shown, as in the case of economic interest groups and tariff policy, their power may be diluted because not all economic interest groups view the issues in the same way. Some favor freer trade, whereas others may prefer protectionism, depending on their specific competitive circumstances.

Among the more salient interest groups affecting foreign policy are those that have special links to foreign nations through a common ethnicity or ideology; they form what has been called a *linkage group* between nations that may facilitate reciprocal influence. Linkage groups have been known to influence governments in the direction of the policy preferred by the foreign government with which a group identifies. One study based on the voting behavior of twenty-five African states in the United Nations found a statistically significant relationship between states with highly active communist groups and their similarity to Soviet voting behavior.[54] Foreign-policy decisions may be made explicitly to placate domestic linkage groups, as in the case of the Malaysian government's decision to recognize the People's Republic of China in order to obtain the support of the large numbers of Malaysian Chinese who favored such an action.[55] Politicians in the United States have often sought domestic political support from Eastern European refugees by endorsing Captive Nations Week. Speeches favoring a united Ireland or opposing Fidel Castro can be expected to gain support among Irish and Cuban voters, respectively. More often than not, such ethnic groups have been exploited by politicians for their own ends rather than being able to manipulate the political process themselves.

Although linkage groups may be exploited for political purposes, their existence may create some problems both domestically and internationally. The large number of overseas Chinese in Southeast Asia places serious strains on relations between those nations and the People's Republic of China. Similarly, India has been concerned about Pakistan's ability to influence the millions of Muslims residing within Indian borders, and the Philippines has been sensitive to the encouragement and aid provided by Islamic states to Philippine Muslim

---

54. Dan C. Heldman, "Soviet Relations with the Developing States: An Application of Correlation Analysis," in Roger E. Kanet, ed., *The Behavioral Revolution and Communist Studies* (New York: Free Press, 1971), pp. 339–63.

55. Michael Leifer, "South-East Asia," in Clapham, *Foreign Policy Making in Developing States*, p. 30.

minorities in support of the latter's revolutionary goals. Suspicion is likely to be aroused, however, regardless of whether or not the linkage state does anything to encourage its linkage groups, and in order to reassure another state it might be necessary actively to discourage linkage groups located in foreign countries.

Interest groups have an impact only on issues that are allowed to gestate over time. As a result, their role during crises is considerably limited. One of the more interesting illustrations of pressure groups attempting to influence a foreign-policy issue involved efforts to obtain a favorable Senate vote in support of ratification of the SALT II Treaty. Dozens of pro-SALT interest groups were organized under the rubric of Americans for SALT. Opposing the treaty were groups like the Committee on the Present Danger and the National Strategy Information Center. Extensive lobbying among senators and their staffs, as well as elaborate public information campaigns, were organized both for and against the treaty.

The flow of information and pressure, however, was not unidirectional. The White House, aided by the Arms Control and Disarmament Agency and the State Department, provided considerable assistance to the public education efforts of the pro-SALT groups. Literature, spokespersons, mailing lists, and the like were shared with these groups in an effort to gain public acceptance for the treaty. All such efforts were to little avail, however, for the treaty was never brought up for a vote.

Generally, interest groups cannot compete effectively against governmental groups, for the latter have the advantage of authoritative information. Governmental officials can determine which information and how much of it will be made available to the public. As a result, it is more likely that the government will be able to manipulate and influence the interest group than the reverse. On the whole, interest groups have had a limited impact on foreign policy even in democratic polities, but since such groups are at least organized, it might be suggested that they have a greater impact on foreign policy than the mass public, to which we now turn our attention.

PUBLIC OPINION

One of the criticisms of democratic foreign-policy decision making noted earlier is the notion that an uninformed public has too much influence on foreign-policy matters, which results in unwise decisions. Although research on the precise linkage between public opinion and foreign policy is limited, as most such research surveys only public attitudes toward various international issues, we can make some generalizations about the role of public opinion. Among these are the following:

1.   The mass public is generally ill informed and uninterested in foreign-policy matters.

The consensus of experts is fairly high regarding the general lack of knowledge about international affairs among the mass public, which is generally viewed as consisting of 75 to 90 percent of the adult population even in an advanced state like the United States. To illustrate the basically ill-informed quality of the American public, a survey conducted in the late spring of 1964 found that 25 percent of the population was unaware that China was ruled by a communist government and a like number was not even cognizant of the fact that the United States was fighting in Vietnam at the time.[56] Readership of world news stories tends to be limited among the mass public, and with respect to news, domestic affairs tend to receive the most attention. Hadley Cantril has reported that even at the height of World War II the public's interest in domestic affairs was almost twice as intense as its interest in foreign affairs.[57]

This lack of information and interest is not confined to the American public by any means. A 1967 survey conducted in Japan, which has one of the world's highest literacy rates and newspaper readerships, showed that one out of three respondents did not know about the existence of a communist government in China, while only half knew that China at the time had no diplomatic relations with Japan and that China was not a member of the United Nations at the time.[58] Interest in international affairs also appears to be limited, as another study found 27.1 percent of the West Germans "very interested in international affairs" as compared to 16.9 percent of the English, 11.9 percent of the French, 8.7 percent of the Japanese, and 4.4 percent of the Italians.[59]

56.   Lloyd A. Free and Hadley Cantril, *The Political Beliefs of Americans* (New York: Simon and Schuster, 1968), p. 59.

57.   Cited in Ralph B. Levering, *The Public and American Foreign Policy, 1918–78* (New York: William Morrow, 1978), p. 32.

58.   Chae-Jin Lee, *Japan Faces China* (Baltimore: Johns Hopkins Press, 1976), p. 9.

59.   Daniel H. Willich, "Public Interest in International Affairs," *Social Science Quarterly,* 50 (September 1969), 274.

2. Decision makers have considerable latitude in the making of foreign policy.

Empirical studies of the impact of public opinion on foreign policy, albeit few and based primarily on data from the United States, appear to be in agreement that decision makers have a considerable degree of latitude within which to operate. A cross-national study by Martin Abravanel and Barry B. Hughes concluded that in the short run, "changes in attitudes and shifts in policy are correlated at a relatively low level. And to the degree that a short-term relationship can be found, it is the public that responds to governmental action rather than vice versa."[60] This was particularly true for France and Great Britain, where the relationship between foreign-policy changes and subsequent changes in public opinion showed positive correlations of .47 and .41, respectively. The results were not significant for West Germany and Italy, which lack long-term democratic traditions. The pattern for the United States has tended to follow that of Britain and France.

The latitude of decision makers is especially high in times of crisis, since the public tends to rally around the flag at such times. Presidential popularity appears to peak with crises whether governmental policies are effective or not. Kennedy's popularity rose from 61 to 74 percent after the Cuban missile crisis, but it stood at an even higher 85 percent following the Bay of Pigs fiasco in 1961; Truman had an impressive 81 percent of the public supporting his commitment to South Korea in 1950, despite his low popularity at the time, and Nixon's escalation of the Vietnam War in 1972 also enhanced his public support despite the increasing opposition to that war.[61] But the most dramatic rise in presidential support occurred in response to the Iranian seizure of the United States Embassy in Teheran in November 1979. As a result of the crisis, President Carter's popularity rating rose from 32 to 61 percent in one month—the most dramatic turnaround in a President's rating since Gallup polling began in the late 1930s.

Public-opinion polls have generally shown that the American public favors an active role in foreign policy, despite periodic frus-

60.   Martin Abravanel and Barry B. Hughes, "The Relationship Between Public Opinion and Governmental Foreign Policy: A Cross-National Study," in Patrick J. McGowan, ed., *Sage International Yearbook of Foreign Policy Studies*, vol. 1 (Beverly Hills, Calif.: Sage Publications, 1973), p. 126.

61.   Barry B. Hughes, *The Domestic Context of American Foreign Policy* (San Francisco: W. H. Freeman, 1978), pp. 38–39.

trations like Korea and Vietnam. Some 60 to 80 percent of the respondents in public-opinion polls conducted from 1949 through 1969 have favored an active role for American foreign policy. Even after the disaster in Vietnam, the figure still remained at 66 percent of the respondents surveyed in 1974.[62] With such a high level of support, few decision makers need to be concerned about taking decisive action in foreign affairs. Public opinion seems to be far from the millstone around the necks of decision makers portrayed by Walter Lippmann; it is more likely to be highly supportive.

If there is a lack of congruence between governmental preferences and public opinion, it is generally the former that tend to prevail. According to studies by Warren E. Miller and Donald E. Stokes, United States legislators appear not to be overly responsive to public preferences, particularly in the foreign-policy area.[63] The 1978 Senate vote on the Panama Canal Treaties, which call for eventual reversion of the canal to Panama, is indicative of congressional efforts to place perceived national interests above constituency interest. Similarly, interviews conducted among State Department officials have documented how little such officials perceive themselves to be influenced by public opinion.[64] Former Secretary of State Dean Rusk made it clear to his subordinates that he did not want them to take domestic opinion into account in making their decisions.

If public opinion has had a minimal impact on American foreign policy, it seems to have had even less effect on the foreign policies of other democratic states. Donald C. Hellmann writes that decision makers in Japan "have paid little attention to public opinion on major foreign-policy issues."[65] Despite overwhelming opposition in the press and among the public to the United States–Japanese Security Treaty of 1960, in which some ten million persons signed a petition opposing the treaty, the Japanese Diet supported its ratification. Absent from that vote as a result of their boycott of the Diet, however, were all of the members of Japan's second-largest party, the Japanese Socialist party. Similarly, Kenneth Younger, who has served as minister of state for

62. Ibid., p. 31.

63. Warren E. Miller and Donald E. Stokes, "Constituency Influence in Congress," *American Political Science Review*, 57 (March 1963), 45–56.

64. Bernard C. Cohen, *The Public's Impact on Foreign Policy* (Boston: Little, Brown, 1973), pp. 58–70.

65. Donald C. Hellmann, *Japanese Foreign Policy and Domestic Politics* (Berkeley: University of California Press, 1969), p. 15.

foreign affairs in the United Kingdom, has written that he could think of no occasion when he or his superiors "had been greatly affected by public opinion in reaching important decisions."[66] Public opinion in Britain was overwhelmingly against British membership in the Common Market, yet the government still chose to join, and despite strong public opposition to *Ost-Politik,* the Brandt government proceeded toward normalizing West German relations with the Soviet Union and Eastern Europe.

Although mass public opinion can hardly be viewed as a significant input into the foreign policy of authoritarian states, considerable energy is expended in such states to educate—or, perhaps more accurately, indoctrinate—the mass public on foreign-policy issues. Mao Zedong was particularly anxious to make foreign relations part of the daily life of the Chinese citizen through the use of slogans, propaganda campaigns, and mass demonstrations. In fact, the *People's Daily* devotes a higher percentage of space to foreign affairs than any other mass circulation newspaper in the world.[67]

In developing states the role of public opinion in the foreign-policy process has also been limited. This is partially due to the seriously uniformed nature of the public and the high level of illiteracy in such polities. It probably also has something to do with a general lack of concern about such issues among the mass public, whose loyalties and identifications are more likely to be directed toward the local level and who are more concerned about survival than grand politics. This general lack of knowledge and interest on the part of the public has meant, for example, that political parties in Latin America seldom campaign or pursue consistent positions on international issues, and the same can be said for most African and Asian polities.

Despite considerable evidence that the general public exerts very little influence on daily foreign-policy decisions, there is still a pervasive belief that public opinion sets general limits beyond which decision makers may not go. The refusal of the United States to intervene in Vietnam after the French defeat at Diem Bien Phu in 1954 was strongly influenced by public concern about becoming involved in a major land war in Asia, particularly after the recent bitter experience of Korea. Similarly, the frustration surrounding the Vietnam fiasco made Con-

66.   Cited in Leon D. Epstein, "British Foreign Policy," in Roy C. Macridis, ed., *Foreign Policy in World Politics,* 5th ed. (Englewood Cliffs, N.J.: Prentice-Hall, 1976), p. 53.

67.   Allen S. Whiting and Robert F. Dernberger, *China's Future: Foreign Policy and Economic Development in the Post-Mao Era* (New York: McGraw-Hill, 1977), p. 40.

gress and the American public reticent to support American involvement in the Angolan crisis in 1975, despite the urgings of President Ford and Secretary of State Kissinger. The public's mood appears to change over time, however, as such unpopular events become more remote.

3.   Public opinion is easily manipulable.

Those who are concerned about public opinion swinging widely and adventuristically and thus affecting foreign policy adversely might find some solace in the fact that mass opinion is easily manipulated and can be marshaled to serve the interests of those in power even in the most democratic of polities. This position has been cogently argued in William Lederer's *Nation of Sheep*, which outlines a number of reasons why the democratic press tends to report what the national elites desire.[68] Among these are the desire of reporters to retain access to their sources of information, which may be possible only if they report stories that are favorable to government officials; reliance on official press releases owing to lack of time or resources to investigate a story in person; the sparse geographic distribution of reporters throughout the world, so that one reporter often covers several countries; and the fact that much information about foreign-policy issues is classified.

It may well be that the ability to manipulate public opinion is greater in a democratic polity than in an authoritarian polity because defense mechanisms have been built up in the latter to protect the individual against manipulation. This can be seen in the fact that it was primarily young people who revolted against communism in Hungary in 1956—presumably those who had been fed the party line and were not familiar with the more democratic days prior to the invasion of Hitler and the subsequent establishment of a Soviet-dominated government. The elder Hungarians, whose early education had not been manipulated to the same extent, tended to sit on the sidelines and to accept the party position. Evidence suggesting the tendency of those who are provided with a single viewpoint to protect themselves against what are perceived as propagandistic messages is found in various social-psychological experiments involving such things as efforts to get military recruits to practice better dental hygiene. Respondents who are

68.   William Lederer, *A Nation of Sheep* (New York: W. W. Norton, 1961).

given two views of the subject tend to accept the message more readily than those who are presented with only one side of the issue and consequently feel manipulated.

Political elites may attempt to manipulate public opinion for both domestic and international purposes. Just as political decision makers have been known to use external conflict to divert attention from internal problems, they have sought to demonstrate their peacemaking capabilities in the international arena in order to bolster sagging public support. Both Presidents Nixon and Carter actively sought to play a peacemaking role while in office. The former sought to counter his deteriorating position at the time of Watergate by attempting to negotiate a SALT II agreement and to hold a summit conference with the Soviet Union in 1974. Many have speculated that Carter gambled on success in negotiations with Menachem Begin and Anwar Sadat at Camp David in September 1978 as a way of improving his standing with the public, which was lower than that of any President since Harry S. Truman. Indeed, Carter's successes at Camp David raised his popularity rating some 13 percent. It has also been asserted that Chancellor Willy Brandt of the Federal Republic of Germany activated his *Ost-Politik* policy, calling for better relations with Soviet bloc states, in the late 1960s because of his declining popularity within West Germany. Since Brandt's Socialist party was in coalition with the Free Democratic party, it was impossible to press a domestic success, for there were too many philosophical differences between the two parties on domestic issues. Leaders of developing countries also tend to exert considerable energy on foreign-policy issues, as in the case of the late Prime Minister Jawaharlal Nehru of India. Domestic problems in such countries have often seemed so intractable that the leadership, perhaps in the desire to feel that it is at least doing something useful, tends to become preoccupied with foreign-policy issues.

Decision makers also attempt to influence public opinion in order to improve their bargaining position in the international arena. Demonstrating that the public is behind them on a given policy and suggesting that the state has no other options given the pressure of public opinion can be a useful strategy in international bargaining. Franklin D. Roosevelt used this strategem so much that Stalin began to rationalize his own foreign-policy positions on the basis that a given move that he opposed would be unacceptable to the Soviet public. As the SALT II negotiations entered their final phase, the Carter administration sought to take advantage of the Senate's hostility toward a SALT agreement as a way of inducing the Soviets to be more conciliatory in the negotiations.

One of the most striking examples of the use of public opinion for diplomatic ends occurred in October 1975, when more than one hundred thousand protesting Moroccans marched into Spanish Sahara to demonstrate support for Moroccan territorial claims against Algeria. The case illustrates how governmental propaganda can be utilized to rally public opinion to demonstrate against unpopular international moves. The use of such mass demonstrations has been a fairly common practice, particularly in countries with authoritarian and personalist regimes.

4.   Efforts to manipulate public opinion may backfire.

In attempting to manipulate public opinion to support a given policy, whether for internal or external objectives, decision makers need to be aware of latent predispositions that exist within a target population; otherwise, their efforts to mobilize public opinion might be counterproductive. Two cases in which the United States sought to educate the American public on foreign-policy issues demonstrate this point very well. These consist of governmental efforts to generate support for freer trade in the 1950s and to increase public support for foreign aid in 1961.[69]

In both instances what might be called the "iceberg effect" resulted from the official educational efforts to sell a more liberal policy on the issue. Visualize if you will an iceberg, of which only a small portion exists above the water level. This portion might represent the informed public, whereas the much larger portion that is submerged could reflect the uninformed mass public. The informed public was found to be better educated and more liberal on the issues of foreign aid and trade, as is generally true of better-educated people. When the public campaign to lower the water level of ignorance began to show some success, the larger public, represented by previously submerged portions of the iceberg, brought with it a group whose latent attitudes were hostile to a more liberal policy on trade and aid. Consequently, the administration only increased the amount of antagonism

69. Raymond A. Bauer, Ithiel de Sola Pool, and Lewis A. Dexter, *American Business and Public Policy: The Politics of Foreign Trade* (Chicago: Aldine-Atherton, 1963); James N. Rosenau, *National Leadership and Foreign Policy: A Case Study in the Mobilization of Support* (Princeton, N.J.: Princeton University Press, 1963).

toward the policies it was trying to persuade the public to accept. In 1978 the Carter administration risked similar negative responses in attempting to generate mass public support for the Panama Canal Treaties, as such publicity made the issue salient to a broader public whose latent predisposition was to oppose any such action, which was viewed as a policy of weakness. Of course, if one's adversaries make a major point of an issue, an administration may have little choice but to engage in a counterattack in support of its position.

5. Public opinion will be effective only if it is organized, but even then foreign-policy pressure groups tend to be less effective than vested-interest groups that attempt to affect domestic policy.

Perhaps the greatest deficiency of the foreign-policy pressure group lies in the fact that it has greater difficulty in making credible and legitimate claims on foreign-policy matters than a pressure group does in making such claims on domestic matters. Decision makers tend to question the legitimacy of a group's claims on generalized foreign-policy issues, since its stake in such an issue is no greater than that of any other group of citizens. A special expertise or vested interest needs to be demonstrated in order for such a pressure group to have much influence. Thus, it is somewhat easier for the National Farm Organization to have an impact on farm legislation than it is for the United States Association for the United Nations to influence the United States' policy at the United Nations.

6. Public opinion, or at least the decision makers' perception of that opinion, places certain constraints on the making of foreign policy.

Research seems to indicate that the decision makers in a democratic society generally operate on the basis of what they perceive to be the public will. The historian Ernest R. May has noted that one can almost count on one's fingers the number of occasions when American statesmen made major decisions that they thought contrary to the public will.[70] Franklin D. Roosevelt felt constrained in taking the United States into World War II, given the strong antiwar sentiment at the time; American decision makers were also reluctant to recognize the

---

70. Cited in Levering, *The Public and American Foreign Policy*, p. 152.

People's Republic of China, since a lobby group, the Committee of One Million, had made it appear that such a move would be unacceptable to the public; and according to Daniel Ellsberg, the insistence of American decision makers on remaining in Vietnam even after they recognized that the effort was futile was largely due to their belief that the American public would not tolerate a defeat in war and that such an event might mean certain electoral defeat.[71]

In order to generate support for a policy, decision makers find it necessary to oversimplify issues and to express complex issues in simple slogans. In turn, this tends to become a millstone around the necks of the decision makers, sometimes impeding flexible foreign policy. Decision makers who have made a career out of anticommunist statements, for example, are going to find it difficult to shift gears and press for detente when circumstances suggest the desirability of such a change.

That democratic decision makers have felt constrained by public opinion from time to time cannot be doubted, but there has also been a tendency to believe one's own state to be constrained more than another state. Thus, a French academic once complained at a conference in London that although the British exercised effective freedom in foreign policy, the French government had to pay more attention to public opinion.[72]

7.   Public opinion generally does not incite a nation to war.

There has been some concern that public moods, perhaps fired by the mass media, may induce a state to go to war or behave in a bellicose fashion. This was alleged to have been the case in 1898, when the United States declared war on Spain despite the fact that the latter had acceded to all of its demands. The Hearst newspapers in particular were accused of practicing yellow journalism in an effort to fuel emotional support for war with Spain. A study of the relationship of public opinion to the outbreak of war in the United States and Britain, however, suggested that such incitement has not usually been the case. Public opinion seemed to follow policy changes with respect to more militant postures rather than preceding such changes.[73]

71. Daniel Ellsberg, *Papers on the War* (New York: Simon and Schuster, 1972), p. 122.

72. Wallace, *The Foreign Policy Process in Britain*, p. 271.

73. Joel T. Campbell and Leila S. Cain, "Public Opinion and the Outbreak of War," *Journal of Conflict Resolution*, 9 (September 1965), 318–28.

8. Public opinion on foreign-policy issues plays a minor role in electoral politics.

If public opinion is to have an impact on foreign policy, it would seem that its effect would be felt most emphatically around election time as candidates and governments seek to be more responsive to public needs and desires. The fact of the matter is that in most countries that hold democratic elections, foreign policy has not been much of an issue, or at any rate the positions of the candidates have not been clear enough to turn an election into a referendum on a foreign-policy issue. Even the 1968 presidential election in the United States did not become a referendum on Vietnam, despite the high salience of the issue at the time. This was due primarily to the fact that the two contenders for the presidency, Richard Nixon and Hubert Humphrey, were not perceived as taking radically different positions on the issue. Indeed, this appears to be a general pattern in American electoral campaigns, in which there is a tendency to blur differences on foreign-policy positions. In contrast, struggles for power in the Soviet Union have tended to accentuate such differences.[74]

Foreign-policy issues tend to be of even less significance in the political campaigns of other democratic states. Dorothy Pickles, for example, has suggested that it is commonplace that French elections are never won on foreign-policy issues.[75] Michael Brecher noted that even for a state like Israel, where national security is the foremost issue, foreign-policy issues dominated only two of five elections through 1965.[76] He concluded that there is no evidence to suggest that Israeli elections have influenced either the strategy of foreign policy making or its implementation. Similarly, decision makers in Japan have paid little attention to public opinion on foreign-policy issues, primarily because the Liberal Democratic party, with its vastly superior numbers, has dominated the decision-making process most of the time since 1951. Major foreign-policy controversies such as the Japanese–American Security Treaty in 1960 and the Okinawa reversion issue had a minimal impact on electoral outcomes. According to Chae-Jin Lee,

---

74. Zbigniew Brzezinski and Samuel P. Huntington, *Political Power: USA/USSR* (New York: Viking Press, 1964), p. 193.

75. Dorothy Pickles, "French Foreign Policy," in F. S. Northedge, ed., *The Foreign Policies of the Powers* (New York: Praeger, 1968), p. 189.

76. Michael Brecher, *The Foreign Policy System of Israel* (New Haven, Conn.: Yale University Press, 1972), p. 125.

personality and party have been more important than the issues in recent Japanese elections.[77]

Part of the reason that public opinion tends to become less activated on foreign-policy issues than on domestic issues may be the fact that foreign policy has a less immediate and visible effect on the electorate. Supporting a disarmament agreement or negotiating a human rights document can be viewed as a relatively safe action for a decision maker, for it often takes time for any adverse effects to show themselves, whereas decisions related to domestic allocations of resources or actions designed to affect employment or inflation are likely to be more immediately felt. Moreover, there may be a general feeling on the part of the public that it lacks appropriate information on which to base a judgment. Information is more closely controlled on foreign-policy matters, given its sensitive nature; as a result, there is greater willingness to defer to those who are closer to the situation.

As international decisions come increasingly to be perceived as affecting domestic well-being, one can expect an intensified effort on the part of the public to become more involved. The implications of the 1972 grain deal with the Soviet Union, which substantially increased wheat prices for the American consumer, as well as the OPEC oil boycott of 1973–74, demonstrated how a nation's well-being is affected by foreign-policy decisions.

THE DECISIONAL CONTEXT

Although it is possible to develop certain generalizations regarding the role played by various actors (bureaucrats, legislators, the public) in the decision-making process, it is still necessary to explore the specific circumstances surrounding a given decision in order to comprehend why certain choices are made. The most extensively researched of these contextual factors is the existence or nonexistence of crises, which can affect decision making in several ways. In the first instance, crises tend to provide decision makers with greater decisional latitude. Political leaders can generally anticipate that the public will support them during periods of crisis as the nation rallies around the flag. As has been pointed out, crises like the Cuban missile crisis and the seizure of the American Embassy in Teheran added several

77. Chae-Jin Lee, *Japan Faces China*, p. 11.

points to the President's popularity. Even failures like the Bay of Pigs and the abortive attempt to free the American hostages from Iran in April 1980 had the immediate effect of increasing presidential popularity.

During periods of crisis the decision-making group is generally smaller, as only the central decision maker and his or her top associates become involved. This is so not only because of the need to make rapid decisions, but also because of concern about secrecy as a plan is developed. Such constraints would seem to lessen the impact of the bureaucracy on the making of foreign policy, providing support for the rational-actor model. It has been suggested that decisions made during crises are more likely to be in accord with the broader national interest than those made during more placid times. Decisions made in the context of a crisis are less likely to be watered down through bureaucratic compromise, and the decision makers themselves may be less concerned with the sometimes uninformed and selfish demands of the mass public and special interests. On the other hand, Steven Krasner argues that because of the time constraints that prevail at such a time, central decision makers must rely on the expertise, predetermined preferences, and contingency plans already developed by the bureaucracy.[78]

Because of the limited time available and the psychological stress inherent in a crisis situation, there will be less searching for alternatives. During an emergency one can anticipate that decision makers will grasp the first historical analogy that comes to mind and then proceed to collect information to support it. Crises also tend to lead to rigid and stereotypic thinking, which has serious negative implications for rational foreign-policy choice.

Communication difficulties both within the nation and between nations are more likely to occur during crisis periods. Since crises produce a sense of national emergency, one is likely to find greater concern about secrecy in the decision-making process. Agencies of government, even if they have adequate time to communicate during the crisis, fail to do so for fear that such communications might be intercepted. Consequently, important events are not anticipated, as in the case of Pearl Harbor, and inappropriate responses based on incomplete information will result.

---

78. Steven D. Krasner, "Are Bureaucracies Important," *Foreign Policy*, 7 (Summer 1972), 176.

Communication failures during crises are even more likely to occur when inter-state communication is involved. A serious difficulty is created by the problem of information overload as decision makers become exercised about an issue. Separating out the most salient messages coming from several sources may be especially difficult. Communication is also impeded by the determined efforts of the adversary to mislead its opposition. Poor communication also results from the perceptual difficulties confronting individual decision makers during periods of stress, as discussed in Chapter 2. Because of these communication problems and others like them, one study of sixteen international crises found that the chances of a message getting through untarnished to someone in the receiving government were only about four in ten.[79]

Periods of persistent crisis like the cold war have serious implications for foreign policy. Chief among these is the likelihood that recurrent crises may dull one's reactions to danger. As people live with tension for long periods, they are less likely to be vigilant when new and dangerous situations arise. Crises may present a particular problem if recent history has involved a number of false alarms. This seems to have been the case with respect to the Western failure to anticipate the North Korean invasion of South Korea in June 1950. Several previous border incidents had led those involved to miscalculate and underestimate the massive strike from the north.

Whether recurrent crises tend to increase or decrease the probability of war has been assessed differently by two distinguished scholars. Quincy Wright has suggested that the probability of war is a function of the additive effect of the probability of war erupting in a series of crises.[80] The inevitable result of such a formulation is that sooner or later a 100-percent probability of war is reached. Charles A. McClelland, on the other hand, explicitly rejects this formulation, arguing that states learn how to routinize their behavior in conflict situations.[81] Having learned how to deescalate one crisis, they can apply what they have learned to another situation involving the same state. It may be,

79. Glenn H. Snyder, *Conflict Among Nations* (Princeton, N.J.: Princeton University Press, 1977), p. 316.

80. Wright, *A Study of War*, p. 1272.

81. Charles A. McClelland, "The Acute International Crisis," in Klaus Knorr and Sidney Verba, eds., *The International System: Theoretical Essays* (Princeton, N.J., Princeton University Press, 1961), pp. 182–204.

however, that when a state has gone to the brink several times, it will become less cautious and go beyond the point of no return.

The size and range of the foreign-policy agenda provides a second major set of illustrations of how contextual factors can affect foreign-policy choices. The number of issues clamoring for attention determine the time that can be spent on each issue by top-level decision makers. This may mean in some instances that certain issues will not reach the decisional stage regardless of how important they might seem, or that they will be decided at lower decisional levels, either of which can make a difference in the choices that are made.

Decision makers are sensitive about becoming involved in too many crises at one time, particularly if this might result in a two-front war. The differing responses of the United States government to the North Korean seizure of the *Pueblo* in 1968 and to the Iranian hostage situation in 1979–81 are most instructive on this point. The Iranian seizure became a nightly news item in the United States, and President Carter, on the pretext of having to stay in Washington to deal with the crisis, did not venture out of the city for several months. On the other hand, the United States government, as well as the public, seemed almost to forget about the naval personnel who were imprisoned in North Korea for a period of more than a year. A major difference between the two situations that might help explain the different reactions was that the United States was involved in Vietnam at the time of the *Pueblo* incident and was therefore concerned about the danger of creating a two-front war if it were to take strong action against North Korea. Similar concerns preoccupied German decision makers in both World Wars as they sought, at least initially, to move against one group of states while neutralizing the other.

It is necessary in effective decision making to develop priorities rather than attempt to deal with many issues simultaneously. Only great powers can afford the luxury of an extensive foreign-policy agenda, and even they may run into difficulties if the agenda is too full. Part of Kaiser Wilhelm's problem around the time of World War I arose from the fact that he was seeking too many foreign-policy objectives concurrently and, as a result, was making too many enemies.[82] Certain objectives would have to be relinquished or deferred for the kaiser to

---

82. Robert Jervis, *Perception and Misperception in International Politics* (Princeton, N.J., Princeton University Press, 1976), p. 140.

gain a sufficient number of allies to aid him in achieving his most important goals.

How simultaneous events can affect foreign-policy choices can also be seen in United States policy toward Taiwan. It is quite probable that the Carter administration would have moved more rapidly toward recognition of the People's Republic of China but for the fact that efforts to obtain ratification of the Panama Canal Treaties in 1977 had already alienated a significant number of Americans. To have introduced another policy to which a large portion of the population would be opposed would only have produced further domestic division. Hence the administration waited two years before recognizing the People's Republic of China and simultaneously rejecting American defense commitments to Taiwan.

The kinds of issues found on a state's foreign-policy agenda will make a difference in terms of which domestic groups are able and willing to assume a more active foreign-policy role. Britain's successive economic crises have tended to strengthen the role of Treasury in the British decision-making process. In many other states the increasing salience of international economic issues is providing a more significant role for economic ministries, as noted previously. Similarly, continuing military crises will result in the military's playing a more prominent role, and military options will receive more serious consideration than they might otherwise have obtained.

Although other contextual factors that are relevant to decision making might be noted, the critical factor is how the decision makers themselves define a given situation. Do they see it as a crisis that threatens their basic values, or is it viewed as an issue that does not require immediate attention? There are obviously hundreds of events occurring throughout the world that might suggest the need for some sort of response. For all but the superpowers, most of these events will be seen as quite irrelevant. Moreover, within the decision-making unit some people may view a given issue as important while others may not. This in turn will affect both who decides and what action, if any, is taken.

CONCLUSION

Evidence has been presented in this chapter to suggest that the structure of the decision-making process and who makes the decisions can make a difference in foreign policy. A major debate surrounds the question of whether authoritarian or democratic structures are superior in the making of foreign policy. In terms of effectiveness and efficiency, there are reasons to support the primacy of authoritarian regimes, for such governments ought to be able to make decisions more rapidly, ensure domestic compliance with their decisions, and perhaps be more consistent in their foreign policy. Yet such ideals have not always been realized, and authoritarian regimes often are less effective in developing an innovative foreign policy because of subordinates' pervasive fear of raising questions. Although authoritarian governments appear to have certain advantages in diplomatic negotiations, the evidence is divided on the question of which type of regime is likely to pursue more peaceful policies.

How power is distributed in the decision-making structure was also seen to make some difference. Generally speaking, central governments and the executive branches dominate foreign policy in both authoritarian and democratic governments. Legislatures do little more than ratify executive decisions; despite efforts to redress the balance, as in the case of the 1973 War Powers Act, the executive remains dominant.

More interesting in terms of explaining foreign policy are the relative roles of central decision makers and bureaucrats. Despite some very persuasive arguments in support of the bureaucratic politics model, which sees a key role for bureaucrats at both the formulation and implementation stages, the central decision makers determine who their key advisers will be and which advice to heed. Given the importance of national security issues and control over the instruments of coercion, the military is one bureaucratic group that can have a significant impact on foreign policy. However, divisions among the military, along with tradition, and the sharing of common values with the broader society, have operated to restrain the military from dominating the decision-making process.

Political parties, interest groups, and particularly the mass public appear to have the least impact on foreign-policy choices. Since the latter is so easily manipulated, its importance as a determinant of foreign policy is highly limited even in democratic polities. At the same time, we know that democratically elected leaders often seem to have their eyes on the popularity polls when certain foreign-policy decisions are being made. The evidence does suggest, however, that there is little reason to fear an uninformed and emotional public interfering with rational foreign-policy calculation by forcing ill-conceived policies on reluctant decision makers.

Finally, it has been suggested that the context in which a decision is made makes a difference in both the process and the substance of foreign policy. Decisions made during a crisis, for example, involve fewer decision makers and a less active search for alternatives. What specific issues are being considered and the size of the foreign-policy agenda were also found to influence which individuals and groups are activated in the policy process and, therefore, what decisions are ultimately made.

6

ECONOMIC DETERMINANTS

Economic factors have long been viewed as possible explanations of why states behave as they do. Plato, for example, saw money as a cause of war and even went so far as to suggest that a republic should remain poor so that it would not be worth attacking. But perhaps the most deterministic economic theory explaining the behavior of states is found in Marxist literature, in which economics is viewed as the driving force that determines political behavior. Classes and nations are seen as responding to events in the external world on the basis of their position in the economic system, and there is believed to be a certain inevitability in those responses.

In recent years there has been considerable interest in the role of economic factors. Such factors have become a vital part of foreign policy, given the increased involvement of nations in economic foreign relations. But it is not only the enhanced relevance of economic interdependence that has made economic factors so important in foreign policy; the decline in the cold war has also provided an opportunity for nations to become more concerned about their economic relationships and less preoccupied with security issues.

In a very basic sense economic considerations are central to foreign-policy choices, for economic resources are required for the implementation of most policies. The economic resources of a state influence whether that state can be a donor or must be a recipient of foreign aid; resources also affect the state's ability to enter costly armament races, engage in trade, or achieve a favorable balance of payments. Although the distribution of resources in the international system may not actually determine the precise policies that are adopted, it certainly places a limit on the range of foreign-policy options. A state with a paucity of resources will not be able to play the role of a great power, however much it might wish to do so. On the other hand, having considerable economic resources does not mean that a state *must* play such a role.

In attempting to assess the relative impact of economic factors, in contrast to politico-security factors, on foreign policy, it becomes difficult to separate the two, for often economic means are utilized to obtain political and security objectives. Such was the conclusion reached in a study of Soviet economic penetration in China during the period 1945–60.[1] The Soviet Union's primary concerns in China were seen as involving security interests. However, economic instruments were used to further security goals, sometimes at great expense to the Soviet Union. It is probable that similar politico-security motivations inspired Soviet imperialism in Eastern Europe. Klaus Knorr has argued that "there is no case of Communist aggression on record which even faintly suggests the presence of economic objectives."[2] This tendency to diminish the role of economic factors as a determinant of Soviet foreign policy is particularly interesting given the emphasis Marxist–Leninist theory gives to economic determinism. It should be noted, however, that empirical studies indicate that the Soviet Union has derived economic rewards from its imperialism in Eastern Europe. Paul Marer concluded that if reparations cancellations were excluded, six Eastern European countries provided a $20 billion subvention to the Soviet Union. With reparations cancellations included, the positive balance for the Soviet Union still stood at $14 billion.[3]

Despite the fact that a number of economic moves are motivated primarily by national security interests, it may be that many policies

1.   Roy T. Grow, "Soviet Economic Penetration of China, 1945–60," in Steven J. Rosen and James R. Kurth, eds., *Testing Theories of Economic Imperialism* (Lexington, Mass.: D. C. Heath, 1974), pp. 261–81.

2.   Klaus Knorr, *Power and Wealth* (New York: Basic Books, 1973), p. 117.

3.   Paul Marer, "The Political Economy of Soviet Relations with Eastern Europe," in Rosen and Kurth, *Testing Theories of Economic Imperialism*, pp. 231–61.

that are rationalized on such grounds are inherently motivated by economic interests. A group may be seen as behaving too selfishly if it gives the appearance that it is motivated primarily by profit or economic reward. As a result, it will often seek to justify its policies, however crassly they are motivated, on the basis of their alleged contribution to the national security interests of the state. Thus, oil interests may seek to generate support for a policy of making the United States energy independent by suggesting that such independence is vital to American national security interests, whereas the oil interests' primary motivation is to increase profits by encouraging the government to take actions that would reduce outside competition. This can be accomplished by instituting import controls or providing positive economic rewards for increased oil exploration and production. Intervention in the affairs of other governments has also frequently been justified as a way of facilitating representative government when the real motivation has been to protect overseas economic interests.

While recognizing that it is sometimes difficult to separate economic explanations of foreign policy from other determinants, in the remaining sections of this chapter we will explore a number of different viewpoints that place considerable emphasis on economic factors. These include radical theories related to economic imperialism and the existence of a military–industrial complex to more conservative theories suggesting the benefits of global economic interdependence.

IMPERIALISM

Explanations of imperialism in international affairs are many and varied, although economic theories tend to dominate. Some writers have suggested that imperialism has historically been associated with capitalist classes interested in improving their profits. For example, the British theorist J. A. Hobson, writing in 1902, blamed British imperialism on special-interest groups composed of capitalists.[4] Borrowing from Karl Marx, Hobson asserted that imperialism resulted when capitalist groups, confronted with an oversupply of capital and goods, sought to obtain markets abroad in order to divest themselves of that surplus. The economically underdeveloped areas of the world provided particularly useful investment opportunities, given their chronic

4. J. A. Hobson, *Imperialism: A Study* (London: George Allen and Unwin, 1938).

lack of capital and their untapped markets. For Hobson, the imperialism of the British government became "a vast system of outdoor relief for the upper classes." Unlike Marx, however, Hobson did not recommend eliminating capitalism and the capitalist; instead, he believed the means of purchase should be placed in the hands of the workers in order to reduce the incentive for economic imperialism. This could be done by strengthening unions and by using the taxing powers of government to place more money at the disposal of the domestic consumer.

V. I. Lenin adapted the notions of Marx and Hobson in his own theory of imperialism, which he regarded as the last stage of capitalism.[5] Like his predecessors, Lenin saw capitalist states engaging in imperialist activities in order to distribute the oversupply of capital and goods that capitalist economies inevitably produced. By engaging in such imperialistic endeavors, the capitalist systems were able to forestall their inevitable collapse. But this imperialism brought them into conflict with other capitalist states, and the end result was war between imperialist nations, as evidenced by World War I.

There are a number of persuasive reasons for rejecting the notion that capitalism necessarily leads to imperialism or conflict between imperialist states, as suggested by such theorists as Hobson and Lenin. In the first place, imperialism *preceded* the rise of capitalism and was a common feature in many ancient empires and feudal systems. Second, most of the wars that occurred in the age of mature capitalism were not fought primarily for economic motives, according to Hans J. Morgenthau, who cites as examples such wars as the Austro-Prussian War, the Franco-German War, the Crimean War, the Spanish–American War, the Russo-Japanese War, and the two World Wars.[6] Raymond Aron has specifically rejected Lenin's efforts to explain World War I as motivated by competitive capitalist states, since the competition for colonies had declined prior to the onset of the war, having peaked a couple of decades earlier.[7] Another authority objected to the notion that imperialism leads to conflict between imperialistic nations by noting that, with the exception of the Boer War, all the colonial conflicts were

5. V. I. Lenin, *Imperialism: The Highest Stage of Capitalism* (New York: International Publishers, 1939).

6. Hans J. Morgenthau, *Politics Among Nations*, 5th ed. (New York: Knopf, 1967), p. 46.

7. Raymond Aron, *Peace and War*, trans. Richard Howard and Annette Baker Fox (Garden City, N.Y.: Doubleday, 1966), p. 261.

settled through diplomacy, and at any rate, two of Britain's fiercest colonial competitors were its allies during World War I.[8] Quincy Wright found that "wars have occurred during periods of capitalistic dominance, but they have been least frequent in the areas most completely organized under that system."[9] Even if one were to find that capitalist states tended to behave in an imperialistic fashion, this would not necessarily mean that capitalism *induces* imperialism. It might be due simply to the tendency of great powers to be imperialistic, and in modern times most of the powerful states have been capitalist states.

The alleged need on the part of capitalist states to invest surplus capital and to find markets in the less developed world generally seems not to be supported by the facts. Overseas investments often constitute only a small fraction of the total capital investments of a state. The foreign investments of most capitalist states represent less than 10 percent of the domestic book value of most corporations. Even in terms of overseas investments, developed countries tend to make most of their investments in the developed world rather than in less developed countries (LDCs). Some 70 percent of American investments abroad are made in other economically advanced countries, and during the nineteenth century, the heyday of British imperialism, some three-fourths of British investments went to the United States, the Commonwealth, and other developed states, in contrast to the developing regions of Asia and Africa.[10] Investments directed toward other developed states would seem to contradict Leninist theory, for presumably other capitalist states should also be confronted with the problem of surplus capital and accordingly could hardly be expected to be receptive to foreign capital investment in their states.

Perhaps a major factor explaining the preference for investments in the developed world is the fact that the return is frequently higher while the risk is substantially lower. It has been suggested that the profitability of investments by multinational corporations in less developed countries is uniformly lower by about 2 percent except for the

8. Robert Gilpin, *U.S. Power and the Multinational Corporation* (New York: Basic Books, 1975), p. 74.

9. Quincy Wright, *A Study of War*, 2nd ed. (Chicago: University of Chicago Press, 1965), pp. 1163–64.

10. Bruce M. Russett and Elizabeth C. Hanson, *Interest and Ideology* (San Francisco: Freeman, 1975), pp. 31, 41.

pharmaceutical industry, in which it is about even.[11] Also, it takes longer for a new operation to break even in a less developed state. Another study has indicated that over the period 1959–69 the return on American manufacturing investments averaged 12.4 percent while returns on investments abroad amounted to only 11.8 percent.[12] India, the showcase of the colonial empire, also failed to yield as high a return on investments as was obtained in Britain itself.[13]

When one adds the economic costs of defending the overseas interests of imperial powers and the expense of governmental foreign-aid programs to improve literacy, transportation, communication, and economic well-being in LDCs, the staggering price of imperialism becomes even more apparent, raising serious questions regarding economic motivations for imperialism. As a result, a number of writers place less emphasis on economic interests in explaining imperialism and look to such factors as power, security, and prestige. For Joseph Schumpeter, the major pressure for imperialism came from military and governmental circles, whose authority and position depended on continued warfare.[14] Schumpeter even claimed that imperialism was a holdover from precapitalist society and would eventually disappear as capitalism matured, as indeed seems to have happened in the current postcolonial period. Eugene Staley has suggested that economic interests have merely been used as an excuse for imperialism, since private interests and investments have more often been subjected to general political and military goals rather than being able to shape those goals.[15] According to one authority, it is probably only in smaller countries whose security seems somewhat assured, such as Switzerland and the Netherlands, that foreign investment and trade decisions tend to be made purely on economic grounds rather than on political and security grounds.[16]

Loss of territory, rather than its acquisition through imperialism,

11. Peter F. Drucker, "Multinationals and Developing Countries: Myths and Realities," *Foreign Affairs*, 53 (October 1974), 124.

12. Steven J. Rosen and Walter S. Jones, *The Logic of International Relations*, 2nd ed. (Cambridge, Mass.: Winthrop, 1977), p. 57.

13. Kenneth Boulding and Tapan Mukerjee, "Unprofitable Enterprise: Britain in India, 1800–1967," *Peace Research Society (International) Papers*, 16 (1971), 11.

14. Joseph Schumpeter, *Imperialism and Social Classes*, trans. Heinz Norden (New York: Meridian Books, 1955).

15. Eugene Staley, *War and the Private Investor* (Garden City, N.Y.: Doubleday, 1935).

16. Gilpin, *U.S. Power and the Multinational Corporation*, p. 5.

may in some instances provide economic benefits. Charles P. Kindleberger has noted how the separation of East and West Germany actually increased the real standard of living for the population located in the West.[17] The loss of East Germany permitted the Federal Republic to buy its grain in world markets at prices below those charged by *Junker* farms in the eastern sector. The influx of refugees from East Germany also stimulated economic development, for with a high level of demand and high investment, the availability of more labor helped hold down wages and raise profits, savings, investment, and growth.

While colonialism has virtually ended as one colony after another became independent since World War II, and there appears to be a general recognition that efforts to control another territory are costly, a group of neo-Marxist writers, particularly in the United States, has sought to revive economic explanations for actions taken by allegedly imperialistic capitalist states. Prominent among these is Harry Magdoff, who interprets American foreign policy from the perspective of the need for governmental action to make the world secure for the operations of American capital.[18] Given dependence on foreign resources and on profits from sales abroad, there is a continuing effort by the wealthy states to keep the less developed world in a dependent relationship. This is accomplished through international investment and economic domination, rather than through the direct political control of the age of colonialism. Magdoff also notes that the developed state is highly dependent on a number of specific strategic materials, such as nickel, chrome, cobalt, bauxite, and oil, which are often located in the developing regions. The developed state has an interest not only in ensuring continued access to these materials but also in discouraging industrialization by the developing state, for the latter would then have an increasing desire to retain such resources for itself.

Radical theorists have developed a number of arguments in their attempt to refute the notion that imperialism is not a profitable activity for the capitalist state and the concomitant assumption that imperialism consequently is not motivated primarily by economic considerations. In the first place, they argue that even if imperialism is a costly venture for the nation as a whole, certain individuals and corporations gain considerably from imperialistic actions designed to ensure raw materials, markets, and protection for overseas investments. These

17. Charles P. Kindleberger, *Power and Money* (New York: Basic Books, 1970), p. 89.
18. Harry Magdoff, *The Age of Imperialism* (New York: Monthly Review Press, 1969).

benefits, and the actions taken by governments to guarantee them for specific economic interests, will be examined in some detail in our discussions of the military–industrial complex and the role of the multinational corporation in foreign policy.

Second, radical theorists have argued that even though imperialism may be costly for a state, the state may engage in imperialistic actions in order to deny a given territory to an adversary that might be able to benefit economically and militarily from its acquisition.[19] Thus, the Open Door policy of the United States around the turn of the century was designed to deny economic trade benefits in China to European powers unless the United States could share in those benefits.

Third, even though there are no immediate economic rewards from acquiring control over territory abroad, such rewards may come later through the discovery of unexpected resources or future marketing prospects that will follow economic development in the area. Few people anticipated the recent discovery of enormous oil reserves in Mexico, which appears to place that state second only to Saudi Arabia in known oil reserves.

Finally, efforts to ensure continued control and influence in an area might be motivated not so much by the desire to protect economic interests in that specific area, interests that might be minimal at best, as by the need to protect more significant economic interests elsewhere. United States' action in Vietnam was viewed as a deterrent to a communist takeover that would threaten American economic interests in neighboring regions. By themselves, the United States' interests in Vietnam could not come close to justifying its expenditure of resources and lives in the war—an expenditure that amounted to some $150 billion and fifty thousand American lives. But when viewed in terms of the implications for other territories, a more plausible justification can be offered for the sacrifice. At least this is what a number of decision makers believed as they accepted the domino theory, which visualized country after country in Southeast Asia falling to communist forces if the latter were successful in Vietnam. Nevertheless, Vietnam is an extremely weak case in support of the relationship between capitalism and war, for the wealthiest citizens in the United States were more dovish than the poor. Business groups were often quite outspoken

19. Paul M. Sweezey, *The Theory of Capitalist Development* (New York: Monthly Review Press, 1968), p. 303.

against the war, and during the 1972 primaries George McGovern, the antiwar candidate, received more support in the affluent suburbs than in the cities.

THE MULTINATIONAL CORPORATION

In an effort to revive economic theories of imperialism and exploitation, radical writers have paid particular attention to the spectacular rise in recent years of the multinational corporation, which threatens to overwhelm many nation–states in terms of both size and global control. These corporations, often in collusion with their home governments, have been blamed for many of the world's economic, social, and political ills. Part of the concern about the multinational corporation arises simply from its mammoth size. Some of the larger multinational corporations (MNCs) have assets and sales that far surpass the gross national products of an overwhelming majority of the world's nation–states.

Given the resources at their command, multinational corporations have assumed the role of dominant actors in the international system, sometimes operating at the expense of their own home governments. By controlling enormous assets cross-nationally, decisions made by MNCs as to where to buy and sell products and where to make foreign investments have a major impact on the balance of payments and the value of currency. It has even been suggested that the currency speculations engaged in by MNCs, many of which are American, undermined the dollar and led to its devaluation in February 1973.[20]

Despite having their headquarters in a given country and being staffed by citizens of that country, multinational corporations and their subsidiaries bave been known on many occasions to disregard the directives of their home governments.[21] For example, after the briefest hesitation, a subsidiary of Gulf Oil turned several hundred million dol-

20. David H. Blake and Robert S. Walters, *The Politics of Global Economic Relations* (Englewood Cliffs, N.J.: Prentice-Hall, 1976), p. 76.

21. These and subsequent illustrations of the interactions between governments and multinational businesses are gleaned from the following studies: Raymond Vernon, *Sovereignty at Bay* (New York: Basic Books, 1971); Raymond Vernon, *Storm over the Multinationals* (Cambridge, Mass.: Harvard University Press, 1977); and Gilpin, *U.S. Power and the Multinational Corporation.*

lars over to the winning side in the 1976 Angolan civil war even though the United States had opposed the new regime and had yet to recognize it. More serious digressions from governmental policy occurred among American subsidiaries that sold arms to Hitler and American multinational oil companies that failed to provide needed petroleum supplies to the United States during the 1973–74 oil boycott, preferring instead to sell their products in more profitable markets.

With the extensive resources they control, multinational corporations have also been exceedingly active in extracting special considerations from their home governments in support of their overseas activities. Neo-Marxist writers have tended to portray the relationship between big business and government as one in which the latter, owing to bribery and political pressures, simply does the bidding of the former. Foreign policy is seen by such writers primarily as an effort to protect and further the economic interests of the MNCs and other businesses at home and abroad.

Some governments have been more active than others in meshing governmental and corporate interests. In socialist states, with their state-owned enterprises, the two policy levels are virtually inseparable. Among democratic states, the Japanese government has been exceedingly active in protecting and furthering the overseas interests of business, as have Britain and France. The United States government, in contrast, has been less preoccupied on this score. Nevertheless, there are a number of instances in which the United States intervened on behalf of specific economic interests. The United Fruit Company clearly gained from the intervention of the United States Marines in the banana republics of Central America during the early part of this century; the United States government was also instrumental during the 1920s in obtaining access for American oil companies in areas reserved for France and Britain; and the government has placed considerable pressure on Japan from time to time in an effort to force it to unilaterally restrict exports to the United States as an aid to various American economic interests. A similar pattern of protection and efforts to further the overseas economic interests of business can be seen in the behavior of less developed countries. For example, the Indian government has provided subsidies of 20 to 30 percent to aid its businesses in the export of capital equipment.

In order to dispel the notion that multinational corporations have all the advantages and governments only do their bidding, examples are listed below to demonstrate that the United States government has often pursued foreign economic policies that have been disadvantageous to big business:

Legislation designed to make foreign subsidiaries of American companies subject to American law

Restrictions on trade with communist countries

Restrictions on capital outflows

Taking a strong pro-Israeli stance, which impedes the interests of the large oil companies and other American corporations doing business in the Middle East

Continuation of the Vietnam War despite the overwhelming reservations of big business

Promotion of Japanese expansion into the United States market while tolerating Japanese exclusionist policies

Encouragement of the integrative efforts of the European Economic Community, which only resulted in increased protectionism against American products

There are also many instances on record in which governments have attempted to utilize their control over MNCs to further specific foreign-policy goals, as the following list indicates:

During the 1960s the Canadian government pressured American auto manufacturers with subsidiaries in Canada to lobby before Congress for free trade in automobiles. Those efforts were successful, thanks largely to Canadian government promises and threats directed at American subsidiaries located in Canada.

The United States sought to stop subsidiaries in Canada from selling flour to Cuba, drugs to Vietnam, and trucks to China. (The Canadian government was often able to counter these pressures by utilizing other Canadian firms in such transactions.)

In 1964 the United States attempted to forestall nuclear development in France by refusing to allow IBM to transfer specialized computer technology to its French subsidiary.

The United States was able to forestall Britain from selling British Viscount aircraft to the People's Republic of China simply because the planes were equipped with American navigational equipment.

Arab governments have sought to influence MNCs in the Arab–
Israeli conflict by boycotting corporations that trade with Israel.

It would be inappropriate to view even a small LDC as being
consistently at the mercy of the larger MNC. As a result of the global
spread of MNCs, a country can shop around for a foreign business that
is more compatible with its needs and is willing to share more of the
profits. At the same time, the increase in the number of LDCs in need of
outside capital and technology has provided bargaining advantages for
the MNC, which frequently finds nations competing for its technology
and capital. No longer are business interests restricted by the imperial
boundaries of the colonial empire; businesses now have an opportunity
to sell themselves to the highest bidder in a greatly expanded market,
particularly since the number of independent nation–states has almost
tripled since World War II.

Whether the multinational corporation exploits the weaker nation
remains a point of controversy. In arguing that there is an exploitative
relationship between the two, the more radical writers note that the
MNC and other business interests tend to decapitalize the LDC. Although foreign businesses may provide investment in a country, they
often take out more in profits than they invest. For example, in the
period 1960–68 American multinationals annually provided fresh capital totaling approximately $1 billion to their subsidiaries in LDCs, but
they withdrew approximately $2.5 billion in income alone.[22] The fact
of the matter is that multinational corporations rely heavily on indigenous capital for many projects and in the process deprive potential
domestic interests of such capital.

Second, the technological dependence created by outside business interests means that a country is less likely to develop its own
innovative capacity, relying instead on technology borrowed from the
MNC. In the short run this can be very useful, but it is hardly productive as far as the long-term growth of a state is concerned.

Third, foreign investment by multinationals and others distorts
the economic structure of the host country, encouraging consumption
patterns that hinder long-term growth.[23] As a result, scarce resources
are used to purchase well-advertised consumer products and luxuries

22. Vernon, *Sovereignty at Bay*, p. 172.
23. Gilpin, *U.S. Power and the Multinational Corporation*, p. 252.

rather than being invested in products that can lead to the long-range development of the state.

Fourth, the establishment of subsidiaries enables an MNC to gain access to a market that is protected by tariffs or other forms of discrimination designed to restrict importation. Indeed, a major motivation for the rise of MNCs has been the desire to elude restrictive trade practices, and the easiest procedure for doing this is through the establishment of a subsidiary abroad.

Fifth, MNCs have a vested interest in discouraging industrialization in LDCs, for the industries thus created would begin to compete with them. As a result, multinationals are reluctant to turn over the necessary technology and capital to local interests that might be able to exploit their own country's resources. The MNC is also fearful that new industries in the LDC will demand to retain their own raw materials, thus decreasing available supplies and increasing prices.

Sixth, since LDCs are often forced to concentrate on extractive industries for export, they are denied the added value derived from processing their own resources. The LDC often finds it necessary to import the finished product, paying for the processing and transportation as well as the profits skimmed off at various stages of production.

Despite the alleged exploitation of less developed countries some conservative writers have argued that the MNC has much to offer in the developmental process. First, the MNC can provide needed capital investment in the LDC; without such assistance, the LDC can hardly hope to improve its economic position.

Second, if a state's productive capacity is increased, more jobs, which are scarce in most LDCs, can be provided. A majority of those jobs often go to the indigenous labor supply, sometimes by governmental requirement, and those jobs, in turn, stimulate the entire economy.

Third, at the request of the local government MNCs often provide a number of public services for their employees, including education, health, transportation, and communication. Some of these facilities can be enjoyed by the larger population as well.

Fourth, MNCs provide the latest technology through subsidiaries located in the less developed states. Such technology would come at a high cost if it had to be purchased directly from a multinational corporation, but research and development costs are often absorbed by the parent company.

Fifth, foreign subsidiaries are able to provide substitutes for imports by producing products within the state. Import substitution becomes vitally important to most less developed countries, which already suffer severe balance-of-payments problems and need to reduce imports as much as possible. Products that can be produced locally, thanks to foreign capital and technology, may be used for export once domestic needs are met. The distribution of such exports can also benefit from the foreign country's marketing system.

Sixth, MNCs generate royalties and taxable income, which provide badly needed revenues for the LDC. As educated elites within the LDCs gain more knowledge and experience with respect to the production and marketing of their state's basic commodities, they no longer need to rely on the judgments and accounting procedures of the MNCs in order to know what is a fair rate of return for the state. Ultimately this training and the revenues obtained will enable local interests to purchase and, thus, gain control of foreign-owned subsidiaries.

For these various reasons more conservative writers conclude that the multinational corporation is an important instrument that will aid a number of third world countries in their efforts to become developed. The diffusion of technology and the increased availability of capital should enable LDCs to shorten the time required for industrialization—a process that in the past has often taken centuries. There have been a few real success stories among third world countries, notably South Korea, Taiwan, Singapore, and Brazil.

Rather than being exploited by MNCs and capitalist states, conservatives note that the frustration of the less developed state is more likely to lie in the fact that it is so little needed. The development of synthetic materials and substitutes and the discovery of new sources of exploitable raw materials have made the LDCs less relevant as suppliers of raw materials. The third world has also become a less vital market for developed states; it accounted for over 30 percent of the latter's exports in 1950 but less than 20 percent by the late 1960s.[24] Investments and earnings in the third world have also been declining relative to corporate totals. Coupled with the seemingly unending problems of governmental instability, inter-state conflict, famine, and overpopulation that one finds among many LDCs in the Southern Hemisphere, the danger is that the North may turn its back completely on that part of the world, leaving it to solve its own problems as best it can. Accusations of

---

24.   Benjamin J. Cohen, *The Question of Imperialism* (New York: Basic Books, 1973), p. 135.

exploitation by capitalist interests would probably be considerably muted if this were the case, and the leadership of LDCs would be more likely to complain about neglect.

Several systematic studies have been undertaken to determine the extent to which capitalist governments pursue policies designed primarily to protect and further the economic interests of domestic business, but their findings have been inconclusive. According to research conducted by John W. Eley and John H. Peterson, American foreign aid seems to have been motivated not so much by concern with defending overseas economic interests as by the need to protect security interests.[25] The researchers found that for the United States there was not a strong relationship between foreign aid, on the one hand, and investment, exports, and the protection of raw materials, on the other. In other words, foreign aid seems not to have been given to the states in which the United States' economic interests were greatest but, rather, to those in which security interests predominated. During the period 1945–60 more aid was provided to communist Yugoslavia in an effort to keep it independent of the Soviet Union than was given to the whole of Latin America. On the other hand, support for the notion that aid follows economic interests is provided by the work of Steven J. Rosen, who examined the patterns of American aid, trade, and investment in five countries over a number of years and concluded that "the consistency of the aid curves with trade and investment suggests a harmony of policies between private traders and investors and public dispensers of foreign assistance."[26] Similar conclusions were reached by John S. Odell, whose statistical studies indicated that the level of United States military assistance given to LDCs during the cold war varied with the importance of the nation as a supplier of raw materials and as a target for private investment and trade.[27]

The same patterns were not found with respect to military intervention, for in the postwar era the United States has been reluctant to use that instrument in support of its economic interests. Despite the importance of oil, the United States has never intervened militarily to

25. John W. Eley and John H. Peterson, "Economic Interests and American Foreign Policy Allocation, 1960–69," in Patrick J. McGowan, ed., *Sage Foreign Policy Yearbook*, vol. 1 (Beverly Hills, Calif.: Sage Publications, 1973), pp. 161–86.

26. Steven J. Rosen, "The Open Door Imperative and U.S. Foreign Policy," in Rosen and Kurth, *Testing Theories of Economic Imperialism*, p. 134.

27. John S. Odell, "Correlates of U.S. Military Assistance and Military Intervention," in ibid., pp. 143–63.

offset an act of nationalization, save perhaps in Iran in 1953, when Mossadegh threatened to nationalize the assets of foreign oil companies.[28] Even then, the United States was involved only indirectly, through the Central Intelligence Agency, in forcing Mossadegh out and replacing him with the Shah. According to one assessment, Argentina, Cuba, Chile, Peru, Egypt, Libya, Indonesia, Sri Lanka, and Iran have all succeeded in nationalizing foreign property, in some cases without payment of compensation, but the United States failed to intervene on behalf of the affected corporations.[29]

Perhaps there has been some willingness on the part of the business community to accept nationalization in view of the fact that some compensation is received in the form of tax write-offs, direct governmental aid, or insurance. Since business interests are more concerned about continuing commercial relations with the country, they may not want to press their opposition to nationalization too vigorously. The United States Congress did attempt to discourage nationalization by passing the Hickenlooper Amendment, which declared that foreign aid would be withdrawn from any state that nationalized American property abroad without appropriate compensation. The Pelly Amendment, adopted in 1968, required suspension of military sales and credit to nations that seized American fishing vessels more than twelve miles off the coast of any state. Despite the obligatory nature of both pieces of legislation, each has been applied only once—the Hickenlooper Amendment against Ceylon in 1962 and the Pelly Amendment against Peru in 1969.[30] It has been persuasively argued, however, that the restricted application of the Hickenlooper Amendment corresponds with corporate preferences, since business is concerned that formal sanctions would only strengthen nationalist hostility to foreign investment in Latin America.[31] Even when economic interests are as vitally affected, as they were during the 1973–74 oil boycott, the United States has failed to act decisively. The limited discussion of direct military action that oc-

28. James R. Kurth, "The Multinational Corporation, U.S. Foreign Policy, and the Less Developed Countries," in Abdul Aziz Said and Luiz R. Simmons, eds., *The New Sovereigns* (Englewood Cliffs, N.J.: Prentice-Hall, 1975), p. 147.

29. Charles V. Reynolds, *Theory and Explanation in International Politics* (London: Martin Robertson, 1973), p. 235.

30. Stephen D. Krasner, *Defending the National Interest* (Princeton, N.J.: Princeton University Press, 1968), p. 223.

31. Charles H. Lipson, "Corporate Preferences and Public Policies: Foreign Aid Sanctions and Investment Protection," *World Politics*, 28 (April 1976), 410.

curred at the time seemed to have been influenced more by national security concerns than by economic considerations.

The general lack of enthusiasm for military intervention on the part of many business interests has been underscored by the work of Russett and Hanson. Utilizing data based on questionnaires returned by 567 business executives, along with an analysis of fluctuations in the stock market and a content analysis of business publications, these scholars concluded that none of the sources showed substantial economically based enthusiasm for Vietnam or other military interventions since 1945. Economic interests were basically neutral or contradictory.[32]

THE MILITARY – INDUSTRIAL COMPLEX

Although one might provide evidence suggesting that business as a whole is not highly imperialistic and has much to gain from peace, a number of writers have asserted that the segment of business that is concerned with producing weapons has an economic interest in war or the threat of war. This view was particularly evident in the period following World War I, as George Bernard Shaw wrote biting satirical plays condemning the arms manufacturer, the Nye Commission was established by the Senate to inquire into the profits of the arms industry, and Charles A. Beard expounded on his "devil theory" of war, accusing economic interests of driving the United States dangerously close to war.[33] Additional concern about a military-industrial complex was raised in 1957 when the sociologist C. Wright Mills published his treatise on the so-called power elite.[34] Among Mills' power elite were three groups that were believed to be involved in a conspiratorial effort to keep military spending high—the military, business, and political leaders. Collusion among these three groups was facilitated by the interchangeability of roles as military officers became government officials (Eisenhower and de Gaulle) and also assumed roles in the corporate hierarchy. According to an official United States government estimate, in 1969 some 2,000 retired military offi-

32. Russett and Hanson, *Interest and Ideology*, p. 264.

33. See, for example, Shaw's "Major Barbara" and "Arms and the Man." The relevant study by Charles A. Beard is *The Devil Theory of War* (New York: Vanguard Press, 1936).

34. C. Wright Mills, *The Power Elite* (New York: Oxford University Press, 1956).

cers occupied key corporate positions in the civilian munitions area.[35] Another estimate has suggested that 50–60 percent of military retirees who are employed have positions that are directly dependent on the defense and aerospace industries.[36] The flow between the corporate world and government has also tended to be extensive; one estimate suggested that between 1940 and 1967, 70 out of 91 secretaries and undersecretaries of defense and state, secretaries of the three branches of the armed forces, chairmen of the Atomic Energy Commission, and directors of the CIA came from large corporations and investment houses.[37]

Most of the research on the military–industrial complex in the United States has centered on possible collusion between members of Congress—who ultimately vote on the military budget—and various economic interest groups, particularly those among their constituents. Several studies seem to suggest that members of Congress have not always voted in accordance with the economic interests of their state or district and its share of military–industrial facilities. Robert A. Bernstein and William W. Anthony found that the basic ideological orientation of members of Congress had a greater impact on the way they voted on the ABM issue than party commitment or potential economic benefits to their constituencies.[38] This finding was reinforced by another study, which found that the position of members of Congress on issues of military spending and foreign policy was explained much better by their general ideological perspectives than by the dependence of their districts on military contracts.[39] Similarly, Stephen Cobb found that the amount of defense spending within a state seemed not to have affected the votes of senators on foreign-policy issues.[40] On the other hand, it

35.   U.S. Congress, Joint Economic Committee, *The Economics of Military Procurement* (Washington, D.C.: Government Printing Office, 1969), p. 28.

36.   Albert Biderman, "Retired Soldiers Within and Without the Military–Industrial Complex," in Sam C. Sarkesian, ed., *The Military–Industrial Complex* (Beverly Hills, Calif.: Sage Publications, 1972), p. 113.

37.   Richard J. Barnet, *The Economy of Death* (New York: Atheneum, 1969), p. 88.

38.   Robert A. Bernstein and William W. Anthony, "The ABM Issue in the Senate, 1968–70," *American Political Science Review*, 68 (September 1974), 1198–1206.

39.   Wayne Moyer, "House Voting on Defense: An Ideological Explanation," in Bruce M. Russett and Alfred Stepan, eds., *Military Force and American Society* (New York: Harper & Row, 1973), pp. 106–42.

40.   Stephen Cobb, "The Impact of Defense Spending on Senatorial Voting Behavior," in Patrick J. McGowan, ed., *Sage International Yearbook of Foreign Policy Studies*, vol. 2 (Beverly Hills, Calif.: Sage Publications, 1973), pp. 135–60.

was discovered that members of Congress from districts with *disproportionately high* military employment were more likely to favor high levels of military spending and also to approve of more hawkish foreign-policy acts than those from districts with low military employment.[41] Data for the period 1952–72 have also shown that the congressional districts of members of the Armed Services Committees and the Appropriations Subcommittee on Defense and Military Construction received a higher proportion of additional military procurement expenditures than districts that were not similarly represented.[42]

That economic considerations tend to influence decisions related to military procurement is suggested by research conducted by James R. Kurth, who examined contracting procedures in the United States' aerospace industry during the 1960s.[43] On the basis of which corporations received prime contracts, Kurth developed what he called the bail-out imperative and the follow-on imperative. Contracts tended to be awarded either to contractors that were in deep financial trouble, as in the case of Lockheed, or to contractors that were just completing a previous contract. The primary motivation appeared to be keeping the lines of production open rather than any rational calculation of need or even cost-effectiveness.

Further evidence suggesting the existence of a military–industrial complex in the United States can be found in the extensive cost overruns of most weapon systems. The cost of the Trident submarine, for example, increased by more than 50 percent in a span of a few years. It is claimed that military and industrial interests conspire to negotiate military procurement contracts with low bids, only to have the costs rise sharply once Congress, the bureaucracy, and the American public are committed to the program. Weapons systems have also been developed to a level of sophistication far beyond what is necessary to fulfill their mission, and are used to replace weapons that are far from obsolete. Given the destructive capability of nuclear weapons, for example, does it really make much difference whether the accuracy of a nuclear missile is improved by a hundred feet? Billions of dollars have

41.   Bruce M. Russett, *What Price Vigilance?* (New Haven, Conn.: Yale University Press, 1970), pp. 56–90.

42.   Barry S. Rundquist and David E. Griffith, "The Parochial Constraint on Foreign Policymaking," in Richard L. Merritt, ed., *Foreign Policy Analysis* (Lexington, Mass.: D. C. Heath, 1975), p. 40.

43.   James R. Kurth, "Why We Buy the Weapons We Do," *Foreign Policy*, No. 11 (Summer 1973), 33–56.

been spent for just such purposes. Moreover, according to an official government report, "billions of dollars have been wasted on weapons systems that have had to be canceled because they did not work."[44] In the rush to production, many technical problems simply have not been resolved.

Should one assume that high military spending is a result of an elite conspiracy, it ought to be remembered that the mass public has been a vocal advocate of military expenditures, and this support helps explain the significant relationship between high military employment in a state or congressional district and hawkish voting patterns, as noted earlier. One need only reflect on the tremendous public outcry that erupts any time the Defense Department decides to close a military installation. The most vocal opponents are those employed by the defense industry itself, and they turn out to be most supportive of high military spending, as was shown by a survey of 381 men in Connecticut.[45] Since length of time spent in defense-related employment seemed to make a difference in the strength of the relationship, the author of this study concluded that there was a causal relationship between defense experience and belligerent attitudes on foreign policy; it was not simply a matter of self-selection. Among the general public, an analysis of polls conducted in the United States from 1945 through the 1960s reveals that "majorities of 60 percent or more of those with an opinion generally favored maintenance or increase in the defense budget size."[46]

Although most of the research related to the military–industrial complex argument has focused on the United States, this does not mean that similar complexes do not exist in other societies. Certain elite groups in the Soviet Union, for example, have joined together in support of higher defense spending. According to Vernon V. Aspaturian, these include the armed forces, the defense industry, heavy industry, and the conservative wing of the Communist party apparatus.[47] These groups were effective in expelling Nikita Khrushchev from

44. U.S. Congress, Joint Economic Committee, *The Economics of Military Procurement*, p. 3.

45. Nancy Edelman Phillips, "Militarism and Grass Roots Involvement in the Military Industrial Complex," *Journal of Conflict Resolution*, 17 (December 1973), 625–55.

46. Barry B. Hughes, *The Domestic Context of American Foreign Policy* (San Francisco: W. H. Freeman, 1978), p. 203.

47. Vernon V. Aspaturian, "The Soviet Military–Industrial Complex: Does It Exist?" *Journal of International Affairs*, 26, no. 1 (1972), 1–28.

power in 1964, primarily over the latter's Cuban missile policy, and increasing Soviet military spending to the point where the superior position of the United States has been threatened.

The military–industrial complex in the Soviet Union does not operate as a monolithic unit, despite the aggregative role that the Ministry of Defense may play for the military. The complex is composed of some eight defense–industrial ministries, which turn out weapons systems for five different military services. The competition that results, however, is likely not to reduce overall defense spending but, rather, to expand it as each coalition seeks to increase its part of the budgetary allocation. In some instances a military-industrial interest group may even collude to support another coalition's interests in return for support for their own spending objectives. The power of the eight defense–industrial ministries is indicated by the fact that full membership in the party's Central Committee is routinely accorded to these ministers. One long-time manager in the defense–industrial sector, D. D. Ustinov, even succeeded Marshal Andrei Grechko as defense minister in 1976, and was also elected a full member of the Politburo.[48]

One authority has noted that it would be only partly in jest to suggest that the United States *has* a military–industrial complex whereas the Soviet Union *is* a military–industrial complex. Among the factors that enhance the power of military–industrial interests in the Soviet Union, according to the same source, are tradition, insecurity, commitment to retaining the Soviet Eastern European empire, the fact that the military is the most modernized and skilled sector of the society, the ability of this sector to mobilize support through glorification of past and present military strength, and the association of the defense complex with all segments of the elite and the leadership.[49]

Evidence suggesting the existence of military–industrial complexes has also been provided for such states as Hitler's Germany and both prewar and postwar Japan.[50] With respect to postwar Japan, it has

48. Karl F. Spielmann, "Defense Industrialists in the USSR," in Dale R. Herspring and Ivan Volgyes, eds., *Civil–Military Relations in Communist Systems* (Boulder, Col.: Westview Press, 1978), pp. 108–9.

49. Seweryn Bialer, "The Soviet Political Elite and Internal Development in the USSR," in William E. Griffith, ed., *The Soviet Empire* (Lexington, Mass.: D. C. Heath, 1976), p. 37.

50. Albert Axelbank, *Black Star over Japan* (New York: Hill and Wang, 1972); Yale Maxon, *Control of Japanese Foreign Policy: A Study of Civil–Military Rivalry, 1930–1945* (Berkeley: University of California Press, 1957); William Manchester, *The Arms of Krupp* (Boston: Little, Brown, 1968).

been noted that business has not dominated the views of the defense industry, since the largest munitions manufacturers in Japan carry on most of their business in the nonmilitary sector.[51] The fact that Japan has diverted only about 1 percent of its GNP to the military sector in recent years suggests that the military–industrial complex has not been overly effective.

One of the most dangerous trends in the arms area has been the phenomenal increase in arms sales abroad. In terms of constant dollars, annual sales more than doubled between 1969 and 1978. An increasing number of weapons are finding their way to third world countries, as African imports were twenty-one times higher in 1978 than in 1969, and Middle Eastern imports were five times larger. Latin American imports tripled during the period, with Asian figures not far behind.[52] This is particularly troublesome because of the volatile nature of these regions, which have accounted for most of the violence in the world in the postwar era.

The extensive increase in the arms trade cannot be attributed exclusively to the greed of private munitions manufacturers, for in a number of states the defense industry is nationally owned. In the free-enterprise system of the United States, some 70 percent of the sales made in recent years have been handled directly by the government. With respect to the remaining exports, one study indicated that out of a total of 1,500 American arms manufacturers, all but twenty had been encouraged by the government to sell weapons abroad.[53]

Despite the destabilizing effect that arms sales abroad might have on various regions of the world, governments have been persuaded to continue the practice for a variety of reasons. These include arguments that the arms trade will help solve balance-of-trade problems, aid in balancing the budget, and provide full employment. Externally, arms exports can create friends and strengthen alliances. And of course, if these arguments fail to persuade, one can always point out that if we do not sell the arms, another nation will.

It would be easy to assume that states that have become major

51. F. C. Landon, *Japan's Foreign Policy* (Vancouver: University of British Columbia Press, 1973), p. 202.

52. U.S. Arms Control and Disarmament Agency, *World Military Expenditures and Arms Transfers 1969–1978* (Washington, D.C.: Government Printing Office, 1980), pp. 8–10.

53. Cited in Jonathan F. Galloway, "The Military–Industrial Linkages of U.S.-Based Multinational Corporations," *International Studies Quarterly*, 16 (December 1972), 505.

arms exporters have contributed extensively to global conflict, yet the matter is not that simple. Efforts to restrict the arms trade may only increase the incentive for potential recipients to develop their own military production facilities. Having invested in such facilities, they would be subject to continuing pressure from the newly created industrial–military complex to keep the factories in operation. The supply of armaments would then be increased beyond what it might have been had arms shipments been allowed. Second, failure to bolster the military capability of the weaker state in a regional conflict may only encourage aggression on the part of its enemy. Military assistance can be used to restore a regional balance of power and thus act as a deterrent. It might also be noted that arms embargoes to both sides in a conflict often favor the aggressor, which is usually militarily superior to the victim. This was particularly true in the case of the 1936 Italo-Ethiopian arms embargo, which clearly worked to the disadvantage of Ethiopia.

A recent study provides partial support for the notion that foreign military assistance does not increase regional conflict, but may even act to deter such conflict. In examining great-power aid to some fifteen states in Asia, Davis B. Bobrow and colleagues unexpectedly discovered that military assistance had a pronounced positive relationship with more cooperative international interactions among the Asian states themselves.[54] This was not true with respect to economic or human resources assistance, which had little impact upon intra-Asian cooperation.

Not all writers attempt to blame high military spending on the corporate heads, for whom military contracts are sometimes a mixed blessing; instead, it is argued that the military or the government itself is responsible. John Kenneth Galbraith asserts that the military suppliers are merely captive contractors dominated by the military services, which call the shots.[55] Seymour Melman seconds this view by suggesting that governmental managers have actually taken over corporate decision making with respect to the manufacture of weapons.[56]

Finally, it ought to be noted that neither evidence of support for higher military spending by a number of groups in a society nor high

54. Davis B. Bobrow et al., "The Impact of Foreign Assistance on National Development and International Conflict," *Journal of Peace Science*, 1 (Autumn 1973), 39–60.

55. John Kenneth Galbraith, *How to Control the Military* (New York: Signet Books, 1969), p. 10.

56. Seymour Melman, *Pentagon Capitalism* (New York: McGraw-Hill, 1970).

profit margins are necessarily evidence of a conspiratorial effort, but rather may be a genuine reflection of a perceived need to provide for the national defense. If one's economic interests are likely to benefit, it makes it that much easier to accept the notion that the more weapons one has, the better off one is, and that it is preferable to have too many than to have too few.

THE DISTRIBUTION OF RESOURCES

The availability of resources and the willingness to use such resources for given purposes have an important impact on both military and economic policies. The choice of which weapons system to emphasize and what level of armaments to strive for is influenced by available economic resources, which are not unlimited even in the wealthiest of states, and hard choices often have to be made. The United States' decision in 1954 to emphasize a massive nuclear retaliation strategy was influenced primarily by the desire to provide an effective deterrent at a less expensive price. Troops and conventional armaments are costly, and the hope was that nuclear threats might deter all wars, obviating the need for establishing a large conventional capability. The desire expressed at the time was to obtain a bigger bang for a buck. Similar considerations appear to have influenced Khrushchev's 1960 decision to reduce Soviet troops by some 1.2 million and rely more on strategic nuclear capability. Economic considerations also affected the decision of the People's Republic of China to support a People's Liberation Army instead of developing an expensive military structure. More resources for economic development could be provided if military spending could be kept low, and this would be more likely with a lightly armed People's Liberation Army, which could also be assigned to construction activities in rural areas. The Nixon doctrine, presented in Guam in 1969, in which the United States asked the states of Asia to take more responsibility for their own defense, appears to have been motivated as much by economic considerations, particularly the adverse balance of payments confronting the United States, as by growing public opposition to the use of American troops abroad in ventures like the Vietnam War. And Britain's military withdrawal from its bases east of Suez in the 1960s was a response to serious economic dislocation at home and to balance-of-payments difficulties.

Economic resources play a particularly important role in whether a state is able to produce nuclear weapons. To the extent that a state has its own supply of fissionable materials, its prospects of producing nuclear weapons are greatly enhanced, especially in view of the fact that imported fissionable products are likely to be subject to strict controls to make certain they are not diverted to military use. Consequently, states like Brazil and South Africa, which have thus far refused to ratify the Nuclear Nonproliferation Treaty and also have important supplies of fissionable materials, are in an excellent position to develop their own nuclear arsenals. The high capital cost of producing nuclear weapons precludes a number of LDCs from developing an extensive nuclear capability. India, although clearly an economically underdeveloped state in terms of per capita income, was able to divert sufficient resources to become the sixth state to explode a nuclear device by virtue of its high gross national product, which ranks tenth in the world.

The availability of resources also affects decisions on whether to fight or continue fighting wars. One writer has suggested that "in the century between the Napoleonic Wars and the First World War it was almost an axiom among major European powers that lack of finance was a strong deterrent against war."[57] The cycles in international conflict, in which one finds wars erupting every generation or so, may be due not only to weariness of war on the part of a given people but also to the fact that resources are depleted in war and it takes time to rebuild before a new military adventure can be undertaken.

Although a state might be hesitant to undertake war if its resources are limited, the same deficiencies may lead it to covet the economic assets of others, providing sufficient incentive for the attack, whatever the risks. Such behavior has occurred throughout recorded history as groups suffering from an inadequate hunting or harvest season have simply added to their food supplies by conquering neighboring peoples. Raymond W. Copson has cited a number of economically inspired aggressions in contemporary Africa, including Libya's annexation of part of northern Chad—a move motivated by the presence of uranium ore and other minerals; Nigeria and the Cameroons have fought over the Cross estuary because of fisheries and oil; Libya came into conflict with Tunisia over oil exploration of the continental shelf;

57.   Geoffrey Blainey, *The Causes of War* (New York: Free Press, 1973), p. 90.

and similar conflicts over economic interests have arisen between Nigeria and Chad, Mali and Upper Volta, and Somalia and Ethiopia.[58] One could add many examples from other parts of the world, but these examples from Africa suffice to make the point that economically motivated conflict is still very prevalent.

Attempting to retain access to raw materials that are in short supply also tends to be a major objective of states and can lead to conflict between them. One authority concluded that American policy makers generally place broader foreign-policy aims above the security of the supply of raw materials, and an assured supply is viewed as more important than the ideological goal of guaranteeing competitive markets.[59] That the United States can make the protection of supplies secondary to broader national interests may be partially due to its limited dependence on the importation of strategic materials. In the mid-1970s the United States was dependent on foreign sources for only 15 percent of its supply of critical nonfuel minerals, while Western Europe and Japan had to import, respectively, 75 percent and 90 percent of their supplies.[60]

International conflict has also been blamed on the disparities between rich and poor states in the international system. Such disparities have been accelerating rather than decreasing in recent decades. Whereas at the beginning of the nineteenth century the ratio of the economic position of the average citizen of the wealthiest states to that of the average citizen of the poorest states might have been about 2 to 1, today that disparity has been estimated at 40 to 1 in nominal terms and 20 to 1 in real terms.[61] For part of the developing world the economic situation has recently become so desperate that economists are beginning to speak of a "fourth world" representing the poorest of the poor states, which can look forward only to periods of mass starvation. Some have even suggested the possibility of pursuing a policy of triage based on the lifeboat concept, in which some people are allowed to die in order to assure the survival of the remainder.

The picture may not be entirely bleak for the less developed coun-

58.   Raymond W. Copson, "African International Politics: Underdevelopment and Conflict in the 70s," *Orbis*, 22 (Spring 1978), 227–45.

59.   Krasner, *Defending the National Interest*, p. 148.

60.   Ibid., p. 9.

61.   Cited in James W. Howe, *The U.S. and World Development: Agenda for Action, 1975* (New York: Praeger, 1975), p. 166.

tries if one recalls that the industrialized states themselves required several centuries to reach their current standard . Less time might be required for developing the third world, for it is able to obtain knowledge and technology at a relatively low cost. The greatest cost of technological development occurs early in the stage of invention and development, as many blind leads are taken before the most efficient means of production are developed. The LDC will be able to skip this phase and concentrate on proven methods.

But the critical question in terms of war and peace is whether a more equal sharing of the earth's resources will alleviate the problem of international conflict. It might be argued that war between wealthy and poor states is less likely than between states at similar levels of development, for the weaker will fear to attack the stronger, and the stronger will have no need to engage in military conflict since they will be able to obtain their basic foreign-policy goals without using force. There are still those who fear the prospect of poorer states obtaining nuclear capability—a move that would enable them to blackmail the northern states into providing a more equitable distribution of the world's resources. If confronted with a desperate economic situation, they would have little to lose in such a confrontation.

Empirical research dealing with the question of whether the developed or less developed states are more likely to engage in external conflict behavior appears to be divided. Major aggregate data studies conducted by Rudolph J. Rummel and covering the period 1955–57 found no relationship between various indicators of the level of economic development and the amount of foreign conflict in which the state engaged.[62] A similar study by East and Gregg discovered that economic development is not related to either conflict or cooperation.[63] The lack of a positive relationship was also found by Lewis F. Richardson in his study of three hundred deadly conflicts covering the longer period 1820–1945.[64]

On the other hand, the Feierabends, after categorizing some

62. Rudolph J. Rummel, "Some Attributes and Behavioral Patterns of Nations," *Journal of Peace Research*, 4, no. 2 (1967), 197; and "The Relationship Between National Attributes and Foreign Conflict Behavior," in J. David Singer, ed., *Quantitative International Politics* (New York: Free Press, 1968), p. 204.

63. Maurice East and Phillip M. Gregg, "Factors Influencing Cooperation and Conflict in the International System," *International Studies Quarterly*, 11 (September 1967), 266.

64. Lewis F. Richardson, *Statistics of Deadly Quarrels* (New York: Quadrangle/The N.Y. Times, 1960), p. xi.

eighty-four nations in terms of their level of development and relating these categories to the conflict behavior of each state for the period 1955–61, found that there is a tendency for "modern" countries to be peaceful and "nonmodern" nations to be externally aggressive.[65] Michael Haas analyzed some seventy nations and concluded that "rich countries have more foreign conflict than most of the economically developing nations of the world."[66] Finally, a study of the conflict behavior of 107 nations conducted in 1963 found that the more modernized states were more likely than the nonmodernized ones to respond militarily to their environment.[67]

The divergence in findings may be due to the different times analyzed, to the variation in the states included, or perhaps to the way conflict and economic development were measured. But despite disparate results from studies examining the effects of level of economic development on international conflict, it is clear that the overwhelming majority of conflicts in the postwar world have occurred within the third world. Edward E. Azar, who coded 596 domestic and international hostilities on a yearly basis for the period 1950–70, found 93 percent, or 525, of the coded events occurring in or involving small and poor states.[68] However, one or more middle or super powers were involved in 30 percent of these cases. A number of these instances involved the United States and the Soviet Union engaging in proxy conflicts through their respective allies. At least two empirical studies indicate that states that are more highly developed economically tend to be less enthusiastic about supporting international organization and engaging in international cooperation.[69] Apparently, the wealthier states are not willing to undertake the burden of supporting the poor as

65. Ivo Feierabend and Rosalind Feierabend, "Level of Development and Internation Behavior," in Richard Butwell, ed., *Foreign Policy and the Developing Nation* (Lexington: University of Kentucky Press, 1969), p. 158.

66. Michael Haas, "Societal Approaches to the Study of War," *Journal of Peace Research*, 2, no. 2 (1965), 323.

67. Warren R. Phillips, "The Conflict Environment of Nations: A Study of Conflict Inputs to Nations in 1963," in Jonathan Wilkenfeld, ed., *Conflict Behavior and Linkage Politics* (New York: David McKay, 1973), p. 143.

68. Edward E. Azar, *Probe for Peace: Small-State Hostilities* (Minneapolis: Burgess, 1973), p. 3.

69. Jack E. Vincent, "An Application of Attribute Theory to General Assembly Voting Patterns and Some Implications," *International Organization*, 26 (Summer 1972), 576; James P. Lester, "Technology, Politics, and World Order: Predicting Technological-Related International Outcomes," *World Affairs*, 140 (Fall 1977), 127–51.

would be required in a more integrated world. This suggests that world government will probably remain an unattainable goal as long as a high level of economic inequality among nations persists.

With respect to the argument that economic deprivation in itself leads to aggression, one should note that research on economic cycles seems to suggest the reverse in that conflict does not occur when deprivation is greatest but, rather, when things begin to improve. The British economic historian A. L. Macfie examined economic indicators for Britain during the period 1805–1914 and concluded that Britain's involvement in conflict was more likely to occur when an economic recovery was well under way.[70] Similar patterns were found for the United States in a study by Dexter Perkins, which showed that belligerent feeling in the United States tended to coincide with recovery from economic disturbances.[71] In support of this argument he offers the following examples: the War of 1812 came after a commercial upturn; the Mexican War came after the depression of 1837–42 had been succeeded by a period of improvement; the Spanish–American War came after the return of prosperity following the depression of 1893; entry into World War I came after some improvement following the economic decline of 1913–14; and World War II came after substantial recovery from the depression of the 1930s.

Noting a predictable regularity is far from explaining why such a pattern exists. Perhaps it is, as Perkins suggests, a result of an ebullient mood that naturally erupts as conditions begin to improve, or maybe it is simply due to the restraint shown by governments that lack resources to engage in warlike activity when the economy is in a dismal state, or perhaps the pattern persists only because increased external hostility has stimulated the economy as a nation prepares for war. Whatever the explanation, the pattern is highly compatible with James C. Davies' theory of revolution, in which revolutionary fervor within a state was seen to increase after economic conditions improved rather than during the periods of greatest economic deprivation.[72]

70. A. L. Macfie, "The Outbreak of War and the Trade Cycle," *Economic History*, February 1938.

71. Dexter Perkins, *The American Approach to Foreign Policy*, rev. ed. (New York: Atheneum, 1968), pp. 136–55.

72. James C. Davies, "Toward a Theory of Revolution," *American Sociological Review*, 27 (April 1962), 5–19.

POPULATION PRESSURE

Overpopulation has been a major factor contributing to the problem of economic deprivation, which in turn has been alleged to exacerbate international conflict. The problem has been examined by the eighteenth-century writer Thomas Malthus, who noted that the world's food supply grows only at an arithmetic rate, whereas population tends to increase at a geometric rate. What this means is that the threat of overpopulation will be an unceasing problem and, according to some, can be "solved" as Malthus suggested only by war or starvation.

The magnitude of the global population problem can be seen by noting that at present the world's population is doubling every 35 or 36 years. This means that the world's current population of 4 billion will increase to 8 billion by 2015 and 16 billion by 2050. Some 70 percent of that population resides in the less developed world and is subjected to frequent famines and malnutrition. Generally speaking, the world's food supplies are extensive and can support several billion more people, particularly if the ocean's rich food resources are properly exploited. The problem of food is largely a distributional one, in which some regions have great abundance and others suffer deprivation. Redistributing foodstuffs is not an easy task, though. If a state provides food to LDCs at nominal or no cost, the opportunities for others to sell to that state are correspondingly decreased. Thus, humanitarian gestures of food aid can create serious conflict with other states that export agricultural products. Governments have not always distributed available food in accordance with their own domestic needs. Part of a state's population may be starving, but the government of a less developed country, desiring to increase exports and gain vitally needed development funds, may encourage a large agricultural export market.

Dietary habits also affect the supply of food. For example, the insistence of people in the United States and other developed countries on eating substantial amounts of beef undermines the potential global supply of grain, since it takes nearly seven pounds of grain to produce one pound of beef.

Richard A. Falk has gone somewhat beyond Malthusian theory in explaining just why one might expect increasing violence in the global system as population grows. These reasons include the following:

1. Crowding creates pressure for expansion into emptier spaces.

2. Increased resource demands create incentives to assure resource supplies.

3. Overpopulation generates mass misery, which in turn leads to repressive systems of government and gives rise to extremist ideologies.

4. The widening gap between rich and poor induced by population pressures tends to intensify a sense of injustice.

5. Population pressure in rich countries reinforces existing barriers to migration across boundaries and reduces willingness to provide food assistance.[73]

Despite some plausible arguments that population pressure might lead to increased violence, statistical studies of the nineteenth and twentieth centuries find little relationship between population growth and density, on the one hand, and international conflict, on the other.[74] In his *Study of War* Quincy Wright concluded that more than overpopulation is necessary to explain international violence. Whereas population pressure might lead to imperialistic wars, France behaved in a bellicose fashion in the late nineteenth century primarily because its population was declining relative to that of Germany, creating concern about the balance of power.

Throughout history mass migrations have occurred as a means of dealing with overpopulation and a contracting food supply. Such expansions have resulted in war and conflict with neighboring states whose territories have been affected. Some writers have suggested that a major factor in the present Sino-Soviet rivalry is population pressure from China, which is seen as having designs on sparsely populated areas in the Soviet Union. The Soviet Union may well have visions of a modern Genghis Khan sweeping through the steppes of Russia in order to provide land for his people.

Mass migration through territorial conquest, however, is not the

73. Richard A. Falk, *This Endangered Planet* (New York: Random House, 1971), p. 156.

74. J. David Singer, "The 'Correlates of War' Project: Interim Report and Rationale," *World Politics*, 24 (January 1972), 267; Nazli Choucri and James Bennett, "Population, Resources, and Technology: Political Implications of the Environmental Crisis," *International Organization*, 26 (Spring 1972), 183–84.

only way for a state to come to terms with an ever-increasing population that places severe demands on its limited resources. In the past, Mexico, Japan, and Italy have been quite successful in resolving such pressures through peaceful mass emigration to other countries. Moreover, improved technology may help minimize population pressure by providing more food and resources for the increasing population.

Despite the argument that technological growth might help resolve the problem of population growth, Nazli Choucri and Robert C. North have developed a theory of lateral growth that holds that the growth of technology creates pressure for expansion rather than reducing such pressures.[75] Technological growth, combined with a growing population, is seen as creating pressure for lateral expansion because it requires increased kinds and quantities of resources to sustain and advance the technology. At the same time, not all lateral pressure results in imperialism or international conflict. Trade might be used to satisfy demands, as in the case of Sweden and other Scandinavian countries that have been subjected to such pressures. Britain, France, and Germany, on the other hand, responded with efforts to expand their colonial empires during the period 1870–1914. Between 60 and 85 percent of the variance in colonial expansion for these three states can be explained by population growth, technological growth, and military preparedness. Since more manipulable variables, such as leadership and diplomatic interaction, contributed little to such expansion, it may be somewhat difficult to control expansionist pressures. The major consequence of overseas expansion, of course, has been the accompanying violence, in terms of both colonial wars and wars between colonial powers.

There has been at least one other attempt to test the lateral pressure theory. This dealt with the behavior of ten Central Asian states during the period 1950–70.[76] Utilizing indicators of population growth, technological growth, and military preparedness to measure lateral pressure, the study concluded that violent states did indeed have higher lateral pressure scores than disputing states, which in turn

75. Nazli Choucri and Robert C. North, "Dynamics of International Conflict," in Raymond Tanter and Richard H. Ullman, eds., *Theory and International Relations* (Princeton, N.J.: Princeton University Press, 1972), pp. 80–122.

76. Frederick S. Pearson, Kenneth E. Rudd, and Robert A. Baumann, "Critical Analysis of Two-System Level Approaches to the Study of War," *Peace Research Society (International) Papers*, 27 (1977), 59–66.

scored higher than peaceful states. The relationships, however, were not overwhelming, and power seemed to predict the occurrence of conflicts and military clashes in Asia better than population and technological growth.

Several economic theories, including those related to imperialism, the role of a military–industrial complex, and relative deprivation, have been examined, yet there seems to be little consensus on whether economic factors help explain the occurrence of international conflict. Lewis F. Richardson, analyzing wars that occurred during the nineteenth and twentieth centuries, concluded that only 29 percent of those wars resulted from economic causes.[77] Economists themselves have often played down the role of economic factors in explaining war. The distinguished international economist Charles P. Kindleberger concluded that "war is not predominantly an economic affair. Economic causes of war do not dominate."[78] This view is seconded by another eminent economist, Jacob Viner, who sees war as "essentially a political phenomenon, a way of dealing with disputes between groups."[79]

Perhaps a major reason for the lack of agreement on how or whether economic factors contribute to international conflict is the belief that economic interdependence will contribute to peace rather than war. It is to such issues that we now turn our attention.

ECONOMIC INTERDEPENDENCE

There is little doubt that the world has been growing smaller and more interdependent in recent years. It is now possible, through the use of satellites in outer space, to be in instant contact with other peoples throughout the world. The age of jet travel has enabled people to visit distant lands in ever-increasing numbers. Economic transactions involving trade and the establishment of foreign subsidiaries and branch banks have accelerated at a rapid pace. One estimate has shown world trade increasing by more than 7 percent per year during the postwar period, and direct foreign invest-

---

77. Richardson, *Statistics of Deadly Quarrels*, p. xi.
78. Kindleberger, *Power and Money*, p. 101.
79. Cited in Cohen, *The Question of Imperialism*, p. 247.

ment and overseas production have grown at an even faster pace.[80] Despite the worldwide recession of recent years, there has been little effort to resort to the heavy-handed protectionist policies that predominated during the 1930s, extending the depression from one state to another.

A number of positive outcomes are expected from an increasingly interdependent world. In the first place, interdependence is viewed as a device for lessening conflict between states. A state contemplating hostile activities may be deterred for fear that its foreign assets may be seized in retaliation and its economic interaction disrupted. As states invest more and more in foreign areas or increase their trade with another state, they become increasingly dependent on the economic and political stability of the foreign state. A major restraint on the willingness of OPEC countries to raise the price of oil is the existence of billions of dollars in investment located in developed countries like the United States. The OPEC countries fear that increased oil prices will further weaken the economies and the value of the currency of the states where substantial OPEC investments are located. As a result, OPEC states, along with other foreign and domestic investors, would suffer substantial losses on their investments in those countries. Corporations with large overseas foreign investments may also work to restrain the conflict behavior of their respective governments for fear that such conflict might increase the likelihood of nationalization by host governments or the removal of special business incentives extended to overseas investors, not to mention the fear of losing a major source of raw materials. States that are interested in protecting their economic interests abroad are likely to choose more subtle and covert means of influence rather than overt military action.

Free-trade theorists envision a peaceful world evolving from economic specialization, in which each state produces the products in which it has a comparative advantage. Such a system would work to the economic benefit of all, but more important, it would generate such interdependence that conflict between states would have to be reduced for fear of disrupting important external sources of supply. Economic interests would find it necessary to lobby in favor of peace in order to survive in an interdependent and specialized world.

Functionalists and neo-functionalists have also theorized that

---

80. Robert O. Keohane and Joseph S. Nye, *Power and Interdependence* (Boston: Little, Brown, 1977), p. 39.

economic interdependence will induce those involved in international interactions to replace narrow nationalist loyalties with broader, transnational loyalties. According to the functionalist notion, involvement in economic transactions across states will tend to generate common ways of looking at issues and new loyalties in which one begins to recognize the interests one shares with people in other societies. One is most likely to see such functional loyalties developing between businesspeople as well as between international labor groups. Loyalties that are now directed toward the nation–state might gradually be transfered to multinational corporations or other supranational institutions. The MNC is viewed as facilitating the integration of peoples of different nations as they involve themselves in a common cause. This in turn should aid in developing an international outlook on the part of those who participate in international activities.

Despite these hopes, involvement in MNCs and international business in general appears not to have a significant impact on the development of supranational attitudes. In one of the few studies examining the impact of employment in an MNC on international attitudes, Bernard Mennis and Karl P. Sauvant concluded, on the basis of 2,766 questionnaires returned by German business executives, that "corporate internationalization, transnational contact, and value priorities are not at all correlated with any of the nine integration variables."[81] Similar results were discovered in an earlier study by Bauer, Pool, and Dexter, which found that transnational participation by business elites did not change their basic attitudes with respect to foreign-trade legislation.[82]

Economic interdependence may help reduce international conflict in yet another way. Because there are presumed rewards in an interdependent economy, states may be more willing to tolerate undesirable policies on the part of other states, recognizing that long-term cooperation is worth a temporary setback. Participants in an integrated society are likely to accept the notion that they cannot win in every instance, and will compromise with the expectation that others will reciprocate in the future.

Finally, it might be noted that the Soviet and Chinese need for technology, credit, and certain trade items, which the Western states

81.   Bernard Mennis and Karl P. Sauvant, *Emerging Forms of Transnational Community* (Lexington, Mass.: D. C. Heath, 1976), p. 116.

82.   Raymond A. Bauer, Ithiel de Sola Pool, and Lewis A. Dexter, *American Business and Public Policy: The Politics of Foreign Trade* (Chicago: Aldine-Atherton, 1972).

can provide, has contributed to detente and normalization of relations with the West. The People's Republic of China is willing to forgo the Maoist prescription of self-reliance in order to modernize; and prior to the Afghan incursion the Soviet Union, given its perceived need for American trade and technology, was more conciliatory on a host of issues ranging from SALT to the treatment of Soviet Jews.

There is far from a consensus regarding the benefits of free trade and economic interaction as a means of increasing interdependence and well-being among the nations of the world. The inequities in the trade structure between the developed and developing countries have come under considerable criticism, most notably from the Latin-American economist Raul Prebisch.[83] According to Prebisch, free trade favors the North, or the developed states, in contrast to the South, or the less developed states, because of economic structural differences between countries at different stages of development. The South must engage in trade largely in terms of primary products, given its nonindustrialized status. Because of this, LDCs are confronted with a situation of continuing weakness in the balance of trade, since the value of the primary products that they are able to sell has declined relative to the value of manufactured products, which they are forced to import. Three basic reasons are given for this phenomenon:

1. Because of strong labor unions in the developed countries, prices tend to rise substantially more rapidly there than in the South. This is due to the fact that labor unions are able to demand higher wages, which are reflected in higher prices.

2. Primary products suffer in contrast to manufactured products because the demand for such products is inelastic. People can eat only so much and consume only so much energy. This means that unlike the case of many manufactured products, which have not yet saturated the world's markets, efforts to increase productivity of primary products will not increase income but, rather, will tend to lower the price per unit.

3. The value of primary products has tended to decrease in many instances because of the development of synthetic substitutes for many such products.

83. Raul Prebisch, *Towards a New Trade Policy for Development* (Geneva: United Nations, 1964).

Not all economists agree with Prebisch's basic argument that the value of raw materials has been declining relative to that of manufactured products. The experiences of the OPEC states with their quadrupling of oil prices in 1973–74 demonstrates quite the reverse. Raymond Vernon notes that a review of recent studies seems to show an indeterminate relationship between the price of raw materials and the price of manufactured goods and that, if anything, it might be easier to argue that the prices of manufactured goods have declined in relative terms.[84]

Johan Galtung has also called attention to the structural inequality that forces the LDCs, or what he calls the periphery, to concentrate on the production of raw materials for export.[85] In turn, this means that such states are denied the added value that comes from processing their own products and are also forced to pay the transportation costs required to import the processed goods. Dependency theorists, as these writers have come to be known, argue further that the developed countries attempt to keep the LDCs dependent on external trade through the use of foreign aid and investment policies that discourage domestic capital formation and uneven development across various economic sectors.

Several studies have sought to test various aspects of dependency theory, but their results have been inconclusive. R. Dan Walleri, who analyzed 88 countries during the 1960s, found that the greater the trade dependence of the LDC, the lower its level of development, as predicted by the theory.[86] In fact, he found that some 48 percent of the variance in level of economic development achieved in 1970 could be explained by the three measures of trade dependence that he used for 1960. On the other hand, empirical studies involving Latin America and Africa in the mid-1960s found that economic dependency actually promoted economic growth.[87]

It has been argued that LDCs will be forced to remain dependent and unable to accumulate the capital necessary for industrialization

---

84. Vernon, *Storm over the Multinationals*, p. 152.

85. Johan Galtung, "A Structural Theory of Integration," *Journal of Peace Research*, 5, no. 4 (1968), 375–95.

86. R. Dan Walleri, "Trade Dependence and Underdevelopment," *Comparative Political Studies*, 11 (April 1978), 94–127.

87. Robert R. Kaufman et al., "A Preliminary Test of the Theory of Dependence," *Comparative Politics*, 7 (April 1975), 303–30; Patrick J. McGowan and Dale L. Smith, "Economic Dependence in Black Africa: An Analysis of Competing Theories," *International Organization*, 32 (Winter 1978), 179–235.

unless certain trade preferences are provided. In the initial stages it is impossible for the infant industries of the South to compete with the well-developed manufacturing industries of the North. Tariff protection and special preferences will have to be given to allow these industries to develop so that they may become competitive. It has also been suggested that a system of indexation be instituted in order that the price the LDC receives for its exports will not be out of line with the increasingly higher prices it must pay for importing manufactured products. However, a general indexing of the prices of all raw materials may be of little use, since the developed countries as well as the poor ones export primary products.[88]

These structural inequities in the international trading system directly affect the foreign policies of states that perceive themselves to be disadvantaged. The United Nations Conference for Trade and Development has been a major organ seeking to obtain structural change, and the developing countries have also pressed for a new international economic order through the General Assembly of the United Nations. Some of these pressures are beginning to bear fruit: Japan and a number of European states adopted a preferential trading system for the developing world in 1971, and the United States followed suit in 1976.

The success of OPEC in increasing oil prices throughout the world is indicative of the improved position of third world countries in obtaining an increasing share of the profits from their raw materials. Similar cartels have been developed with respect to bauxite and coffee and have been able to raise world prices on those products. Most countries with economies based on the export of raw materials have also had some success in renegotiating concessionary agreements to their own advantage.

It is by no means clear that economic interdependence decreases conflict, for with such interdependence there are more issues over which to differ. If there were little or no need to interact with other political entities, international conflict might be considerably reduced. Economic interdependence may only heighten antagonism, particularly on the part of a state that feels itself to be in an unequal economic relationship. For example, economic interdependence between Canada and the United States has tended to increase Canadian nationalism as

---

88. Raymond Aron, "Europe and the United States," in David S. Landes, ed., *Western Europe: The Trials of Partnership* (Lexington, Mass.: D. C. Heath, 1977), p. 50.

American investments have intruded into the Canadian economy, bringing with them a fear of economic and, ultimately, political and cultural control. An examination of the participants in some forty postwar conflicts with fatalities exceeding one hundred led one analyst to conclude that countries within the same trading group are "more than twice as likely to fight than are nations which belong to different groups, or to none."[89] Similarly, another study revealed that among major powers of the nineteenth and twentieth centuries, trade partners were more likely than non-trade partners to engage in war against one another.[90] At the same time, a study based on trade statistics for thirty countries revealed that the states "with the greatest levels of economic trade engage in the least amounts of hostility. In fact, a doubling of trade on average leads to a 20 percent diminution of belligerence." When statistical adjustments were made for causality, the relationship between trade and decreased conflict proved to be even more robust.[91]

International economic interdependence also means that the nation–state is more vulnerable to crises originating in other parts of the system. If an outside state is dependent on investment, trade, or raw materials, the incentive to intervene in foreign conflicts will be very high whenever economic interests are threatened. Such interdependence could either exacerbate the conflict by encouraging other outside powers to exploit it, or minimize the conflict by increasing the effectiveness of deterrence. In examining seventeen cases of international conflict during the period 1935–61 in which deterrence was relevant, Bruce M. Russett concluded that "economic interdependence may be virtually essential to successful deterrence."[92] In such instances the defender's credibility was enhanced in the mind of the would-be attacker, who might logically assume that a defender would be more likely to take effective deterrent or defensive action to protect an area where important economic interests are at stake than one where they are less significant.

89. Bruce M. Russett, *International Regions and the International System* (Chicago: Rand McNally, 1967), pp. 198–99.

90. Charles S. Gochman, "Military Confrontation and the Likelihood of War: The Major Powers, 1820–1970." Paper delivered at the Annual Conference of the North American Peace Science Society (International), Cambridge, Mass., 1975.

91. Solomon William Polachek, "Conflict and Trade," *Journal of Conflict Resolution*, 24 (March 1980), 55.

92. Bruce M. Russett, "The Calculus of Deterrence," *Journal of Conflict Resolution*, 7 (June 1963), 97–109.

CONCLUSION

Our discussion has indicated that major differences exist between conservative and radical theorists with respect to interpretations of the role of economic factors in the making of foreign policy. Radical theorists generally see economic factors as highly deterministic, believing that one can trace most international conflicts to economic origins. They have expounded on the relationship between capitalism and imperialism, and have tended to support a conspiratorial view of the role played by multinational corporations and capitalist governments, particularly with respect to military spending and economic aid and trade. Radical theorists view the wealthy states as structurally and actively exploiting the less developed states in an effort to keep them economically dependent. They anticipate that things will only get worse for the LDC unless there is a genuine Marxist revolution.

Conservative theorists, on the other hand, challenge many of the causal linkages suggested by radical theorists. Imperialism, after all, is much older than capitalism, and only a small group of business interests has profited from war and imperialism. Instead, the conservatives see a growing economic interdependence between states, which they feel will produce a more conciliatory and integrated world. They also see a positive reward for the LDCs arising from foreign aid and investment, making possible a contraction in the time required for industrialization, a process that took centuries for some of the existing developed states.

Our review of other economic variables revealed that resource availability makes a difference in how active a policy a state can pursue, for a state with limited resources can ill afford to pursue a global foreign policy. Studies of whether developed or less developed states engage in more international conflict have not been conclusive, but it is clear that most of the violence in the postwar period has occurred among third world countries. Resource availability must be related to population, which can serve as either a liability or an asset as far as the power of a state is concerned. Recent statistical evidence, however, does not support the Malthusian theory of overpopulation as a major explanation of war.

Many observers have viewed economic interdependence as a way of damping international conflict, but since such interdependence increases the involvement of states with each other, it also expands the number of issues over which they might clash. The relationship appears to be curvilinear, as conflict is lowest when states are not interdependent and therefore are engaging in little interaction, or when their economies are so intertwined that conflict would threaten a highly desirable relationship. Extensive economic interaction is perhaps most threatening to peaceful relationships when states feel completely dependent on an economically superior group, as in the case of the North–South cleavage.

No final answers are possible, but it is clear that economic factors influence foreign policy in a variety of ways. Perhaps most important, such factors have a critical role with respect to the amount of power a state can exercise in the international system—an issue to which we now turn.

7

NATIONAL
POWER
CAPABILITIES

Perhaps no concept is more central to an understanding of foreign policy than that of power. Yet no concept has stirred up more controversy regarding what it means and how it ought to be measured. There is a general consensus that in terms of capabilities the United States is the most powerful state that has ever existed, yet we have seen it unable to prevail over small states like Cuba and North Vietnam; it was neutralized into seeming ineffectiveness in the Iranian hostage situation; and it has often had small, fledgling states snub its attempts to influence votes in the United Nations. The same might be said of the Soviet Union, which, despite its obvious power advantages, has had trouble prevailing in Afghanistan and in controlling the behavior of its neighboring satellite states of Poland and Rumania. But to be able to explain just how such circumstances can arise, it is first necessary to examine what is meant by this elusive term.

THE CONCEPT OF POWER

Power has generally been thought of as the capacity to control or influence the behavior of others. Much of the confusion with respect to this concept arises over the failure to distinguish between the capacity to act and the actual exercise of power. A state may enjoy a number of tangible assets of power, such as a strong industrial base, a large population, advanced technology, and important resources; it may also rank high in various intangible factors of power, such as high morale, effective leadership, and high educational levels, yet be unable or unwilling to translate these components into actual influence. One researcher, for example, in estimating the differential between capability and influence during the period 1925–30, suggested that in terms of capabilities, the following rank order would be appropriate: (1) United States, (2) Germany, (3) Great Britain, (4) France, (5) Russia, (6) Italy, (7) Japan. But in terms of impact on the international system and the responses the state was able to evoke in seeking to change the behavior of other states, the rank order was: (1) France, (2) Great Britain, (3) Italy, (4) Germany, (5) Russia, (6) Japan, (7) United States.[1] On the other hand, leaders like Tito of Yugoslavia, Nasser of Egypt, and Nehru of India probably exerted far more influence than the limited capabilities of their respective states would justify.

Even in situations in which a state is clearly interested in exercising power, its capabilities are not always translated into influence. Several factors help explain this failure. In the first instance, power is a perceptual relationship. A state may have abundant capabilities that would allow it to prevail in most situations, but that capability must be perceived as both available and likely to be utilized before another actor will be influenced by it. Perceptions may often be in error as a result of a variety of blinders and communication problems, as shown in Chapter 2, but rightly or wrongly this is the information on which states will act in determining their responses. The consequence has been, according to an estimate by Quincy Wright, that states have miscalculated their own and others' power more than 50 percent of the time.[2]

Second, it should be noted that power is a relative and reciprocal relationship. A state may be able to exercise power over one state but not over another. One authority has suggested that there is a loss-of-power gradient, for a state finds it more difficult to influence states at

1. K. J. Holsti, *International Politics: A Framework for Analysis,* 3rd ed. (Englewood Cliffs, N.J.: Prentice-Hall, 1977), pp. 170–71.

2. Cited in Morton Berkowitz, P. G. Bock, and Vincent J. Fuccillo, *The Politics of American Foreign Policy* (Englewood Cliffs, N.J.: Prentice-Hall, 1977), p. 286.

greater geographic distance than those close at hand.[3] This may be partially an element of resolve, as a state is less concerned with marshaling all of its power in regions that are perceived as remote to its interests. This would certainly help explain the United States' failure in Vietnam. Power is also relative and reciprocal in the sense that in any influence situation each party has some impact on the other. Such is true of even the weakest states, which, if nothing else, can threaten collapse, thus providing a vacuum that a larger state's adversaries can penetrate.

Third, power tends to be issue oriented. A state may have power over another state on one issue but not with respect to others, for sources of power other than reward and punishment become operative. A state may be influenced because it sees a given request as legitimate. A nation that is perceived as an alliance leader is more likely to be seen as making an appropriate influence request than one that is not. But even in this instance an influence attempt by the alliance leader is likely to be more effective if it involves issues affecting the common defense than if it is concerned with economic or ideological issues, which may be viewed as beyond the scope of the alliance commitment. If a state perceives an act as threatening its domestic sovereign rights, it is likely to be highly resistant to influence efforts. A state that is perceived as having expertise or as able to serve as an appropriate role model will also enjoy greater influence than the mere measure of its national power capabilities would suggest.

Fourth, power is affected by one's expectations in relation to another state. The Soviet Union may actually benefit from expectations of a rather heavy-handed style. As a result, when it makes conciliatory moves it is more likely to get credit and a responsive reaction from other actors than the United States would if it made similar moves.[4] Concessions tend to be expected of the latter and therefore are more likely to be taken for granted.

Fifth, a discrepancy between national power capabilities and influence is likely to arise by virtue of the tendency of both decision

3. Kenneth E. Boulding, *Conflict and Defense: A General Theory* (New York: Harper & Row, 1962).

4. Frederick W. Frey, "The Perception of Power: A Developmental Perspective," paper delivered at the Annual Meeting of the International Studies Association, Los Angeles, 1980, p. 24.

makers and analysts to ascribe high power positions to nations that are perceived as more aggressive, rather than those that have the most significant national power capabilities. Both the People's Republic of China and the Soviet Union, during their more assertive days in the 1950s and early 1960s, were generally seen as more significant and powerful than their capabilities at the time would have indicated.

The elusiveness of power can be seen in the fairly rapid changes in the power fortunes of states in the last few years. Take, for example, the rising power of the OPEC states and contrast it with the dramatic fall in the power fortunes of the highly energy-dependent states. The latter, particularly Japan and a number of highly industrialized European states, have been forced to tread a delicate line with respect to Middle Eastern issues, and several were even willing to abandon Israel in order to placate the oil-rich states of the Middle East. Domestic events can also unsettle the power position of a state, as in the case of the 1968 riots in France and the subsequent resignation of President de Gaulle.

Given these problems in conceptualizing power, it is small wonder that students of international relations have not been very successful in developing agreed-upon measures of power. Perhaps the most satisfying operational conceptualization has been that of Robert A. Dahl, who suggested that power is equal to the ability of A to get B to take action X minus the probability that B would take action X anyway.[5] Despite the logic of such a formula, no attempt has been made to apply it in analyzing influence attempts in international relations. The difficulties of measuring just what B would do in the absence of the influence attempt by A are almost insurmountable.

Following the lead of Harold Lasswell, who saw power as determining who got what, when, and how, Deutsch and Edinger have suggested measuring power in terms of ascertaining satisfaction with the final output of the foreign-policy process.[6] To do this they examined a range of foreign-policy issues confronting the Federal Republic of Germany. Various internal groups such as parties, pressure groups, and public opinion, along with external national actors, were rated on a three-point scale indicating relative satisfaction and dissatisfaction with each issue. For example, on the issue of the Paris Agreements of

---

5.   Robert A. Dahl, "The Concept of Power," *Behavioral Science*, 2 (July 1957), 201–15.
6.   Karl W. Deutsch and Lewis J. Edinger, *Germany Rejoins the Powers* (Stanford, Calif.: Stanford University Press, 1959).

1955, which allowed the Federal Republic to become a member of the Western European Union and NATO, the German military was in high agreement, scoring a +3, whereas the Soviet Union was given a −3, indicating overwhelming opposition. Although high satisfaction with the results may suggest only followership rather than influence, the measure can be useful in indicating which actors have little power in influencing the outcome, since their scores tend to be negative.

Most efforts to measure power in the international system have focused on developing indicators of national power capabilities, including such tangible factors as population, industrial capability, and military budgets and forces. A. F. K. Organski and Wilhelm Fuchs gave considerable weight to population in their indexes of power, each of which consisted of only two or three items.[7] As a result, projective data collected in the early 1960s predicted that the People's Republic of China would become the most powerful actor in the world in the 1980s. Such is hardly the case, as the Chinese leadership itself admits to a status more equivalent to that of the developing world especially in terms of economic development. Giving too much weight to population overlooks the negative aspects of having too many mouths to feed, which impedes capital savings and economic growth.

The most popular indexes for industrialization and economic power are gross national product, energy consumption, and iron and steel production. Recent events, however, have demonstrated that high energy consumption can create power vulnerability, particularly if it requires extensive importation from abroad. Some analysts also include measures of modernization in their indexes of economic power. These might include such indicators as urbanization, technology, and a relatively small agricultural work force.

Most neglected in the construction of indexes of power are the so-called intangible factors. The label "intangible" is indicative of the feeling that such factors are difficult, if not impossible, to measure. The problem may not be insurmountable, for one might utilize measures of governmental stability or public support as measured by public-opinion polls to get some notion of morale. Leadership quality might be tapped in a similar fashion. However, what cannot always be ascer-

7. A. F. K. Organski, *World Politics*, 2nd ed. (New York: Knopf, 1968). Fuchs' work is discussed in Karl W. Deutsch, *The Analysis of International Relations*, 1st ed. (Englewood Cliffs, N.J.: Prentice-Hall, 1968), p. 23.

tained in advance is the degree to which a people will rally around a flag or a leader when attacked from the outside. It was hardly expected that the Soviet population would develop such unity in supporting its government as it did after the battle of Stalingrad. Some even speculated that the Ukranians and other non-Russians would defect to the invading Nazis. Morale was the factor that turned the war around.

The difficulty of measuring power can also be seen in attempts to assess relative military capabilities. Such efforts have often led to acrimonious debates over the question of whether the Soviet Union or the United States is ahead in the strategic arms race. The fact that the two powers emphasize different delivery systems makes the problem especially difficult, as the United States has preferred bombers and submarine-launched ballistic missiles, whereas the Soviets have emphasized intercontinental land-launched missiles. But how does the United States' lead in cruise missiles, MIRVed missiles, and the accuracy of its missiles affect the power equation? On the other hand, the Soviet Union has missiles that will each deliver a substantially heavier payload of nuclear destruction. Yet others will remind us that the Soviet Union must be concerned not only with adequate defense against the United States but also with defense against a hostile China—a threat that is not currently shared by the United States. And the debate goes on and on, complicating not only decisions about how large a military budget, and what kind, to adopt but also about how to determine military equivalence in the Strategic Arms Limitation Talks.

Measuring military capability is not much easier when it comes to nonnuclear weapons. Comparisons of overall defense budgets are misleading because of the differing budgetary procedures used in various states. Soviet military budgets have always been viewed as undervalued, since they exclude a number of budgetary items included in American defense budgets. Comparing numbers of troops is difficult because divisions within the Soviet Union are considerably smaller than those in the United States. Equivalence would require that the United States count reserve and National Guard troops in its force totals.[8] In addition, it must be remembered that an aggressor needs larger numbers than a defender does, since the former must normally

---

8.   Edward N. Luttwak, "The Missing Dimension of U.S. Defense Policy: Force, Perceptions, and Power," in Donald C. Daniel, ed., *International Perceptions of the Superpower Military Balance* (New York: Praeger, 1978), p. 23.

operate with longer supply lines. One should also try to account for qualitative differences in conventional weapons.

Since power involves perception, some observers, such as Kissinger and Nixon, believe that the most important way to increase power is simply to increase aggregate military spending. As a result, they often seem less concerned about which specific military programs benefit but, rather, are interested primarily in communicating resolve. Soviet leaders also tend to think in terms of the overall military balance, defined as the "correlation of world forces," which includes factors like ideology. At present they appear to believe this correlation to be in their favor.

Despite the elusiveness and complexity of the concept of power, it remains central to the study of foreign-policy behavior. In the following sections we will examine how certain geopolitical capabilities might affect power, as well as the role played by military and economic capabilities. Efforts will be made to explain why, when, and where certain states are able to prevail over others in the international system and how relative power capabilities affect foreign-policy choices.

GEOPOLITICAL SOURCES OF POWER

Certain states enjoy national power capabilities by virtue of the geographic conditions they are endowed with or are able to obtain. States vary considerably in terms of the availability of resources, size, arable land, and location, all of which can influence the power of the state as well as the role it is able to play in the international system. The resources that a state enjoys influence its wealth as well as its ability to pursue an independent foreign policy. No state in today's complex industrial world has adequate resources to pursue a completely independent policy. Although the United States comes perhaps the closest of any state to being able to pursue a policy of autarchy, the oil crisis has underscored the vulnerability even of superpowers.

Occupying a large expanse of territory not only is likely to increase the probability that a state will enjoy more resources and arable land; it will also provide an opportunity to retreat in a war situation and then regroup and reverse an invasion, as the Russians did after the Napoleonic invasion in 1812 and the German invasion in 1941. Small states do not have such an opportunity and can be conquered and occupied rapidly, as is shown by Hitler's invasion of the lowland countries of Europe. At the same time, a large area poses serious transportation problems, which make it difficult to integrate an efficient national economy. It has been suggested that Japan's highly successful economic development was possible because its population of a hundred million lives in a small area. This provided a sufficient domestic market for industrial products as well as a "densely meshed communications network that worked to heighten the efficiency of economic activities."[9]

The location of a state is also likely to affect both its power and its policies. Sea powers historically have been protected from invasion by the water surrounding them. Even the narrow British Channel provided some protection from Hitler during World War II. Although modern military technology, which allows destruction at great distances, has undermined the security of insular states, conquering and controlling such a state remains difficult to the extent that troops must be landed on its beaches.

The topography of a state also has power and security implications. Mountains traditionally have provided barriers to invasion. It is much simpler to move modernized armies through flat lands, and as a result, certain invasion routes, such as those through Poland or across the lowlands of Western Europe, have been popular. The Soviet Union became aware of the drawbacks of inhospitable terrain in its 1979 incursion into Afghanistan, and this situation helps explain some of the difficulties it has had in controlling that area.

A number of geopolitical writers have developed theories regarding the implications of the geographic setting of a state for its foreign policy. Among these is the British writer Sir Halford Mackinder, who suggested in a book published in 1919 that the critical element in world power was control of the heartland of the Eurasian continent, which consisted largely of the European part of the Soviet Union.[10] Control of the heartland would enable a state to dominate the world island consisting of Europe, Asia, and Africa, and this would lead to control of the

9. Michio Royama, "Environmental Factors and Japan in the 1970s," in Morton A. Kaplan and Kinhide Mushakoji, eds., *Japan, America, and the Future World Order* (New York: Free Press, 1976), p. 344.

10. Sir Halford Mackinder, *Democratic Ideals and Realities* (New York: Norton, 1962; first published in 1919).

entire world. By 1943, however, Mackinder had noted the frailty of his earlier dictum, suggesting that the North Atlantic region, through the use of air power, could balance the threat that might be posed by the Soviet Union after Germany was defeated.[11]

Explicitly rejecting the Mackinder thesis, a former Yale professor, Nicholas J. Spykman, suggested that control over the region is more likely to go to the rimland powers, such as Great Britain and Japan.[12] The primary limitations on the heartland's being able to assume a dominant position were seen to lie in the area's undesirable climate, its emphasis on agrarian productivity, and its general lack of resources.

Another early-twentieth-century American, Admiral Alfred T. Mahan, advocated expansion of sea power as the most useful approach to providing power and security for a state. He suggested that such an emphasis was particularly relevant for the United States, given its position on two oceans.[13] The United States' acquisition of the Philippines and other Pacific territories made increased naval power a virtual necessity. Britain, with its insular position, also would not require a large standing army and could therefore divert more of its resources to its naval capability. Modern-day disciples of Mahan are found in the Navy and among those who would prefer to see the United States emphasize submarine-launched ballistic missiles.

As a final illustration of geopolitical theory, one might note the work of Karl Haushofer, whose ideas were exploited by Adolph Hitler.[14] It was Haushofer who developed the notion of *lebensraum*, or the need for "living space." Borrowing from Social Darwinist ideas, he formulated the notion of an organic state that must expand or it would die. Although he influenced Nazi policy, it is probable that as a geopolitician he opposed Hitler's invasion of the Soviet Union because of the Soviet advantage of defense in depth and its ability to relinquish space temporarily to gain time to regroup. Instead, Haushofer favored a combination of powers, consisting of the Soviet Union, Japan, China, and India, under German leadership.

11. Colin S. Gray, *The Geopolitics of the Nuclear Era* (New York: Crane and Russak, 1977), p. 34.

12. Nicholas J. Spykman, *The Geography of Peace* (New York: Harcourt Brace Jovanovich, 1944), p. 43.

13. Alfred T. Mahan, *The Influence of Sea Power in History, 1660–1783* (Boston: Little, Brown, 1918).

14. Andreas Dorpalen, *The World of General Haushofer* (New York: Farrar and Rinehart, 1942, reprinted by Kennikat).

The most systematic research concerned with geographic variables has focused on the issue of boundaries. Territorial boundaries have long been viewed as an important factor in international conflict. Evan Luard went so far as to suggest that territorial disputes have been "perhaps the most important single cause of war between states in the last two or three centuries."[15] The prevalence of such conflicts can clearly be seen in the Middle East, in the continuing struggles over boundaries between Israel and its neighbors and in the 1980–81 border war between Iraq and Iran, in which the former sought to regain three small islands in the Persian Gulf that had been seized by Iran in 1971, as well as other territories that would give Iraq greater control over important waterways.

Statistical studies have shown that the states with the largest numbers of boundaries have tended to engage in the greatest number of conflicts. Research by Lewis F. Richardson revealed that, for 33 nations during the period 1820–1945, the number of frontiers shared with other countries was positively related to participation in wars with at least 7,000 war dead.[16] It has been suggested, however, that merely counting the number of boundaries shared is an inadequate measure of geographic contiguity, and that one should consider the length of the borders and the density of the population in order to determine interaction opportunities. When this approach was used, it was discovered that one could better predict the amount of violence even when utilizing Richardson's data.[17] Sharing borders with a larger number of states can also have a contagion effect on war, as studies utilizing data from the Correlates of War project in the nineteenth and twentieth centuries have revealed.[18] Another study suggested that wars were more likely to widen if they began near the hub of Europe than if they started on the perimeters.[19] Contiguity also seemed to make a difference in terms of the likelihood that African states would intervene in liberation

15. Evan Luard, *Conflict and Peace in the Modern International System* (Boston: Little, Brown, 1968), p. 111.

16. Lewis F. Richardson, *Statistics of Deadly Quarrels* (New York: Quadrangle/The N.Y. Times, 1960), p. 176.

17. James Paul Wesley, "Frequency of Wars and Geographical Opportunity," *Journal of Conflict Resolution*, 6 (December 1962), 387–89.

18. Harvey Starr and Benjamin A. Most, "The Substance and Study of Borders in International Relations Research," *International Studies Quarterly*, 20 (December 1976), 581–620; Manus Midlarsky, *On War* (New York: Free Press, 1975).

19. Geoffrey Blainey, *The Causes of War* (New York: Free Press, 1973), p. 232.

movements in other countries on the continent.[20] Penetration is obviously a simpler matter if the state borders on the target state.

In relating geographic proximity to conflict behavior, it would do well to heed the words of Bruce M. Russett, who wrote, "Except in some sense for border disputes, countries do not fight each other *because* they are physically close; they merely have the *opportunity* to fight because they are close. Proximity becomes the catalyst."[21] Given modern technology, geographic distances may even become less important in terms of defining opportunities for attack.

Although contiguity tends to facilitate conflict, a state that borders on a much larger country may actually gain power and security. This is particularly true if the neighboring state is a status quo power that does not threaten the smaller state's survival. Canada, unlike more remote states, can rest assured that the United States will come to its aid any time it is threatened from without. Its strategic location also makes it more likely that the United States will be more responsive to Canadian concerns than it would be to those of more distant allies.

Contiguity can also be important in terms of international political integration. A statistical study of integration conducted by Roger Cobb and Charles Elder found geographic contiguity to be related to high levels of international interaction.[22] States that border each other are also more likely to be allies. If the neighboring state is somewhat larger, neutrality, if not alignment, will generally be required.

The difficulties Pakistan had in generating unity between its eastern and western sectors may be explained in part by the fact that a thousand miles of Indian territory separated the two sections. The union collapsed in 1971 with the Bangladesh war. Similarly, the United Arab Republic, consisting of the noncontiguous states of Egypt, Syria, and Yemen, was short-lived; and recent efforts to unify Libya and Syria into a single political, economic, and military unit do not appear promising, particularly in view of the geographical distance between the two.

20. Vincent B. Khapoya, "The Politics of Decision: A Comparative Study of African Policy Toward Liberation Movements," University of Denver Social Science Foundation Monograph, 12 (1974–75).

21. Bruce M. Russett, *International Regions and the International System* (Chicago: Rand McNally, 1967), p. 200. Emphasis in original.

22. Roger W. Cobb and Charles Elder, *International Community* (New York: Holt, Rinehart and Winston, 1970).

States with good natural frontiers, such as Spain, France, and Britain, have generally been more stable and less threatened by border conflicts than states like those of Eastern Europe, Germany, and Austria.[23] It is therefore small wonder that states have been motivated to extend control to their natural frontiers, as in the case of France's efforts to expand to the Pyrenees, the Mediterranean, and the Rhine River. A common plea on the part of Israel has been that it needs to obtain defensible borders.

It is obvious that certain other geographic variables, such as raw materials, amount of arable land, and even climatological conditions, have an impact on foreign-policy choices. Their importance to foreign policy, however, lies in the contribution they can make to the military and economic power of a state, and it is to these issues that we now turn our attention.

MILITARY POWER

A well-known proposition holds that if you want peace you must prepare for war. An examination of rapidly increasing defense budgets throughout the world suggests that many decision makers have taken this axiom to heart. Between 1865 and 1965, for example, the proportion of the world product devoted to military expenditures rose from 2.6 percent to 6.8 percent. For the great powers the respective figures were 1 percent and 5.4 percent.[24] President Reagan's military budget requests totalled more than $188 billion for fiscal year 1982, and global military spending has now reached substantially above $500 billion.

In examining the role of military power as a determinant of foreign-policy behavior, it might be appropriate to begin our discussion with an analysis of the impact of nuclear weapons, which, according to some writers, may have revolutionized world politics. The acquisition of nuclear weapons may be somewhat of a mixed blessing for a nation. Without doubt, nuclear capability will enhance a state's position within its region and may even provide an entree to disarmament talks that are limited to nuclear powers. At the same time, it is unlikely that nuclear weapons will provide much leverage vis-à-vis the current nu-

---

23.   Robert G. Wesson, *State Systems* (New York: Free Press, 1978), p. 111.

24.   Stanley Hoffmann, *Primacy of World Order* (New York: McGraw-Hill, 1978), p. 209.

clear states, particularly the United States and the Soviet Union, as Britain discovered at the time of its invasion of Suez in 1956. Greater arms sophistication, numbers, and ability to protect their nuclear weapons will tend to keep the superpowers in the forefront of the nuclear arms race; as a result, it would be foolish, if not impossible, to challenge that preeminence.

There are, however, a number of serious negative implications for a state that chooses to develop nuclear weapons. Although it is unlikely that the larger nuclear powers would take action to destroy an incipient nuclear program, as was actually discussed with respect to China's nuclear program, the danger would always remain. There would also be an incentive for the superpower to withdraw its commitments from a newly nuclearized state, for a continuing relationship would only increase the probability that the superpower would be drawn into a nuclear war not of its choosing. Not only is the smaller nuclear power likely to lose whatever superpower support it may previously have enjoyed, but it will be confronted with considerable pressure from that superpower should it use its new capacity to threaten neighboring nonnuclear states. A nuclear guarantee would probably be made by a superpower to the threatened victim in such an instance.

Not only are the gains likely to be limited for a state choosing the nuclear option, but the costs are appreciable. Britain was unable to pursue an independent military policy despite its possession of a nuclear strike capability, and in the process it may have increased its dependence on the United States because of the tremendous cost of the British nuclear program and the attendant weakening of its civilian technological effort. The same might be said of France, which committed some 80 percent of its scientists to its nuclear effort, neglecting scientific and technological progress elsewhere.

Nuclear weapons may be of limited value to the superpowers as well. They raise the specter of nuclear annihilation, and since each side now has enough to destroy the other side several times over, the use of nuclear weapons in war becomes virtually unthinkable. There may even be some hesitancy on the part of decision makers to utilize conventional forces for fear that such action might escalate into a nuclear war.

The primary importance of nuclear weapons lies not so much in their utility as an instrument of war as in their ability to deter war. The relative peace that has prevailed in the postwar world may well attest to the deterrent efficacy of nuclear weapons. This, of course, does not mean that the system may not break down; the risk of a nuclear war started by accident, miscalculation, irrationality, or fear remains a distinct possibility.

Such a prospect arose during the Cuban missile crisis of 1962, when nuclear war was closer than at any other time before or since. President Kennedy himself placed the odds of a nuclear war at better than one in three. Yet even in this instance it was probably not merely the threat of nuclear war that caused Khrushchev to back down. Rather, it had perhaps more to do with the asymmetry of interests between the two superpowers. Since Cuba and the missiles were so peripheral to Soviet interests and so much more central to American concerns, the outcome might have been predictable. Had the national interests of the two parties been more equivalent, the results may well have differed.

Although the acquisition of nuclear weapons may not have eliminated or even reduced the likelihood of war, it may have eliminated the option of a world empire. Any decision on the part of either superpower to utilize such weapons on a massive scale would probably lead to the annihilation of both. Yet conquest of the other superpower would probably be impossible without the use of nuclear weapons.

There has been some concern that as the strategic nuclear balance becomes less favorable to the United States, there will be an adverse impact on American foreign-policy objectives. If the balance of strategic forces should shift toward the Soviet Union, as some believe has already happened, it has been suggested that the Soviets will become more assertive in their foreign policy. Whatever restraint has been achieved to date is thought to be related to the clear military superiority of the United States. On the contrary, there is some evidence to suggest that the increased sense of Soviet military prominence has not led to an increase in risk taking.[25] The Soviet Union engaged in considerable risk-taking behavior during the Stalin period, despite the fact that the United States enjoyed an atomic monopoly until 1949 and considerable superiority for many years thereafter. Stalin sought to deny the efficacy of nuclear weapons by urging that such permanently operating factors as morale, command, and the quality and quantity of conventional forces were more important. In many respects Khrushchev appeared to behave more erratically and to be more willing to take risks than Leonid Brezhnev, yet the balance of forces has been

25. Hannes Adomeit, "Soviet Risk-Taking and Crisis Behavior: From Confrontation to Coexistence," *Adelphi Papers*, 101 (Fall 1973).

far more favorable to the Soviet Union during Brezhnev's tenure. A Brookings study revealed that Moscow engaged more frequently in "coercive actions" in the late 1960s than it did in the mid-1970s, although it was only in the latter period that Soviet strategic nuclear strength had begun to approach that of the United States.[26] The same study, which analyzed the use of Soviet military forces to bolster Moscow's foreign-policy goals in some 190 instances since the end of World War II, also concluded that "the achievement of strategic parity with the United States gave the Kremlin greater confidence about making forward deployments and threatening military intervention in crises."[27] Moscow's efforts to resupply Egypt during the 1973 war in the Middle East, its military support of insurgents in Angola and the Horn of Africa, and even more emphatically, its incursion into Afghanistan are indicative of the Soviets' willingness to use force. At the same time, a study covering the period 1945–63 suggested that the Soviet Union has been willing to use large amounts of force only in situations in which it has viewed the crisis as being less risky.[28]

Despite a strategic balance that has become more favorable to the Soviet Union, an analysis of 215 incidents in which the United States used or threatened the use of force revealed that the outcomes have actually been more favorable to the United States when its military superiority was less extreme. Short-term outcomes were found to be positive for the United States in only 58 percent of the cases when the strategic balance was 100 to 1 or greater in favor of the United States, but this increased to 94 percent when the ratio decreased to less than 10 to 1. If only incidents in which the Soviet Union participated are examined, the respective success rates for the United States under the two conditions were 43 percent and 92 percent.[29]

Since a major function of military weapons, particularly in the nuclear age, has been to deter war, several studies have sought to ascertain how effective they have been in this regard. A study of eight postwar international crises revealed that as United States' strategic and/or

26. Stephen S. Kaplan, *Diplomacy of Power: Soviet Armed Forces as a Political Instrument* (Washington: D.C.: Brookings Institution, 1981), p. 53.

27. Ibid., p. 679.

28. Jan F. Triska et al., "Pattern and Level of Risk in Soviet Foreign Policy Making, 1945–63," Palo Alto, Calif.: Stanford University, 1965, mimeo.

29. Barry M. Blechman and Stephen S. Kaplan, *Force Without War: U.S. Armed Forces as a Political Instrument* (Washington, D.C.: Brookings Institution, 1978), pp. 128–29. A favorable outcome was defined as one in which two-thirds of the American objectives were obtained.

tactical preparedness was perceived by the Soviets to have increased, their perception of American resolve also increased.[30] An examination of American influence attempts in fifteen major crises during the period 1946–75 in which both strategic nuclear and conventional force were threatened revealed that in nearly every instance a favorable outcome was achieved within a span of six months.[31] Success dropped to three-quarters of the fifteen cases during the longer span of three years, suggesting that the deterrent effectiveness of the nuclear threat declines over time.

Studies of successful deterrence during earlier historical periods have revealed that superior strength by itself is not sufficient to deter war. Such was the conclusion of a study that sampled twenty time periods in several cultures going back some two thousand years.[32] The study did suggest, however, that attention to the quality and mobility of armed forces can be effective in minimizing loss of territory even though it may not deter. That superior strength is an insufficient deterrent is also suggested by data collected for the nineteenth and twentieth centuries, which revealed that in five out of nine wars initiated against the great powers, the nations attacked were appreciably stronger than those initiating the war.[33] Japan's attack on the far more powerful United States apparently has not been an isolated phenomenon.

Wayne Ferris, surveying the period 1850–1950, concluded that superior military power made war more likely. Power in this instance was measured by two indexes, one utilizing nine variables, the other six. In relating relative power to war indicators supplied by the Correlates of War project, Ferris noted that once an intense conflict was under way, power capabilities were not sufficient to prevent escalation to the level of military hostilities.[34] The study also suggested that a changing power relationship was associated with more intense conflict. Apparently uncertainty about relative power in a rapidly changing power structure induces efforts to test the power and resolve of the

30. David C. Schwartz, "Decision Theories and Crisis Behavior: An Empirical Study of Nuclear Deterrence in International Political Crises," *Orbis*, 11 (Summer 1967), 485.

31. Blechman and Kaplan, *Force Without War: U.S. Armed Forces as a Political Instrument*, pp. 99–100.

32. Raoul Naroll et al., *Military Deterrence in History* (Albany: State University of New York, 1974), p. 328.

33. Wayne Ferris, *The Power Capabilities of Nation–States* (Lexington, Mass.: D. C. Heath, 1973).

34. Ibid., p. 124.

other party or may create incentives for striking before a possible power imbalance becomes too intolerable. Geoffrey Blainey has suggested that agreement on the relative power balance is an important factor in peace. In his analysis of wars since 1700, he writes, "Wars usually end when the fighting nations *agree* on their relative strength, and wars usually begin when fighting nations *disagree* on their relative strength."[35] If this is true, it can be argued that since war is the most emphatic way to measure power, war itself can serve as a source of peace.

What is interesting from a deterrence perspective is the question of what characteristics were shared by the participants in crises that resulted in war, in contrast to those in which deterrence proved effective. Michael Mihalka investigated this question in connection with 264 military confrontations involving at least one European state as a participant during the period 1816–1970. Of these 264 cases, some 99 resulted in war.[36] By distinguishing great-power from non-great-power participants, Mihalka found that when the sole initiator was a great power the frequency of hostilities was only 33.6 percent, but when the great power was the target, the frequency increased to 87.5 percent. In other words, smaller powers are less likely to respond to attacks and are less able to deter a negative response when they take the initiative. The study also found that hostilities were less frequent when both parties were great powers than when neither was a great power. To the extent that great powers have been more restrained in pushing military confrontations to armed warfare, some evidence for the deterrent effect of mutual destructive capability is provided.

An examination of seventeen cases in which a larger state sought to deter an attack on a smaller state revealed that power superiority, either locally or strategically, was insufficient to prevent war.[37] A more credible deterrent in these cases was the existence of previous military cooperation and economic interdependence between the defender state and the small state. Potential attackers probably assumed that a defender would be more likely to come to the aid of the small state with which the defender shared economic and military links than one where such ties were lacking.

---

35. Blainey, *The Causes of War*, p. 122. Emphasis in original.

36. Michael Mihalka, "Hostilities in the European State System, 1816–1970," *Peace Science Society (International) Papers*, 26 (1976), 100–16.

37. Bruce M. Russett, "The Calculus of Deterrence," *Journal of Conflict Resolution*, 7 (June 1963), 97–109.

Many writers have expressed the opinion that the existence of a power vacuum may be an invitation to intervention from the outside. There appears to be some evidence that the threat of intervention can be diminished if a state is able to present a strong military posture either through its own efforts or through aid from the outside. An examination of military interventions over the period 1948–67 revealed that as the power to resist intervention increased, the probability of intervention decreased.[38] Thus, increasing military spending or taking pains to communicate the threat of a hostile response does seem to have some deterrent value.

Should deterrence fail and direct military confrontation result, there arises a serious need to bring an end to hostilities. An appropriate procedure for doing so has been labeled "coercive diplomacy" in a study examining deterrent efforts in the cases of Laos in 1961, the Cuban missile crisis in 1962, and American involvement in Vietnam in 1965.[39] These case studies revealed that more than force is necessary for coercive diplomacy to be effective, as is shown in Table 7–1. The fact that all eight conditions were met in the Soviet threat to Laos and the Cuban missile crisis helps explain the reason for success in these two instances, in contrast to the failure in Vietnam, where only two conditions (motivation and usable military options) were satisfied.

It might be expected that the state with the superior power capabilities would most often be the victorious one should deterrence fail, but for a variety of reasons this has not been the case. The weaker state may be able to compensate for its limitations through superior strategy. Similarly, willingness to sacrifice and suffer may enable the weaker ultimately to prevail, as is illustrated, again, by the United States' involvement in Vietnam. The Vietnamese, fighting on their own soil, were far more predisposed to sacrifice and to accept damage than were the Americans, located thousands of miles away. Being on the defensive may also be to the ultimate advantage of the weaker state, for the aggressor will have to stretch its supply lines. Those who are concerned about the greater number of Warsaw Pact forces compared to those of NATO often overlook this basic truth when they raise the specter of a massive conventional strike in Western Europe.

---

38.   Frederick S. Pearson, "Geographical Proximity and Foreign Military Intervention," *Journal of Conflict Resolution*, 18 (September 1974), 432–59.

39.   Alexander George et al., *The Limits of Coercive Diplomacy* (Boston: Little, Brown, 1971).

TABLE 7-1. Presence of Conditions Favoring a Successful Outcome of Coercive Diplomacy in Three Crises

	Laos 1961	Cuba 1962	Vietnam 1965
1. Strength of United States motivation	+	+	+
2. Asymmetry of motivation favoring United States	+	+	
3. Clarity of American objectives	+	+	
4. Sense of urgency to achieve American objective	+	+	
5. Adequate domestic political support	+	+	
6. Usable military options	+	+	+
7. Opponent's fear of unacceptable escalation	+	+	
8. Clarity concerning the precise terms of settlement	+	+	

SOURCE: Alexander George et al., *The Limits of Coercive Diplomacy* (Boston: Little, Brown, 1971), p. 227.

Since most indexes of power capability give considerable weight to existing forces, the potential power of the state that is able to mobilize significant resources either internally or externally through temporary alliances can frequently change the initial calculations. Obviously, the significance of actual forces depends on the sort of war being fought; if it is a quick, blitz-type war or a nuclear war, existing forces will be much more critical.

Cross-national data covering the period 1850–1966 reveal that the side possessing the greater power capabilities at the time of the initiation of hostilities was victorious more often than would be expected by chance, but there have been many instances in which this has not been the case.[40] The same study also revealed that a high disparity between the power of the contending sides guaranteed neither a shorter war nor a less devastating one, despite the possibility of bringing overwhelming force to bear on the situation.

Historical studies have also shown that states that initiate wars often fail to win them. Data from the Correlates of War project revealed that although some four-fifths of all wars occurring between 1815 and 1910 were *won* by the governments that started them, three-fifths of the wars fought between 1910 and 1965 have been *lost* by the initiating government.[41]

40. Ferris, *The Power Capabilities of Nation–States*, p. 115.

41. Karl W. Deutsch, "Peace Research: The Need, the Problem, and the Prospect," in Peter Jones, ed., *The International Yearbook of Foreign Policy Analysis*, vol. 2 (New York: Crane and Russak, 1975).

In deciding whether to exercise the military option, a state is concerned about whether the use of military force is likely to diminish its power base. Since the utilization of weapons leads to their destruction, it might seem on the surface that such use would weaken a state's power, perhaps making it more vulnerable to others. This is not necessarily the case, for the willingness to use weapons, as demonstrated by their actual employment, can have a deterrent value with respect to other potential conflicts. The use of force may enhance the credibility of subsequent threats to use force. It is also possible that the use of force may add power through the capture of important resources. If such resources are more valuable than the cost of using force, a net gain may accrue.

Wars have frequently failed to change power balances appreciably. An empirical analysis of power levels after major wars has revealed the tendency for the power distribution to return to its prewar levels.[42] This tendency persists because the power levels of winners and neutrals are usually affected only marginally by the conflicts. After a few years the effects of war are dissipated as the losers accelerate their recovery and resume their antebellum rate of growth.

ECONOMIC POWER

It has been suggested that since nuclear weapons are no longer as significant because the fear of nuclear annihilation limits their use, economic power has increased in importance. There may even be some concern about the use of conventional weapons as an instrument of foreign policy because of the fear that such use may escalate to nuclear war. The importance of economic power has also been enhanced by the increasing economic interdependence among states, as noted in the previous chapter. Economic instruments of power enable a state to reward or punish another state and thereby affect the latter's behavior. Perhaps the best illustration of economic reward is foreign aid.

Economic payoffs to influence behavior have been utilized throughout history. Rulers like those of ancient China demanded tribute from their vassals. According to one authority, "it was quite com-

---

42.   A. F. K. Organski and Jacek Kugler, "The Costs of Major Wars: The Phoenix Factor," *American Political Science Review*, 71 (December 1977), 1347–66.

mon in the eighteenth century to offer statesmen large gratuities in return for an alliance or the favorable conclusion of negotiations."[43] Yet the use of foreign aid as a continuing instrument of policy has been primarily a post-World War II phenomenon.

The threat or actual withdrawal of economic assistance has been used on innumerable occasions in an effort to get one state to do another's bidding. In the late 1940s the United States threatened to cut off Marshall Plan aid to the Netherlands if the latter failed to make a settlement with Indonesian nationalists and relinquish its colonial control over the area. Not only did the United States withdraw economic support from Israel in an effort to get the latter to desist from its aggression in the Suez in 1956, but the Eisenhower administration went a step further the following year by threatening to stop American private investment and charitable support, which amounted to $100 million, if Israel did not evacuate the Gaza Strip.[44]

Beginning with the Arab oil boycott in 1973–74, the most powerful economic weapon has been oil. After the October war Arab leaders began to grasp the potential of oil for getting other states to accept their position regarding Arab–Israeli issues. The oil weapon has been instrumental in obtaining the necessary votes to force Israel out of the International Labor Organization, and has influenced the passage of various resolutions equating Zionism with racism. The leverage was so strong in the summer of 1980 that an anti-Zionist resolution was passed in the General Assembly with only seven negative votes.

Despite the extensive aid provided by Israel to African states during the 1960s, the Arab states were able to obtain a complete reversal of the African leaders' position toward Israel. Oil had become very important to the African states, as had the financial assistance that OPEC dollars provided.[45] Arab leaders also used their economic power vis-à-vis corporations by asserting that any corporation that did business with Israel would not be allowed to engage in business activities with the far more populous Arab states.

The use of trade as an instrument of reward and punishment is not limited to oil-producing states, by any means. Economic sanctions have

43. Wesson, *State Systems*, p. 121.

44. Trygve Mathisen, *The Functions of Small States* (Oslo, Norway: Universitetsforlaget, 1971), p. 218.

45. Victor T. Levine and Timothy W. Luke, *The Arab–African Connection: Political and Economic Realities* (Boulder, Col.: Westview Press, 1979).

been used to influence or punish a variety of states that have been viewed as violating generally accepted international norms. Such sanctions were imposed by the League of Nations on Italy in 1936 in protest of the latter's invasion of Ethiopia. The United Nations has sought to impose similar sanctions on Rhodesia and the Republic of South Africa. Other efforts of this sort have included the United States' attempts to impose economic restrictions upon Cuba and the more recent use of economic sanctions against the Soviet Union with respect to its 1979 invasion of Afghanistan, and against Iran in connection with the seizure of the American Embassy in Teheran.

Despite the prevalence of the use of economic sanctions as an instrument of influence, the results have hardly been satisfactory.[46] The League's efforts to affect the behavior of the aggressor were undermined by the decision of the United States, which was not a member of the League, to make up the shortfall by increasing its trade with Italy. Multinational corporations and other governments have minimized the impact of economic sanctions against such states as Rhodesia and South Africa. When the United States sought to apply economic sanctions against Cuba, Castro merely turned to the Soviet Union. The United States also found it difficult to obtain support among other nations for its 1979–80 economic boycotts of the Soviet Union and Iran.

The general ineffectiveness of economic sanctions has been verified in an examination of ten instances in which economic sanctions were applied during the period 1933–67. The findings suggest that further reductions in trade beyond the initial imposition of the sanction often were not contemplated, and that after two years trade tended to return to its previous levels whether or not the situation that had induced the sanction had been rectified.[47]

After surveying the relative ineffectiveness of trade boycotts as an instrument of economic pressure, one authority suggested that subtle economic weapons, such as reduction of investments, delay in delivering spare parts, snags in licensing, decreasing loans and grants, and refusal to refinance existing debts, tend to be more effective than trade boycotts in influencing the policies of other states.[48] The basic problem

46. See Harry R. Strack, *Sanctions: The Case of Rhodesia* (Syracuse, N.Y.: Syracuse University Press, 1978), and Donald L. Losman, *International Economic Sanctions: The Cases of Cuba, Israel, and Rhodesia* (Albuquerque: University of New Mexico, 1979).

47. Peter Walensteen, "Characteristics of Economic Sanctions," *Journal of Peace Research*, 5, no. 3 (1968), 248–67.

48. R. S. Olson, "Economic Coercion in World Politics," *World Politics*, 31 (July 1979), 471–94.

with the more extreme economic sanctions is that they tend to unify the targeted population, increasing its sense of nationalism and resistance.

Special difficulties arise for pluralistic states that attempt to use trade as a weapon, for often various governmental bureaucracies and interest groups are divided on the issue. Food was not exploited in September 1977 in several sensitive negotiations with the Soviet Union, for those involved in the negotiations discovered only by reading the newspapers that the Department of Agriculture had unilaterally agreed to sell seven million more tons of grain than were called for in United States–Soviet Union agreements.[49] Problems also arise from the fact that many private corporations are beyond the reach of their national governments. Subsidiaries of such companies may sell products that the parent company would be prevented from selling. It has been alleged that even during World War II some armaments were sold to Germany by American firms.

When it comes to bargaining on trade issues, the large developed state, despite its obvious supremacy in terms of economic clout, has not always been able to prevail. A study of twenty-five trade conflicts between the United States and Latin America concluded that the United States was not always the victor. Among these twenty-five conflicts Latin American states were viewed as victorious in seven cases, obtained a compromise in six, and were forced to make unrequited concessions or suffered the imposition of unilateral sanctions in the remaining twelve instances.[50]

Generally speaking, the less developed country will be more vulnerable to economic sanctions than the developed state. It will tend to lose more from trade disruption, since its economy is less diversified. If the state produces only one commodity, curtailing the export of that product could threaten economic ruin. The LDC lacks the opportunity, which is available to the more developed state, of decreasing its vulnerability by stockpiling or producing synthetic substitutes. The unavailability of marketing skills and the lack of diplomatic personnel capable of stimulating exports also makes the developing state more vulnerable to market disruptions. On the other hand, the vulnerability created by economic underdevelopment may make the state more resistant to bombardment and economic deprivation. It has been suggested

49. Samuel P. Huntington, "Trade Technology and Leverage: Economic Diplomacy," *Foreign Policy*, Fall 1978, p. 75.

50. John S. Odell, "Latin American Trade Negotiations with the United States," *International Organization*, 34 (Spring 1980), 207–28.

that a modern state like Belgium would have been less able to resist American pressure than Vietnam, since the economy of the former state can be readily disrupted by destroying or impeding part of the economy because the parts are so interdependent.[51] In advanced economies, where separate pieces of complex machines and other products are manufactured in many locations, dislocation of the transportation system or interference with the production of a single necessary item can shut down an entire industry.

The economic weapon that is most useful to developing states is nationalization. In the 1960s the Philippines was successful in using just such a threat to induce the United States to extend trade preferences.[52] In the previous chapter we noted a number of successful nationalization efforts in which the United States acquiesced without retaliating as the legal requirements of the Hickenlooper and Pelly amendments would seem to require. Governments as well as corporations, fearful of encouraging even more rampant nationalization, have simply been unwilling to press such issues.

THE EFFECTS OF SIZE ON BEHAVIOR

Whether one is speaking of military or economic power capabilities, it seems obvious that great powers behave differently than small powers on several dimensions. A number of studies have concluded that states with greater power capabilities tend to be more active in foreign policy.[53] This, of course, is a function of both more abundant resources and broader global interests. As part of this activity, powerful states have engaged in greater conflict behavior in the postwar era than less powerful ones.[54] During the period 1815–1965, more than half of the smaller powers (77 out of 144) were able to escape war entirely,

51. Franklin B. Weinstein, *Indonesian Foreign Policy and the Dilemma of Dependence* (Ithaca, N.Y.: Cornell University Press, 1976), p. 27.

52. Joseph S. Nye, "Multinational Corporations in World Politics," *Foreign Affairs*, 53 (October 1974), 158.

53. Stephen A. Salmore and Charles F. Hermann, "The Effect of Size, Development, and Accountability on Foreign Policy," *Peace Research Society (International) Papers*, 14 (1970), 16–30; Maurice A. East, "Size and Foreign Policy Behavior," *World Politics*, 25 (July 1973), 556–76.

54. Rudolph J. Rummel, *National Attributes and Behavior* (Beverly Hills, Calif.: Sage Publications, 1979), p. 13.

whereas the great powers participated in at least 19 of the 25 international wars that have occurred since 1914.[55]

Within alliance systems larger states have assumed a disproportionate share of the burden. A major part of the criticism leveled at the People's Republic of China by the Soviet Union in the late 1950s was that China was not adequately sharing in the burden of defense and that it should be grateful for the help it had received from the Soviet Union. Similarly, the United States has been critical of what it has seen as a relatively free ride for Japan and Germany, whose defense efforts have been substantially smaller than those of the United States.

Larger powers have also been found to vote more often than smaller ones in the United Nations, although small powers are more likely to favor multilateral organizations over bilateral ones.[56] A study of 388 mediation efforts during the period 1816–1960 revealed that mediation has been utilized more frequently in the affairs of lesser countries than in disputes among major powers.[57] To a certain extent this has probably been due to great-power efforts to force smaller powers that are engaged in conflicts to have their disputes mediated.

The foreign-policy instruments of large and small states also seem to differ. Large states enjoy superiority in terms of the ability to reward and punish other states. Small states are forced to confine themselves to diplomatic instruments such as protests and verbal persuasion. They are also more likely to use the withdrawal of diplomatic recognition as a tool to influence other members of the international system. Of 211 formal diplomatic ruptures initiated by 72 countries during the period 1945–70, more than 90 percent were found to involve new states or Latin American states.[58]

A study of military intervention by outside powers during the period 1948–67 found that the motivations for such incursions differed between major and minor powers. Interventions by major powers were generally related to strategic power balances, ideology, economic, dip-

---

55. Melvin Small and J. David Singer, "Patterns in International Warfare, 1816–1965," *The Annals of the American Academy of Political and Social Science*, 391 (September 1970), 151–52.

56. Helge Hveem, "Foreign Policy Opinion as a Function of International Position," *Cooperation and Conflict*, 7, no. 2 (1972), p. 70.

57. Edward P. Levine, "Mediation in International Politics," *Peace Research Society (International) Papers*, 18 (1971), 33.

58. P. J. Boyce, *Foreign Affairs for New States* (New York: St. Martin's Press, 1977), p. 162.

lomatic, and military interests; minor powers were concerned with regional disputes over territory, social grievances, regional ideology, or the security of border areas. Even when major and minor powers have participated jointly in a military intervention, the goals of the two types of states were seldom similar.[59]

Decisions on alignment appear to be affected by the relative power of a state. Strategies of alignment seem to be especially relevant for a small state threatened by outside powers. In forging such alliances small states appear not to align with each other but with larger powers. In a study of alliances during the period 1920–57, Bruce M. Russett found that, with the exception of several bilateral alliances among Eastern European states, there were few alliances among relative equals.[60] Instead, smaller states tended to be linked with the great powers. Among the few small-state alliances that have developed, according to Russett, few have shown much political or military integration.

It appears on the surface that it would be particularly useful for small states to join in a common alliance and in so doing become a force in world politics. Small states have demonstrated in the context of the United Nations General Assembly that with coalescence and cooperation they can dominate the voting outcome, particularly since each state, regardless of size, has an equal vote. Despite their voting power, such states have discovered that the resolutions they are able to pass are ineffective, for they have neither the financial nor the military power to support them.

An effective coalition of small states is difficult to achieve not only because of extensive competition among them but also because they are likely to find themselves opposed by groups of larger states that can thwart their objectives. In the 1950s the United States, under the stewardship of President Eisenhower and Secretary of State John Foster Dulles, looked askance at efforts of small states to go it alone or to attempt to pursue neutralist policies either individually or in concert.

There appears to be little consensus on whether or not it is in the best interests of a small state to align itself with a larger state for protection. Machiavelli, for example, suggested that there was little advantage for a small power in remaining neutral, for it risked the enmity of

59. Frederick S. Pearson and Robert Baumann, "Foreign Military Intervention by Large and Small Powers," *International Interactions*, 1 (October 1974), 277.

60. Bruce M. Russett, "An Empirical Typology of International Military Alliances," *Midwest Journal of Political Science*, 15 (May 1971), 262–89.

larger powers; moreover, if a war should occur, alignment would give it a share in the spoils.[61] Even if defeat were to come, one could expect more lenient treatment for the smaller ally. The utility of alignment for the small state is supported by a study undertaken by the Correlates of War project, which found on the basis of data for the period 1816–1970 that "smaller nations without alliance ties tend to be 'aggressed upon' more often."[62] Alignment with a larger state outside of its region is particularly important for a state that would otherwise be dominated by larger states within its region. Israel, threatened by its Arab neighbors, and Brazil, concerned about the dominance of its Spanish-speaking neighbors, have been particularly sensitive about their relations with the United States.

John W. Burton has taken the opposite position, suggesting that nonalignment is an advantageous policy for a small state.[63] Among the possible advantages that might be derived from nonalignment are the following: (1) it ensures freedom and independence; (2) the state can stay out of conflicts that are of little concern to itself; (3) alliances may exacerbate relations with neighbors that do not belong to the same alliance; (4) nonalignment lessens the pressure to divert scarce materials to military obligations; and (5) nonalignment may allow a state to obtain aid from both sides.

Robert Rothstein views nonalignment as relevant only if small states do not threaten to shift the balance of power and are willing to withdraw from active participation in foreign affairs.[64] In other words, the small power should be strategically irrelevant and politically non-provocative.

Whatever the merits of small-state alignment policy, the tendency of small states to align with more powerful states has sometimes had a negative impact on global stability. A study of the behavior of five small neutral states during World War II noted:

Instead of moving to the side of the less powerful and thereby helping to restore the balance they [the small states] tended to

61. Cited in Robert L. Rothstein, *The Weak in the World of the Strong* (New York: Columbia University Press, 1977), p. 33.

62. Cited in Michael D. Wallace, "Early Warning Indicators from the Correlates of War Project," in J. David Singer and Michael D. Wallace, eds., *To Augur Well* (Beverly Hills, Calif.: Sage Publications, 1979), p. 23.

63. Ernest Lefever, "Nehru, Nasser, and Nkrumah on Neutralism," in Laurence Martin, ed., *Neutralism and Nonalignment* (New York: Praeger, 1962), p. 95.

64. Rothstein, *The Weak in the World of the Strong*, p. 32.

comply with the demand of the more powerful and thus accentuate any shifts in the balance of forces caused by changing fortunes of war or prospects of ultimate victory.[65]

In addition to affecting military strategy and alliance behavior, relative power capabilities have an impact on bargaining and negotiation. The relationship between national power capabilities and bargaining behavior is a particularly interesting one, given the recent concern with building bargaining chips and negotiating from strength. But will the existence of superior strength induce the adversary to the bargaining table and make it more accommodating, as the proponents of bargaining from strength assume?

A major problem arises when both sides believe that the proper condition for negotiation is a position of strength. Seldom will both perceive themselves to be in such a position at the same time. As a result, one or the other will refuse to participate until it achieves such a position. This is why interest in negotiation varies, depending upon which side is ahead in a war situation or believes it has achieved an important military breakthrough that momentarily places it in a preeminent position.

The notion of negotiation from strength has been particularly problematic from the standpoint of disarmament negotiations. A review of concession-making behavior in disarmament debates over the period 1945–60 revealed that the United States and the Soviet Union were more likely to make such concessions during periods in which they both had less confidence in their deterrent capabilities as measured by defense expenditures.[66] Since in a dyadic bargaining situation one side's strength is the other side's weakness, this may not occur very often. If either side feels itself to be in a position of clear superiority, there is little incentive to negotiate. The superior state becomes less concerned with searching for alternatives to the existing military system, while the weaker one fears such negotiations, believing that the dominant state will try to dictate the terms. The more likely response on the part of the weaker state is to increase its own military capabilities or look for allies, but not to seek security through disarma-

---

65. Annette Baker Fox, *The Power of Small States: Diplomacy in World War II* (Chicago: University of Chicago Press, 1959), p. 187.

66. Lloyd Jensen, Military Capabilities and Bargaining Behavior," *Journal of Conflict Resolution*, 9 (June 1965), 155–63.

ment. Serious negotiation on strategic arms limitation had to await the advent of nuclear parity in the 1970s.

As states have sought to build weapons to use as bargaining chips (on the assumption that such weapons would help produce agreements favorable to themselves), arms have proliferated without corresponding reductions. During the SALT process itself, which began in 1969 and lasted through the signing of the SALT II Treaty a decade later, the number of deliverable strategic nuclear warheads quadrupled. Weapons systems such as the multiple independent re-entry vehicle (MIRV), the cruise missile, antiballistic missiles, and the Trident and MX missiles have all been advocated largely for their value as bargaining chips at one time or the other. But the history of disarmament negotiations has been such that, once a system is built, it is almost impossible to get rid of it through negotiation. Henry Kissinger himself had pressed the military to develop the cruise missile as a bargaining chip for the SALT talks; unfortunately, this chip could not be cashed, for, as Kissinger admitted, he "didn't realize the Pentagon would fall in love with cruise missiles."[67]

Despite the fact that the strategy of bargaining from a position of military strength often does not work, it is probably true that if agreement is desired, a state must make concessions to a more powerful adversary. Even Neville Chamberlain recognized this in defending the Munich agreement before the British Cabinet:

> *I hope . . . that my colleagues will not think that I am making any attempts to disguise the fact that, if we now possessed a superior force to Germany, we should probably be considering these proposals in a very different spirit. But we must look facts in the face.*[68]

As the weak state confronts the strong state in a bargaining situation, it is by no means obvious that the latter will win. A survey of Soviet and Chinese relations toward the third world concluded that these two states "have made adjustments to the needs of third world countries more often than the latter's decisions have yielded to the

---

67. John W. Finney, "Cruise Missiles Provoke Conflict Within the Military as Well as with Soviets," New York Times, January 21, 1976, p. 30.

68. Cited in Robert Jervis, *Perception and Misperception in International Politics* (Princeton, N.J.: Princeton University Press, 1976), p. 78.

preferences of the Communist countries."[69] The litany of cases in which the United States has been unable to influence the behavior of smaller states hardly needs repeating. Iran and Cuba are but two of the more extreme cases.

A variety of factors help explain why the small state is often able to prevail over the large one, not the least of which is the ability of the small state to concentrate its energies on a single issue. The great power, given its global responsibilities, must deal with many foreign-policy issues concurrently. The issue that assumes primary importance for the small state may be of relative unimportance to a major power preoccupied with an extensive foreign policy agenda.

Second, the small state may be willing to take greater risks and pursue its goals doggedly since it has less to lose than the great power. In some respects a destitute state may be in the best bargaining position, for it has no place to go but up. Moreover, the collapse of such a state is often the last thing a great power would like to see happen, particularly if the great power perceives that the collapse might provide an open invitation to its major adversaries to fill the power vacuum. This became a major concern for the United States in its dealings with Iran over the hostage issue and in its reaction to the Iran-Iraqi war in 1980–81. The possible collapse of the Iranian government was viewed as opening the region to increased influence and control from the Soviet Union, which shares a common border with Iran.

Third, the small power may prevail because of its greater tolerance for sacrifices in a conflict situation. North Vietnam's long history of conflict, first with the French and then with the United States, made it resigned to death and destruction and thus perhaps more willing to suffer than its opponents were. The significance of such acceptance of suffering in a conflict situation is revealed in a study of forty wars that found that almost half were won by the party that lost more lives.[70] Few states, however, will hold out as long as Paraguay, which refused to surrender during the Lopez War of 1865–70 until it had lost some 80 percent of its population.

Fourth, the small state may benefit from a centralized decision-making structure when confronting a larger, pluralistic polity. This might enable the small state to search for allies in various sections of

---

69.   Alvin Z. Rubinstein, "Observations," in Rubinstein, ed., *Soviet and Chinese Influence in the Third World* (New York: Praeger, 1975), p. 223.

70.   Steven Rosen, "War Power and the Willingness to Suffer," in Bruce M. Russett, ed., *Peace, War, and Numbers* (Beverly Hills, Calif.: Sage Publications, 1972), pp. 176–78.

the bureaucracy of the large state and thus perhaps influence the policy directed toward itself or even achieve a reversal of policies already enacted. A small and cohesive bureaucratic structure makes the small state less vulnerable to such penetration.

Fifth, to the extent that the small state enjoys some important natural resources that are in short supply, it may be able to influence larger states. But as pointed out earlier, there are limits to such power, for it requires the cooperation of other states that have extensive supplies of a given commodity to be successful.

Sixth, the small state may gain some leverage by threatening to align with the other side if satisfaction is not obtained. This threat tends to be more effective if the international system is bipolarized. The late Shah of Iran was successful in negotiating better arms deals with the United States because of his threats to approach Moscow if concessions were not forthcoming. The Shah's threat was credible because of his control over both domestic and foreign policy while in power.[71]

CONCLUSION

Power is an important yet elusive concept that plays a vital role in foreign-policy behavior. Much of the confusion over the concept lies in the failure to distinguish between the capacity to act and the actual exercise of power, for the two do not always go together. Capability does not always translate into influence, because perceptual factors may distort one's views of the capabilities and intentions of others. Power is also relative and reciprocal, and has varying effects on different issues, particularly because of the role played by legitimacy, expertise, and role models in affecting influence relationships. Expectations and the tendency to equate aggressiveness with power have led to further confusion between power and influence. As a result, measurement of power is particularly difficult; what is usually measured is national power capabilities.

States may derive some power advantages from their geopolitical position. On the whole, however, such factors tend to be limiting rather than determining, as far as foreign policy is concerned. In this age of nuclear missiles many observers regard geographic factors, particularly

---

71. Shahran Chubin and Sepehr Zabih, *The Foreign Relations of Iran* (Berkeley: University of California Press, 1974), p. 114.

location, as decreasing in importance. Nevertheless, boundaries continue to play an important role, at least in less developed regions.

Most critical in the modern age has been the role of military power. There is evidence suggesting that force has a deterrent value. But there appears to be little consensus on whether superior force makes peace more likely or less so.

Although economic power has become more important, given increased economic interdependence and the fear of nuclear war, the two major instruments of trade and aid have their limitations. Economic boycotts have generally been ineffective in influencing the behavior of other states, although oil boycotts have had some effect.

Relative power capabilities seem to make some difference in the foreign-policy choices of states. Large states have tended to be more active and to engage in more conflict than small states. The latter prefer multilateral forums to bilateral ones and utilize mediation more often. Alliances appear to be composed largely of powers of unequal size. Coalitions of small states have not been effective, nor has nonalignment been a viable option, unless the small state is willing to withdraw from world politics and to be nonprovocative in its foreign policy.

Power is important in bargaining and negotiation, although the strategy of bargaining from strength has tended to reduce the likelihood of agreement. Positions of power parity have been more conducive to agreement, despite evidence suggesting that under certain circumstances, small states may be able to prevail over large states in a bargaining relationship.

8

EXTERNAL AND SYSTEMIC DETERMINANTS

Our discussion so far has focused on factors that are largely internal to the nation–state. The exception has been national power capabilities, which have both an internal and an external component. In this chapter we shall explore the impact of external actors and the structure of the international system on the foreign-policy behavior of a state. In a sense, if there were no external determinants, there would be no foreign policy. In developing a foreign policy, a state is largely reacting to some condition or happening in its external environment. Those who subscribe to the rational-actor model (see Chapter 1) tend to regard this level of analysis as the only significant one.

Much of what is written about international relations is approached from this particular perspective, with little reference to many of the internal calculations already discussed. Despite the extensive use of this approach, there is comparatively little in the way of empirically verifiable work concerning the impact of external variables on foreign policy. The bulk of such research tends to be anecdotal and descriptive. The exception is the recent outpouring of research utilizing what has come to be known as the *event analysis* approach. This approach involves the coding of hundreds of moves, including such activities as threats, promises, protests, violence, and the like, in which states engage on an almost daily basis. These are quantified and analyzed in an attempt to determine changes and directions in the foreign policy of a state. Such data are also useful in examining action–reaction models in foreign policy—an issue to which we now turn our attention.

ACTION AND REACTION IN WORLD POLITICS

Utilizing event data, a number of researchers have documented the tendency of states to reciprocate both hostile and conciliatory behavior. The author of an analysis of the foreign-policy behavior of seventy-eight countries in the developing world concluded that "the international conflict behavior of third world countries conforms very strongly to a simple stimulus response relationship in which the conflict that countries send to other countries in the region is a function of the conflict received from the region."[1] Another researcher analyzing global conflict behavior during 1963 similarly found that the states that initiated relatively large amounts of conflict also tended to be the targets of considerable conflict, at least when the data were aggregated to the yearly level.[2] The same pattern, however, did not persist when the data were analyzed on a monthly basis, perhaps suggesting that reaction is not always immediate. The exception is military violence, in which there may be little choice but to respond punctually in kind.

Several regional studies have confirmed a certain level of reciprocation in foreign-policy behavior. For example, a study of the 1961 Sino-Indian border conflict found a strong correlation between Chinese and Indian actions in the conflict, and an examination of action and reaction in the Cuban missile crisis also proved to be statistically significant as both the United States and the Soviet Union reciprocated each other's hostile and conciliatory actions.[3] Similar results were found in

1.   Stephen G. Walker, "New Nations and an Old Model: The Application of the Garrison State Theory to the Third World," in Sheldon W. Simon, ed., *The Military and Security in the Third World* (Boulder, Col.: Westview Press, 1978), p. 180.

2.   Warren R. Phillips, "The Dynamics of Behavioral Action and Reaction in International Conflict," *Peace Research Society (International) Papers*, 17 (1970), 31–46.

3.   John Osgood Field, "The Sino-Indian Border Conflict: An Exploratory Analysis of Action and Perception," *Sage Professional Papers*, 1 (1972), 47, and Ole R. Holsti, Richard A. Brody, and Robert C. North, "Measuring Affect and Action in International Reaction Models: Empirical Materials from the 1962 Cuban Crisis," *Journal of Peace Research*, 1, nos. 3–4 (1964), 177.

several studies involving the Arab–Israeli conflict, even though different time periods and measuring techniques were utilized.[4] Finally, Dina A. Zinnes found that, with respect to diplomatic messages during the 1914 crisis preceding World War I, there was a high correlation between the perception of hostility and its emission by each state that entered the war.[5]

Charles A. McClelland has noted that states engaged in long periods of acute international crises have a tendency to routinize their behavior. His analyses, drawing on the conflicts over the islands of Quemoy and Matsu and over Berlin, suggest that when one state reacts to the behavior of another over time, some learning goes on that makes subsequent confrontations less dangerous because the states have learned from their handling of past crises.[6] As long as occasional crises do not lead to complacency and lack of adequate caution, McClelland's findings have important implications for the development of a peaceful world as states learn to routinize their conflict behavior without resorting to violence.

Research on cooperative moves also suggests some tendency toward reciprocation. An examination of United States and Soviet concession scores on general disarmament issues during the twenty-one rounds of negotiations that were held in London, New York, and Geneva over the period 1946–60 revealed considerable reciprocation between the two powers. After excluding the erratic year 1955, during which the Soviet Union made numerous concessions and the United States "reserved" all of its past disarmament proposals, the correlation in mutual reciprocation was found to be a statistically significant .57.[7] Similar findings were discovered in coding concession scores for the Nuclear Test Ban talks that began in 1958 and resulted in the Partial

4. Jeffrey S. Milstein, "American and Soviet Influence, Balance of Power, and Arab–Israeli Violence," in Bruce M. Russett, ed., *Peace, War, and Numbers* (Beverly Hills, Calif.: Sage Publications, 1972), p. 152; James M. McCormick, "Evaluating Models of Crisis Behavior: Some Evidence from the Middle East," *International Studies Quarterly,* 19 (January 1975), 17–45; Jonathan Wilkenfeld et al., "Conflict Interactions in the Middle East, 1949–1967," *Journal of Conflict Resolution,* 16 (June 1972), 135–54.

5. Dina A. Zinnes, "A Comparison of Hostile Behavior of Decision-Makers in Simulate and Historical Data," *World Politics,* 13 (April 1966), 474–502.

6. Charles A. McClelland, "Decision Opportunity and Political Controversy: The Quemoy Case," *Journal of Conflict Resolution,* 6 (September 1962), 201–13, and "Access to Berlin: The Quantity and Variety of Events, 1948–1963," in J. David Singer, ed., *Quantitative International Politics* (New York: Free Press, 1968), pp. 159–86.

7. Lloyd Jensen, "Soviet–American Bargaining Behavior in the Post-War Disarmament Negotiations," *Journal of Conflict Resolution,* 9 (September 1963), 522–41.

Test Ban Treaty in 1963.[8] But in the latter instance, as the two approached agreement on a comprehensive test ban in April 1960 with all but three articles of the treaty agreed upon, the Soviet Union began to express avoidance behavior. Such behavior suggests that states may be able to make numerous concessions while results seem remote, perhaps in the expectation that the other side will never accept them, but begin to show avoidance tendencies and may even begin to make retractions as agreement is approached. This setback ultimately led to the conclusion of a partial test ban treaty instead of the desired comprehensive one.

A more detailed content analysis of the debates on the test ban treaty, coding attitudes, behaviors, and responses, revealed similar tendencies toward reciprocation, particularly on the part of the United States. The study also suggested that insofar as external conflict did have an effect, the direction was one in which increased cooperation outside the negotiations contributed to more positive internal interaction. Extensive external conflict was found to have a negative effect on the negotiations.[9] Nevertheless, the results indicated that the negotiations were affected more by the behavior taking place within the negotiations than by the external conflict and cooperative behavior engaged in by the participants.

The importance of reciprocation in resolving international differences is also shown in a study of twenty serious disputes that occurred in the twentieth century. The authors found that a reciprocating strategy was the most effective means of avoiding a diplomatic defeat without going to war, especially when such a strategy was employed against a bullying opponent. They suggested that the success of this strategy was related to its face-saving properties as well as "the universal norm of reciprocity in international affairs."[10] A global crossnational study involving conflict and cooperative behavior during the period 1966–69 concluded that states interact on an exchange basis and are responsive to actors that pay attention to them.[11]

8.   Lloyd Jensen, "Approach–Avoidance Bargaining in the Test Ban Negotiations," *International Studies Quarterly*, 12 (June 1968), 152–60.

9.   P. Terrence Hopmann, "Internal and External Influences on Bargaining in Arms Control Negotiations: The Partial Test Ban," in Russett, *Peace, War, and Numbers*, pp. 313–37.

10.   Russell J. Leng and Hugh G. Wheeler, "Influence Strategies, Success, and War," *Journal of Conflict Resolution*, 23 (December 1979), 655–84.

11.   Charles W. Kegley, Jr., "Selective Attention: A General Characteristic of the Interactive Behavior of Nations," *International Interactions*, 2 (May 1976), 113–16.

Recognizing the importance of concessions to agreement, Charles E. Osgood has suggested that each side in an international conflict situation should gradually reduce international tension by making unilateral conciliatory moves, coupled with verbal and tacit requests that others follow suit.[12] For such a strategy to be successful, he believes the parties should have roughly equal power, be in a stalemate or moving away from a range of acceptable solutions, and be confronted with mutually applied pressure to reach an agreement. Several studies have explicitly tested the Osgood notion of graduated unilateral initiatives and have found the theory to be valid. These include two simulations of strategic arms races and an experiment that utilized dyadic games involving the Prisoner's Dilemma.[13] In the latter study, by S. S. Komorita, Osgood's assertion that the unilateral initiative strategy worked best if utilized subsequent to a competitive stalemate was confirmed. Further evidence of the positive effect of unilateral initiatives was uncovered in a study of United States–Soviet behavior in the test ban talks.[14]

Despite the seeming necessity of making concessions if agreement is to be obtained, such concessions are not without their hazards. A propensity to make concessions may be interpreted by the adversary as an indication that a given issue is not particularly important. Moreover, there is the danger that an adversary may misconstrue the move as an indication of weakness, in which case the adversary is likely to demand more.[15] Experimental studies of bargaining conducted by Siegel and Fouraker suggest that one should begin with hard positions rather than conciliatory moves, which tend only to raise the expectations of others.[16] The end result can only be a less advantageous agreement for the state that begins with the softer position.

Some students of negotiation have rejected the concession/convergence model as a major factor in determining the outcome of

12. Charles E. Osgood, *An Alternative to War or Surrender* (Urbana: University of Illinois Press, 1962).

13. Wayman J. Crow, "A Study of Strategic Doctrines Using the Inter-Nation Simulation," *Journal of Conflict Resolution,* 7 (September 1963), 580–89; Mark Pilisuk and Paul Skolnik, "Inducing Trust: A Test of the Osgood Proposal," *Journal of Personality and Social Psychology,* 28 (February 1968), 121–33; S. S. Komorita, "Concession-Making and Conflict Resolution," *Journal of Conflict Resolution,* 17 (December 1973), 745–62.

14. Amitai Etzioni, "The Kennedy Experiment," *Western Political Quarterly,* 20 (June 1967), 361–80.

15. Charles Lockhart, *Bargaining in International Conflicts* (New York: Columbia University Press, 1979), p. 125.

16. Sidney Siegel and L. E. Fouraker, *Bargaining and Group Decision Making* (New York: McGraw-Hill, 1960).

negotiations. I. William Zartman, in a study based on interviews conducted with some fifty ambassadorial-level diplomats at the United
Nations, concluded that the negotiation process is one of finding an
appropriate formula and attempting to implement it. Minimal attention
tends to be paid to the number of concessions made by the other side.
Instead, concessions are largely symbolic moves made most often toward the end, when agreement is in sight and it is believed that the
other side is likely to accept the package being offered.[17] Interviews
with participants in the Kennedy Round of trade negotiations in 1967,
which resulted in an agreement for substantial tariff reductions, demonstrated that there was minimal awareness of the concessions made by
other particpants, as those involved in the negotiations were unable to
agree on when breakthroughs occurred or whether concessions were
even made.[18] In complex negotiations of this sort, responses seemed to
be related to whether or not a state was predisposed toward a liberal
trade policy than to the specific behavior of the other negotiators.

Several studies have suggested that the past behavior of a state is
sometimes a better predictor of a state's current behavior than the activities of other states in the international system. Whether this is due
simply to bureaucratic inertia or to the fact that one feels more comfort-
able with habitual forms of behavior is uncertain. Still, such research
provides some evidence that action–reaction models may not be the
most appropriate ones. It appears that such models are more relevant to
crisis behavior than to noncrisis behavior. A study of fourteen precrisis
events during the period 1966–69, utilizing data from the World Events
Interaction Survey (WEIS) project, revealed that the action–reaction
model provided "unbelievably and almost universally poor fits."[19] The
past behavior of a state predicted current behavior far more effectively,
and although a combination of the two models increased explanatory
capability somewhat, the variance explained was limited. The past-
behavior model was also found to be superior to the action–reaction
model in explaining communication patterns between India and China
for the period 1959–64 and also the perceptions and expressions of

17.   I. William Zartman, "Negotiation as a Joint Decision-Making Process," *Journal of
Conflict Resolution*, 21 (December 1977), 619–38.

18.   Gilbert R. Winham, "Complexity in International Negotiations," in Daniel
Druckman, ed., *Negotiations: Social-Psychological Perspectives* (Beverly Hills, Calif.:
Sage Publications, 1977), pp. 347–66.

19.   Dina A. Zinnes, "Three Puzzles in Search of a Researcher," *International Studies
Quarterly*, 24 (September 1980), 321.

hostility during the 1914 crisis in Europe.[20] Rather than reacting to the moves of the other side, the parties involved in these two conflicts tended to respond largely as they had in the past. Negotiations between the United States and Nasser over the Aswan Dam also revealed that the parties were more responsive to their own past policies than to each other's moves.[21]

It would be erroneous, however, to conclude that all studies that explicitly compare the predictive value of a state's past behavior with that of moves by the other side find the former to have greater explanatory value. A study of Canadian bilateral relations with other states during the period 1957-70 found significantly higher correlations when applying the stimulus–response model. The overall correlation in bilateral conflict behavior with all countries was .57, with bilateral relations with the United States scoring slightly below the average while those with the Soviet Union scored slightly higher than average. Prior Canadian conflict behavior, on the other hand, scored a correlation of only .18. The study also found that 55 percent of the events coded seemed to have had a specific external stimulus.[22]

Action–reaction models have also been popular in analyzing arms races. That the military spending of one state is related to that of its adversaries is suggested by the work of Lewis F. Richardson, who collected considerable data on defense spending during the nineteenth and twentieth centuries.[23] Although the level of grievance and fatigue also entered into his equations, military spending tended on the whole to be reciprocated during the various periods analyzed.

Efforts to apply Richardson-type arms race models to United States–Soviet military programs have generally been unproductive. Increases in the defense spending of one side seem not to have led to increased spending on the part of the other. As in the case of other action–reaction models, one's own past armament behavior proved to

20. G. Duncan and R. Siverson, "Markov Models for Conflict Analysis: Results from Sino-Indian Relations, 1959–1964," *International Studies Quarterly*, 19 (September 1975), 344–74, and Gordon Hilton, "Expressions of Hostility in Crisis," *Journal of Peace Research*, 8, nos. 3–4 (1971), 249–62.

21. Bertram I. Spector, "A Social-Psychological Model of Position Modification: Aswan," in I. William Zartman, ed., *The 50% Solution* (Garden City, N.Y.: Doubleday/Anchor Press, 1976), pp. 343–71.

22. Don Munton, "Stimulus–Response and Continuity in Canadian Foreign Policy During the Cold War and Détente," in Brian W. Tomlin, ed., *Canadian Foreign Policy: Analysis and Trends* (Toronto: Methuen, 1978).

23. Lewis F. Richardson, *Statistics of Deadly Quarrels* (Pittsburgh, Pa.: Boxwood, 1960).

be a better predictor than that of the other side.[24] Although one study provided some evidence of a positive Soviet reaction to American military spending,[25] Benjamin S. Lambeth has argued that there is little evidence to suggest that Soviet force deployments have in fact been reflex responses to American strategic weapons decisions. As evidence, he cites the fact that the Soviets were talking about maneuverable weapons as early as 1963; Soviet research and development on MIRVs preceded their deployment by the United States; and the Soviets' offensive buildup began in 1962, prior to the United States' decision to establish a strategic posture of 1,054 ICBMs.[26]

Studies of arms races in other parts of the world and in other times have produced divided results. An examination of arms races in the Middle East revealed that for some times and for some states there has been a reciprocal arms buildup. In comparing arms races from 1956 to the 1967 war and from 1967 to the October 1973 war, Hans Rattinger found evidence of an overall arms race only during the first period, whereas in the second period only Israel was seen as reacting to Arab inventories, capabilities, and manpower.[27] The author suggests that one reason for the lack of Arab reaction after 1967 may have been the decision to avenge the 1967 war. In that sense an absence of mutual reciprocation may foreshadow aggression as arms continue to build up, regardless of the behavior of the other side.

A similar study looking at the arms race in Europe during the 1950s and 1960s revealed that reaction processes were significantly more discernible for the NATO nations, especially Britain and France, than for the Warsaw Pact nations.[28] Nevertheless, the author of the study found that bureaucratic momentum had a greater influence on arms spending than action–reaction behavior and international tension.

24.   Charles W. Ostrom, Jr., "Evaluating Alternative Foreign Policy Decision-Making Models," *Journal of Conflict Resolution,* 21 (June 1977), 235–66, and W. Ladd Hollist, "An Analysis of Arms Processes in the United States and the Soviet Union," *International Studies Quarterly,* 21 (September 1977), 503–28.

25.   Zivia S. Wurtele, *A Quantitative Analysis of Arms Competition* (Los Angeles: Pan Heuristics, 1976).

26.   Benjamin S. Lambeth, "The Sources of Soviet Military Doctrine," in Frank B. Horton et al., eds., *Comparative Defense Policy* (Baltimore: Johns Hopkins Press, 1974), pp. 202–3.

27.   Hans Rattinger, "From War to War: Arms Races in the Middle East," *International Studies Quarterly,* 20 (December 1976), 501–31.

28.   Hans Rattinger, "Armaments, Détente, and Bureaucracy: The Case of the Arms Race in Europe," *Journal of Conflict Resolution,* 19 (December 1975), 571–95.

Earlier evidence of arms races is seen in the 1905–16 Anglo-German naval race, in which the British demonstrated a greater propensity to react than the Germans.[29] The two parties also differed in emphasis, with Germany stressing the qualitative race while Britain seemed more concerned with the quantitative race.

There are several reasons why the action–reaction model of arms races is not always descriptive of what happens in the real world, not the least of which are domestic political and bureaucratic factors. Arms expenditures may be explained largely by pressures emanating from the military–industrial complex, as discussed in Chapter 6. Such expenditures may also be motivated by a perceived need to provide for domestic political order, since the military, particularly in developing countries, plays an important role in ensuring domestic tranquillity. Or the level of military spending may be related to interservice rivalry as each military service seeks to maximize its budgetary allocations. This is not to say that increased arms spending on the part of the adversary does not play a role, for such increases provide rationalizations for expanding one's own military efforts and, more important, can aid in obtaining public support for so doing.

Second, there is a tendency for arms spending to reflect past spending levels as opposed to the other side's behavior because of the pressure for military programs to expand in order to absorb whatever money is available. The United States' missile programs after 1954 owed their budgetary existence to the new plateaus of defense spending achieved during the Korean War.[30] Similarly, the end of the Vietnam War failed to result in any appreciable decrease in American military spending but, instead, facilitated the continuation of huge military budgets.

Third, defense spending may not be responsive to the military efforts of the other side because of frequent miscalculation of the latter's capabilities and intentions. The failure to find a good fit in United States–Soviet arms reciprocation may be due partly to the fact that each state has generally reacted to the other's projected strength, not its current strength. Indicative of some of the serious miscalculations that have resulted are the bomber gap of the 1950s and the missile gap of the early 1960s. In the latter instance the United States discovered through

29. John C. Lambelet, "A Complementary Analysis of the Anglo-German Dreadnought Race, 1905–1916," *Peace Science Society (International) Papers*, 26 (1976), 49–66.

30. Colin S. Gray, *The Soviet–American Arms Race* (Westmead, England: Saxon House, 1976), p. 107.

the use of U-2 overflights of Soviet territory that, rather than being far behind the Soviet Union in terms of missile capabilities, the United States was far ahead—so much so that it induced Khrushchev to make the reckless move of sending missiles to Cuba in 1962.

Fourth, arms race calculations are based on expenditures in a bilateral race and therefore do not take adequate account of the military threats of third parties. For example, how much of the Soviet military effort is related to its conflict with China rather than its concern about the threat posed by the United States? An examination of mathematical models of three-nation arms races suggests that two-way races would not escalate infinitely were it not for fear of third-party alliances.[31]

Fifth, work by Paul Smoker suggests that there may be differential rates of submissiveness in an arms race.[32] That is, one party or the other may begin to fear an uncontrollable arms race and, as a result, reduce its military spending when the race seems to be accelerating. If the other side does not share such fears, it is less likely to be responsive to the reduced arms effort.

Sixth, it may even be the case that lowered arms levels will increase the incentive for the other side to add to its military capabilities. According to one authority, the United States probably would not have tried to increase NATO's conventional forces in the 1960s had it not discovered fewer conventional forces in the Soviet Union than previously expected, thereby making it possible to defend Europe without going nuclear.[33] Similarly, the Soviet Union may not have undertaken its determined effort to improve its strategic capability had it not believed that parity with the United States was an achievable goal.

Most interesting from a foreign-policy perspective is the question of whether arms races lead to decisions to go to war. A study of recent wars argues that arms races and hot wars have been largely independent of each other.[34] The Korean War, for example, did not begin with an arms race; if anything, it started with a disarmament race as the United States sought to bring the troops home as rapidly as possible

---

31.   John E. Hunter, "Mathematical Models of a Three-Nation Arms Race," *Journal of Conflict Resolution*, 24 (June 1980), 241.

32.   Paul Smoker, "Fear in the Arms Race: A Mathematical Study," *Journal of Peace Research*, 1, no. 1 (1964), 55–63.

33.   Robert Jervis, *Perception and Misperception in International Politics* (Princeton, N.J.: Princeton University Press, 1976), p. 86.

34.   John C. Lambelet, "Do Arms Races Lead to War," *Journal of Peace Research*, 12, no. 2 (1975), 123–28.

after World War II. That arms races do not always end in war is also suggested by the naval race between England and France, which was widely held to have lasted for sixty-four years (1840–1904) during which no wars occurred. Despite one of the most violent arms races in history, there has been a dramatic decline in the frequency with which military confrontations involving major powers escalate into war. Since World War II only 8 percent of such confrontations were found to have resulted in war.[35]

Several studies have suggested that arms races lead to escalation and increased violence. One such study found that of twenty-six great power military confrontations coded during the nineteenth and twentieth centuries that escalated to war, twenty-three were preceded by arms races. On the other hand, of seventy-two great power confrontations that did not result in war, only five were preceded by arms races.[36] An earlier study using data from the same period discovered a strong relationship between the rate of increase in armament spending and the number of wars begun in the subsequent five-year period.[37] This was so even when the influences of many other factors were controlled.

In a classic study of arms races, Samuel P. Huntington argued that the likelihood of war in such a race varies inversely with the length of time it has been in existence.[38] In effect, war is more likely in the early stage of an arms race, before peaceful patterns of action have been established. Huntington goes on to suggest that quantitative arms races are more likely to lead to war than qualitative ones. Quantitative races are believed to produce inequality, since one only slips further behind as the other side increases its armament. Qualitative races are seen as tending toward equality, for scientific advantages usually do not last very long in a highly technological world. Equality, in turn, is viewed by Huntington as decreasing the likelihood of war. Since quantitative

35. Melvin Small and J. David Singer, "Conflict in the International System, 1816–1977," in Charles W. Kegley, Jr., and Patrick J. McGowan, eds., *Challenges to America: United States Foreign Policy in the 1980s* (Beverly Hills, Calif.: Sage Publications, 1979), p. 107.

36. Michael D. Wallace, "Arms Races and Escalation," *Journal of Conflict Resolution,* 23 (March 1979), 3–16.

37. Michael D. Wallace, "Status, Formal Organization, and Arms Levels as Factors Leading to the Onset of War, 1820–1964," in Russett, *Peace, War, and Numbers,* pp. 49–69.

38. Samuel P. Huntington, "Arms Races: Prerequisites and Results," *Public Policy,* 1958, pp. 41–86.

arms races generally involve a greater financial burden and produce greater tension, powerful pressures are created to end the race through either war or disarmament. Unfortunately, war has been a more frequent outcome than disarmament. Qualitative arms races, on the other hand, are seen by Huntington as involving merely a redeployment rather than an increase of arms budgets and, as such, do not produce the strains leading to war. This does not mean that qualitative arms races are benign, for pressure for war may arise if a state fears that the other side is about to achieve a scientific breakthrough that will dramatically change the military balance. To prevent such a possibility there will be a strong incentive to initiate a strike on the opposing state or its new weapons system, particularly if a state believes itself to be too far behind in the technological race. Qualitative arms races also raise the capacity to wreak greater death and destruction on the world.

THE IMPACT OF THIRD PARTIES

So far we have discussed the action and reaction of states as if such behavior operated in a closed system with little input from the outside. Nothing could be further from the truth; each state is affected by the behavior and reactions of other states. Pressures from the outside in a dispute may include offers of mediation or economic, military, and political assistance. Relevant moves by external actors may also involve such negative sanctions as threats, condemnations, or the withdrawal of military, economic, or political support.

Numerous conflicts have been settled, or at least controlled, by the mediation efforts of third parties, as in the case of Theodore Roosevelt's mediation of the Russo-Japanese War of 1904–5, which ended in the Treaty of Portsmouth; Alexei Kosygin's mediation of the Indo-Pakistani war, which resulted in the signing of the Treaty of Tashkent in 1966; and President Carter's efforts in helping achieve the 1979 Camp David Accords, which established the basis for peace between Egypt and Israel. But just as third powers have played the role of mediator in conflict situations, they have also involved themselves in other states' wars and in so doing have often determined the outcome. Interventions by outside powers in the 1956 Suez war, the October 1973 Middle East war, and the conflict in Rhodesia (Zimbabwe) are but a few illustrations of such involvement.

Since external support, or at least noninterference, is of such critical importance to the military ventures of most states, particularly those with limited power, any calculation regarding a decision to go to war will obviously have to take into account the probable reaction of outside powers. States with extensive alliance support are more likely to initiate aggression, despite an imbalance in power capabilities, in the expectation that they will be aided by their allies. The North Korean incursion into South Korea in 1950 obviously was undertaken with the implicit or explicit approval of the Soviet Union. But just as anticipated support from the outside may encourage a would-be aggressor, an ally may also act to constrain behavior, as in the case of Soviet pressure on the People's Republic of China to end its shelling of the coastal islands of Quemoy and Matsu in 1958.

The decision makers of a state that is confronted with conflict are generally interested in developing as much support for their position in the international community as possible. The decision of the People's Republic of China to end the Great Cultural Revolution in 1969 and resume relations with the outside world was in no small measure related to the Sino-Soviet border conflict that erupted in that year. Within a short time China rejoined the international community by assuming the seat of China at the United Nations and began the process of establishing diplomatic relations with a large number of states, thus ending a long period of isolation. One of the major problems that confronted Iran in its war with Iraq in 1980–81 was its general isolation from the world because it had alienated many nations with its refusal to respect international legal norms by not returning the American hostages. Indeed, the war itself was one of the major factors facilitating the ultimate release of the hostages as Iran became increasingly concerned about ending the economic and military boycott imposed upon it.

Decision makers pay considerable attention to the behavior of other states in order to get clues as to how such states might respond to them in the future. China showed particular concern regarding the Soviet intervention in Czechoslovakia in 1968 and the subsequent pronouncement of the Brezhnev doctrine, which held that the Soviet Union had a right to intervene in the affairs of other socialist states. The credibility of a deterrent threat will often be interpreted on the basis of how the state issuing such a threat carries out similar threats against other states. There has been some speculation, for example, that Khrushchev raised the Berlin issue to the level of a crisis in 1961 because of President Kennedy's minimal support of the Cuban exiles during the Bay of Pigs disaster. Because of the fear of possible misinterpretation of deterrent intentions, efforts to deter a state may be motivated not so much by fear or concern about that particular state as by concern about how such efforts might be interpreted by other, more important states in the system. This is why it is often impossible to calculate what decision makers will do if one focuses narrowly on the concerns and relative capabilities of the states that are immediately involved in a conflict situation.

Third parties can affect the foreign policy of a state by playing the role of intermediary in a conflict situation. Such a role can be particularly important when the two disputing parties are not speaking to each other. In this instance the third party may serve as a messenger by shuttling from one disputant to the other, as former Secretary of State Henry Kissinger did in attempting to bring peace to the Middle East. Also, the third party is able to make suggestions for solving the problem, and can point out where compromise is possible. Such recommendations may be accepted, particularly if the disputing parties view the third party as an objective outsider. In some instances, such as the Rann of Kutch arbitration of 1965 involving a territorial dispute between India and Pakistan, the parties may agree in advance to accept whatever recommendation is made by the arbitrator.

Outside powers have also been known to affect the behavior of the negotiating states by issuing threats and promises of reward, as demonstrated in the previous chapter. Henry Kissinger's manipulation of reward and punishment to try to resolve the Middle East conflict is a case in point. This aspect of third-power leverage does raise the question of whether only great powers can be effective in using such devices to ensure settlements, for most other states lack the necessary resources.

Third parties may also be able to facilitate the reaching of agreements by guaranteeing whatever settlement is made. Third-party guarantees of the Vietnam settlement and the monitoring techniques established after the October Middle East War are but two such examples. Finally, third parties may facilitate agreement by enabling the disputants to save face. In terms of one's own prestige, it may be easier for a state to make concessions to a third party than directly to its adversary. Britain, France, and Israel were able to save face in 1956 after the United States and the Soviet Union pressed them into ending their invasion of Suez by suggesting that they had merely intervened to stabilize the situation until the United Nations was able to take over.

Multiple-party involvement in peacemaking may make the process more difficult, as has been shown in a careful analysis of such efforts since the seventeenth century.[39] The author of that study noted that intervention by outside powers increased the complexity of the peacemaking by multiplying the number of decision makers to be satisfied and the number of decisions and possible settlements that might be reached. Recognizing some of the disadvantages of involving large numbers of states in the conflicts of other states, the founders of the United Nations included a provision in its charter that emphasized that disputants were first and foremost to attempt to resolve their conflicts themselves or regionally; only if those efforts were unsuccessful should the dispute be transmitted to the United Nations for consideration (Article 33).

INTERNATIONAL ORGANIZATION AND FOREIGN POLICY

A third party that has become an important factor affecting the foreign policy of the nation–state in recent years is the international organization. Some idea of the impact of international organizations and the role they play in the foreign policy of states can be gained from the phenomenal increase in the number of such organizations in recent decades. In 1949, for example, there were only 38 international governmental organizations (IGOs), but in 1977 the number had increased to 261.[40]

A number of studies have attempted to determine whether international organizations have affected state behavior by making war less likely or at least ensuring that international conflicts will not escalate. Data from the Correlates of War project for the period 1816–1965 revealed that the amount of intergovernmental organization in the system had no measurable impact on the amount of war. However, that study did find that the rate of increase of such organizations had a slight *negative* association with the magnitude of war in the subsequent five-year period.[41] This would seem to provide some support for the

39. Randle Ripley, *The Origins of Peace* (New York: Columbia University Press, 1974).

40. William D. Coplin, *Introduction to International Politics*, 3rd ed. (Englewood Cliffs, N.J.: Prentice-Hall, 1980), p. 119.

41. J. David Singer and Michael D. Wallace, "Intergovernmental Organization and the Preservation of Peace, 1816–1965," *International Organization*, 24 (Summer 1970), 520–47.

notion that international organization tends to put a damper on international conflict. Another study discovered that the relationship between intergovernmental organizations and war differed, depending on whether IGO membership was aggregated to a system level or merely by country. Thus, for the period 1900–1964 there was a negative relationship between the existence of IGOs and war. On the other hand, the larger number of IGOs to which a nation belonged, the higher its conflict score.[42] What was probably being tapped in the latter instance was the impact of the relative size of states, since other research has shown that larger states tend to belong to more organizations as well as to engage in more conflict behavior.

Several studies have examined the impact of the League of Nations and its successor, the United Nations, on conflict behavior. K. J. Holsti, for example, found with respect to seventy-seven conflicts that occurred during the period 1919–65 that some 23 percent were partially or fully resolved with the help of international organizations. Of the forty-eight cases specifically placed on the agenda of the League of Nations or the United Nations, some 37 percent were successfully settled.[43] In another effort to judge the impact of international organization on peaceful settlement, Quincy Wright found that of the sixty-six political disputes handled by the League of Nations, thirty-five were resolved successfully and twenty were transfered to other agencies for consideration. Most of the eleven failures occurred after 1935, providing the League with a fairly impressive record for fifteen years.[44] A subsequent study by Wright of forty-five cases that came before the United Nations during its first twenty years of operation revealed that nine involved no military action, twenty resulted in the conclusion of hostilities with a formal or tacit cease-fire within the first year, and fourteen escalated for a longer period and with a greater number of casualties, while only two went to the stage of a general war.[45] Although this particular study revealed a fairly good record as far as controlling escalation was concerned, it does not necessarily provide evidence that the conflicts

---

42. James E. Harf, David G. Hoovler, and Thomas E. James, Jr., "Systemic and External Attributes in Foreign Policy Analysis," in James N. Rosenau, ed., *Comparing Foreign Policies* (New York: Wiley, 1974), p. 240.

43. K. J. Holsti, "Resolving International Conflicts," *Journal of Conflict Resolution,* 10 (September 1966), 286–87.

44. Quincy Wright, *A Study of War,* 2nd ed. (Chicago: University of Chicago Press, 1965), p. 1431.

45. Quincy Wright, "The Escalation of International Conflicts," *Journal of Conflict Resolution,* 9 (December 1965), 438.

studied have been resolved. Indeed, a cursory examination of the cases suggests that many conflicts in the postwar world have been perpetuated peacefully, with hostilities erupting over some issues from time to time.

The fact that permanent settlements often are not achieved in conflicts that come before the United Nations is supported by a study of fifty-five such disputes in the pre-1965 period. Almost half of these cases were recorded as unsettled, and only about one-third were settled in part or whole on the basis of the United Nations resolution. Despite the general belief that international organizations are incapable of affecting great-power behavior, the success rate of resolving disputes in which great powers were involved proved to be as high or higher than that of lesser states.[46]

Another evaluation, which is more pessimistic in its assessment of the effectiveness of international organization in peaceful settlement, found that in over one hundred international wars and crises since World War II less than 20 percent of the instances elicited a United Nations resolution calling for a halt to the threat or act of force. Of the cases in which such action was called for, success was achieved in only about half of the cases—success in this instance being defined as compliance by the parties soon after the United Nations directive was issued.[47] This more pessimistic assessment of the effectiveness of the United Nations is undoubtedly due in part to the fact that the cases include instances through 1977. As in the case of the League, the effectiveness of the United Nations in discouraging the use of the military option appears to have declined over time.

The success rates of regional organizations have been found to be not much higher than that of the United Nations. In a study of the collective security successes of the United Nations and three regional organizations, Mark W. Zacher scored only 18 percent of the 116 cases of conflict between members occurring during the period 1946–77 as showing success. In a further breakdown, success was recorded for the United Nations in only 9 percent of the 93 cases examined; for the Organization of African Unity, success was scored at 19 percent (N = 26); the Arab League scored 12 percent (N = 17); and the Organization

46. Ernst B. Haas, "Collective Security and the Future International System," University of Denver Monograph Series in World Affairs no. 5 (Denver, 1967–68), pp. 44, 51.

47. Jock A. Finlayson and Mark W. Zacher, "The United Nations and Collective Security: Retrospect and Prospect," p. 3 (Paper delivered at the Annual Convention of the International Studies Association, Los Angeles, 1980).

of American States (OAS) was successful in 37 percent of its 19 cases.[48] The relatively high success rate of the latter is in no small measure a product of the fact that the United States dominates the organization and can assure adequate force to back up organizational decisions with which it agrees. On occasion it has even been the practice of the United States to decide how to respond to a crisis and only then take the issue to the OAS for approval. Such was the case with respect to the United States' decision to establish a quarantine around Cuba during the 1962 missile crisis.

In an analysis of nineteen conflicts in which the three regional organizations included in the Zacher study participated, it was discovered that these organizations helped settle roughly one-third of the conflicts. In seven of the sixteen cases that involved actual fighting, the regional organization concerned was effective in helping to end the hostilities.[49]

Once a decision has been made, the question arises as to how effective international organization is in obtaining compliance. The record is clearly mixed. Ernst Haas found, on the basis of experiences through 1965, very few cases in which the order to honor a United Nations–sponsored truce was not obeyed by the parties involved.[50] Peace forces were shown to have been effective whenever they were created. A necessary but not sufficient reason for the effectiveness of such peacekeeping forces was great-power involvement, according to a study of seven United Nations peacekeeping cases compared with instances in which peacekeeping intervention was absent.[51]

The ability of international organizations to control the conflict behavior of states would appear quite limited, given the results of the studies just cited. However, there is a fundamental problem involved in such quantitative studies: One cannot count the number of wars or conflicts that did *not* arise because of the constraints decision makers might have felt as a result of the existence of such organizations. In assessing the role of international organizations on foreign policy, one should also keep in mind that such organizations serve as machinery

48. Mark W. Zacher, *International Conflicts and Collective Security, 1946–77* (New York: Praeger, 1979), p. 214.

49. Joseph S. Nye, *Peace in Parts* (Boston: Little, Brown, 1971), p. 170.

50. Haas, "Collective Security and the Future International System," p. 51.

51. N. A. Pelcovits, "Local Conflict and UN Peacekeeping," *International Studies Quarterly*, 20 (December 1976), 533–52.

that can be used by states in pursuit of their foreign policies. It has even been suggested that bringing issues before the United Nations may be viewed as a hostile act. States often use the United Nations in an effort to justify their legal claims, to embarrass the other side, or to rally other members to their own position, motives that have little to do with resolving conflict.[52]

It may be that the importance of international organization for foreign policy lies not so much in its immediate effect on conflict resolution as in its role as a long-term socializing agent that can gradually make the world's decision makers more responsive to the need for international understanding. Several studies have examined the impact of experience in parliamentary bodies on the participants' world-mindedness and support for international solutions to problems. Studies examining the impact of experience with international organizations on members of the United States Congress have generally concluded that the experience was a positive one.[53] Robert E. Riggs discovered that members who had participated in General Assembly meetings tended to pay more attention to the United Nations in subsequent speeches as well as to experience a positive change in affect toward the organization. David A. Karns found that although overall changes in affect were small after attendance at an initial meeting, there were significant positive changes after controlling for party, ideology, and degree of previous isolationism.

A later study comparing American and Norwegian legislators and civil servants revealed that there was no simple linear relationship between participation in international organizations and positive affect. In terms of support for the transfer of sovereignty, the results showed that experience tended only to make the participant more negative on the issue. As a general rule, the study found that international agencies working on specific technical problems tended to win greater approval from national politicians than organizations identified with higher-level political–diplomatic debate.[54]

52.   Abraham Yeselson and Anthony Gaglione, *A Dangerous Place: The United Nations as a Weapon in International Politics* (New York: Grossman, 1974).

53.   Robert E. Riggs, "One Small Step for Functionalism: UN Participation and Attitude Change," *International Organization*, 31 (Summer 1977), 515–39, and David A. Karns, "The Effect of Interparliamentary Meetings on the Foreign Policy Attitudes of United States Congressmen," *International Organization*, 31 (Summer 1977), 497–514.

54.   Robert E. Riggs and I. Jostein Mykletun, *Beyond Functionalism: Attitudes Toward International Organization in Norway and the United States* (Minneapolis: University of Minnesota Press, 1979), p. 159.

Two studies of participation in European parliamentary bodies have uncovered little or no change resulting from the experience. The fact that there may have been little affective change in these instances may have been due to preselection, however, as those who already favored European unity opted for such a role. There was little need to change their attitudes, since they were already positive.[55]

CHARACTERISTICS OF THE INTERNATIONAL SYSTEM

Beyond being affected by the behavior of various other actors in the international system, whether they be nations or groups of nations, foreign-policy decision makers are also influenced by the general characteristics and norms of the international system. That system is not immutable; it changes over time. These changes may even have an impact on the various determinants of foreign policy, some of which may be relevant in one historical epoch but not in another. There is a general belief, for example, that the rise of nuclear weapons has fundamentally changed the nature of the international system, and it may therefore be inappropriate in certain instances to draw analogies with other periods in history. As will be shown shortly, the work of the Correlates of War project has revealed in several instances that such variables as alliances and polarization had different effects in the world of the nineteenth century than they have in the current century. For these reasons it is necessary to examine the implications of the total system on state behavior.

Two recent studies have provided detailed illustrations of various international systems, suggesting the tendency of such systems and their participants to assume certain common characteristics. Robert G. Wesson has noted that state systems like those of classical Greece, pre-imperial China, and the nation–state system of Europe tend to develop a single culture, although with some local variation. He also argues that state systems that are organized as unitary actors are prone to build grandiose monuments, such as the pyramids, the great wall of China, and the Roman Colosseum, while pluralistic state systems are

55. G. Matthew Bonham, "Participation in Regional Parliamentary Assemblies: Effect on Attitudes of Scandinavian Parliamentarians," *Journal of Common Market Studies,* 8 (June 1975), 325, and Henry H. Kern, Jr., "Changing Attitudes Through International Participation: European Parliamentarians and Integration," *International Organization,* 27 (Winter 1973), 45–83.

freer to enrich themselves through trade or to experiment with science or the arts. Although pluralistic state systems may "wear themselves out by warfare, empires choke themselves by unity."[56]

The basic thesis presented by Evan Luard in his study of seven historical international systems, beginning with ancient China and ending with the current age of ideology, is that the system itself shapes the character of the participants so that they become pretty much alike in terms of motives, means, stratification, internal structure, roles, norms, and institutions.[57] Such similarities are not merely a result of copying the styles and modes of behavior of other states in the system; they are also products of systemic structures that affect all participants equally. For example, systems that are dominated by international tension tend to produce states that are suspicious and circumspect in their foreign policies. Such tension may also lead to increased centralization of decision making within the state. States that are in conflict with each other are also likely to adopt similar military strategies. Thus, if guerrilla war is utilized by one side, it will force the other to develop similar capabilities in order to compete effectively.

Those who emphasize systemic factors as a primary explanation of foreign-policy behavior correspondingly tend to deemphasize domestic determinants. Since the system determines the response, differences in economic and political structure or leadership style are seen as largely irrelevant to foreign-policy choices, as each nation tends to behave substantially like any other nation.

Among the most important system characteristics are the norms and laws adhered to by the international society involved. Decision makers want to put on the best face possible, making their decisions appear both moral and legal. If it becomes a choice between two options, both of which are viewed as likely to solve a given problem, decision makers are likely to choose the one they believe to be more moral as well as legal.

Decision makers seem to take international law quite seriously, if the deliberateness with which they engage in treaty making is any indication. This activity seems not to be engaged in frivolously in the belief that it is always possible to renege later. The Soviet record on compliance with international treaties is quite good, according to one statistical assessment. In an analysis of compliance with 2,475 treaties

56. Robert G. Wesson, *State Systems* (New York: Free Press, 1978), pp. 10–15.
57. Evan Luard, *Types of International Society* (New York: Free Press, 1976).

during the period 1918–57, it was calculated that the Soviet infidelity ratio was 11.5 per thousand, or somewhat less than 1.2 percent. This is to say that the Soviet Union fails to honor a political promise, on the average, in only about one month out of every 120 (10 years) over which it is bound, keeping the promise for the other 119 months.[58] If one were to look at the United States' compliance record, it is probable that one would find similar impressive results. At the same time, there are some glaring failures in that record. For example, the United States violated the OAS Charter with its involvement in the overthrow of the Arbenz government in Guatamala in 1954, its Bay of Pigs invasion in 1961, and its intervention in the Dominican Republic in 1965. Former Senator Frank Church estimated that in the latter instance the United States had violated no fewer than eighteen treaty covenants.[59]

Compliance with international law is related not only to living up to treaty commitments but also to observing the customary behavior of civilized states. The advantages of customary rules over treaty law have been summarized by Edward McWhinney: Customary rules do not pin down the prestige of actors in changing circumstances that may require them to reassess the situation; they do not raise the negative problems often involved in formal agreements, such as the embarrassment created when one is trying to renege because of changing circumstances; and they allow decision makers to bypass the bureaucratic process involved in treaty making as well as the need to obtain the approval of alliance partners. On the other hand, such rules are often imprecise, misunderstood, or contradictory.[60]

Since so much of international law is based on customary behavior, the new states feel that they did not participate in its development and are consequently often hostile toward its application. A study of reactions to the negotiations on the law of the seas held in Geneva in 1958 and 1960 is revealing on this point. According to its author, the "dissatisfied" states, which were largely new states, saw international law as a device to camouflage self-interest and allow the few to dominate the many. Legal detail was seen by such states as a trap for them,

---

58. Jan F. Triska and Robert M. Slusser, *The Theory, Law and Policy of Soviet Treaties* (Stanford, Calif.: Stanford University Press, 1962).

59. Cited in Margaret G. Hermann, ed., *A Psychological Examination of Political Leaders* (New York: Free Press, 1977).

60. Edward McWhinney, *Peaceful Coexistence and Soviet–Western International Laws* (Leyden, The Netherlands: Sithoff, 1964), pp. 181–94.

and as a result, they tended to prefer general statements over more exact definitions.[61]

States do occasionally flout international legal decisions, as in the case of Iran's reaction to the hostage decision delivered by the International Court of Justice in 1980. A majority of the states in the international system have also placed reservations on the compulsory-jurisdiction clause of the International Court of Justice, thereby keeping many issues out of the World Court. As a result, the Court has been able to determine only a handful of cases annually.

International law has advanced further with respect to some substantive areas than others. This is particularly true in the case of commercial and transportation policy. Commercial interaction, as in scheduling airlines, railroads, and postal deliveries, requires considerable coordination on an international scale. To achieve such coordination, states have relinquished certain sovereign rights and have been willing to accept the position of the majority in order to accomplish the necessary tasks. The global rise of terrorism has also inspired considerable effort to develop international conventions that will help solve the problem.

The supranational authority of international legal institutions has developed furthest in Europe, where the Court of Justice of the European Communities (the Common Market) has the power to levy fines on individuals and corporations. Individuals who believe that their human rights have been violated by their own national governments may petition the European Commission on Human Rights to investigate the case and perhaps even take the matter to the European Court of Human Rights. This procedure has been particularly successful in compelling states to change laws that are found to be in violation of the Convention on Human Rights. Domestic courts have also often applied provisions of the Convention directly in rulings involving their own citizens.[62]

Although buffeted by the forces of nationalism and other "isms," international law continues to flourish and to expand in scope. States appear to be genuinely concerned with having their moves interpreted

---

61. Robert L. Friedheim, "The Satisfied and Dissatisfied States Negotiate International Law," *World Politics,* 18 (October 1965), 20–41.

62. For a discussion of such instances see Jane S. Jensen and Lloyd Jensen, "The European Convention for the Protection of Human Rights and National Law," paper delivered at the Annual Meeting of the International Studies Association, Los Angeles, 1980.

and justified from a legal perspective. They continue to support international legal structures as useful devices in the execution of their foreign policy.

THE DISTRIBUTION OF POWER

Perhaps the most critical systemic characteristic affecting the foreign policy of a state is the way power is distributed in the international system. Balance-of-power theorists hold that in the pursuit of power states will react to the efforts of others to change the power balance of the system, and in so doing will produce peace and a certain level of international stability. In accordance with the classical balance-of-power theory, some leaders have purposefully undertaken the role of balancer, as in the case of Henry VIII, to whom is attributed the maxim *Cui adhaero praeest* (He whom I support will prevail). According to one story, Henry had a portrait of himself painted in which he held in one hand a pair of scales labeled, respectively, "Austria" and "France." In the other hand he held a weight that was capable of tipping the balance toward one side or the other.[63]

The debate over the optimum distribution of power has revolved around the issue of whether bipolarity or multipolarity provides greater international stability. Kenneth N. Waltz, one of the most prominent proponents of bipolarity, has suggested four arguments in favor of its stabilizing effects:

1. There are no peripheries with only two world powers, as both sides involve themselves in happenings throughout the globe, resulting in a solid and determinate balance.

2. Not only is the competition extensive, it is also intensive, as each power becomes concerned about even minor changes of the balance.

3. There is a tendency to develop schemes for coping with recurrent crises.

4. With preponderant power, minor shifts in the power balance will not be decisive.[64]

---

63. Arthur Cyr, *British Foreign Policy and the Atlantic Area* (New York: Holmes and Meier, 1979), p. 10.

64. Kenneth N. Waltz, "The Stability of a Bipolar World," *Daedalus*, Summer 1964, pp. 881–909.

In examining these arguments, it might be noted that bipolarity does not reduce the motivation for expansion but may increase it, owing to concern with establishing ever-wider buffer areas. One might also question whether peace can be achieved when nations are involved in recurring crises, any one of which may slip over the threshold into violence. Finally, Waltz's suggestion that polarized powers will intervene when minor changes in the balance are threatened may not be entirely accurate. Superpowers may realize that their states enjoy overwhelming force in a bipolarized system, making it unnecessary to be concerned about minor power shifts, as Waltz admits. Instead of intervention, they may prefer isolation, particularly since intervention may lead them into a nuclear war in defense of an ally.

Several arguments favoring multipolarity have been suggested in other studies, which have made the following points:

1. There will be greater opportunities for interaction in a multipolar system, which increases the prospects of achieving national goals by dealing with different states if necessary.

2. With multipolarity, crosscutting loyalties will exist. Every issue will not be viewed as a zero sum game in which everything gained by one participant is immediately assumed to be lost by the other.

3. Multipolarity diminishes the amount of attention paid to other states and conflict situations. By thus limiting preoccupation with any one conflict, the total amount of violence may be reduced.

4. A multipolar system will hold down the arms race. Not every increment of power on the part of other actors will be viewed as directed against oneself, but may be seen as a reaction to one of the many other states in the system.

5. Multipolarity provides mediators who can help in a conflict in a positive way, as suggested earlier in our discussion of the role of third parties.[65]

Those who favor a balance-of-power system tend to support multipolarity as a necessary prerequisite for its successful operation. There

---

65. Richard N. Rosecrance, "Bipolarity, Multipolarity, and the Future," *Journal of Conflict Resolution*, 10 (September 1966), 314–37, and Kjell Goldman, *Tension and Détente in Bipolar Europe* (Stockholm: Esselte Studium, 1974).

must be an opportunity to shift alliances so that threats to the peace can be countered by new aggregations of power. With more than two major powers, there will always be concern that other states in the system will align with one's enemy and thus tilt the balance. The hope is that the uncertainty that is introduced will act to deter the would-be aggressor.

Considerable research has been conducted in recent years on the relationship between alliances and polarization, on the one hand, and the decision of states to engage in conflict behavior, on the other. Much of this work has been conducted under the auspices of the Correlates of War project under the direction of Professor J. David Singer of the University of Michigan. The project has collected data on the frequency, magnitude, and intensity of war in the international system for every year since 1815. This has been supplemented with data related to numerous other variables, such as alliances, international organizations, population, and power. One of the earliest studies emanating from the project found that there was a small positive relationship between the amount of alliance aggregation and the frequency and magnitude of war. When they divided the data between the nineteenth and twentieth centuries, the authors of the study discovered that alliance aggregation did not lead to war during the earlier century, but was closely related to war in the current one.[66] Alliances thus seemed to be a factor for peace in the nineteenth century but a factor for war in the twentieth. The pattern of the twentieth century was confirmed in a later study from the same project, which found that 84 percent of the wars in the present century began in years following rising systemic tightness.[67]

One possible factor contributing to the failure of alliances to deter war in the present century is the reluctance of some states to live up to their obligations. A study by Alan Sabrosky has revealed that alliances were nearly five times as likely to be violated in the twentieth century as in the nineteenth century. However, such violations have not been typical, scoring only 14 percent of the cases in the present century and 3 percent in the previous one.[68]

---

66. J. David Singer and Melvin Small, "Alliance Aggregation and the Onset of War, 1815–1945," in Singer, *Quantitative International Politics*, pp. 247–86.

67. Bruce Bueno de Mesquita, "Systemic Polarization and the Occurrence and Duration of War," *Journal of Conflict Resolution*, 22 (June 1978), 241–68.

68. Alan Ned Sabrosky, "Interstate Alliances: Their Reliability and the Expansion of War," in J. David Singer, ed., *The Correlates of War, Volume II: Testing Some Realpolitik Models* (New York: Free Press, 1980), p. 177.

It appears that the duration of the alliance may make some difference in the likelihood of war, as a reanalysis of the Singer–Small study has suggested. By controlling for duration, the data for the nineteenth century revealed a positive correlation between war involvement and alliance activities.[69] In other words, alliances that persist over longer periods tend to increase the possibility of war. This was confirmed in yet another study, based on events leading up to World War I, which found that if there is a prolonged period of alliance aggregation around the same power center, the system tends to be more prone to war.[70] The existence of alliances with belligerents clearly increases participation in war, but other explanations are also necessary, since almost half of the participants in wars during the period 1815–1965 were not aligned.[71]

Michael D. Wallace, in an analysis involving data from the Correlates of War project, discovered a curvilinear relationship between alliance polarization and the amount of war in the system.[72] Increased war activity was found when polarization was very tight, pulling all members into the war, or when the system was very diffuse, increasing the number of unprotected states that could be attacked.

A survey of the operation of twenty-one international subsystems in Asia, Europe, and Hawaii since 1649 found that the most stable system was a unipolar one, such as an empire. Control in such a case was often retained by the preponderant force of the central decision makers in the system.[73] As in other studies noted earlier, bipolar systems tended to have less frequent but more prolonged wars, often wars of a localized nature around the peripheries. Multipolar systems were found to generate more violence, more countries at war, and more casualties.

Perhaps part of the discrepancy in studies that relate polarization to war is due to the fact, noted by Johan Galtung, that polarization is a

69. William B. Moul, "The Level of Analysis Problem Revisited," *Canadian Journal of Political Science*, 6, no. 3 (September 1973), 494–513.

70. Alan Ned Sabrosky, "From Bosnia to Sarajevo," *Journal of Conflict Resolution*, 19 (March 1975), 3–24.

71. Randolph M. Siverson and Joel King, "Alliances and the Expansion of War," in J. David Singer, ed., *To Augur Well* (Beverly Hills, Calif.: Sage Publications, 1979), pp. 37–49.

72. Michael D. Wallace, *War and Rank Among Nations* (Lexington, Mass.: D. C. Heath, 1973).

73. Michael Haas, "International Subsystems: Stability and Polarity," *American Political Science Review*, 64 (March 1970), 98–123.

two-edged sword. "It serves both escalation, by providing enough distance to organize and deal with antagonists in a highly violent way, and deescalation, by reducing the contact surface to a minimum, possibly even to zero."[74]

There appears to be considerable evidence that a preponderance of power in the hands of a status quo state or group of states can lessen the likelihood that other states will resort to the use of force. Britain's preponderant power in the eighteenth and nineteenth centuries, which allowed it to dominate the seas, was in no small measure related to the relative peace that prevailed during the period. A study of Asian dyads over the period 1950–69 revealed that overwhelming power, defined as a ratio of at least ten to one, substantially reduced the risk of war.[75] Similar results were shown in a study of thirty dyadic interstate wars over the period 1816–1965, which found that when power was closer to parity there was actually more conflict.[76] Findings like these suggest that if one wants international stability it is not a balance of power, defined in terms of an equilibrium, that one should seek but, rather, a preponderance.

Systemic polarity will also affect the way decisions are made, both within alliances and within states. The tighter the polarity, the more centralized the decision-making process in both organizations. Efforts are made to develop a unified position within an alliance before presenting proposals to the other side. This is illustrated by disarmament negotiations, in which, during the years of tight bipolarity, the NATO allies developed their proposals first and then presented them to the Soviet Union. In an age of decreased bipolarity, efforts were not always taken to get the allies' approval first. This was particularly true with respect to the negotiations for the Nuclear Nonproliferation Treaty, which was opened for signature in 1968. In this instance the United States and the Soviet Union had an interest in stopping the spread of nuclear weapons and controlling nuclear energy—goals that were not always shared by American and Soviet allies. Even less consultation was undertaken with respect to the SALT negotiations.

---

74. Johan Galtung, "Peace Thinking," in Albert Lepawsky et al., eds., *The Search for World Order* (Englewood Cliffs, N.J.: Prentice-Hall, 1971), p. 130.

75. Erich Weede, "Overwhelming Preponderance as a Pacifying Condition Among Contiguous Asian Dyads, 1950–69," *Journal of Conflict Resolution*, 20 (September 1976), 395–411.

76. David Garnham, "Dyadic International War, 1816–1965: The Role of Power Parity and Geographical Proximity," *Western Political Quarterly*, 29 (June 1976), 231–42.

CONCLUSION

The importance of the external variable as a determinant of foreign policy is obvious. If there were no external inputs, there would be no need for a foreign policy. Action–reaction models have been found to have some predictive accuracy for both conflict behavior and negotiations. There is also some evidence that such processes may fuel an arms race. At the same time, some studies comparing the predictive value of action–reaction models and past-behavior models have found the latter to be more accurate, particularly as bureaucratic inertia sets in.

Foreign-policy determination is not limited to dyadic interaction, since third parties can also have an impact on the decisions made by a pair of disputing states. Such third parties may either serve a mediating role or may induce greater conflict by siding with one party or the other.

International organizations, which have shown remarkable growth in recent decades, have a special role to play in influencing the foreign policy of a state, particularly in its conflict behavior. It is difficult to make a precise evaluation of the impact of such organizations, for one cannot easily count wars that did not arise as a result of the existence of international organizations. Nevertheless, there is some impressive evidence suggesting that several international disputes were prevented from escalating further. The records of both the League of Nations and the United Nations seem to suggest a decline in their effectiveness over time as conflict managers. Perhaps what may be more salient to foreign policy in the future is the socializing effect of participation in international organizations by national decision makers, since such participation may help develop international understanding among important leaders.

A number of characteristics of the international system appear to shape foreign-policy behavior. States that interact in the same international system tend to assume similar forms of behavior. The system itself has a modifying effect on all states, regardless of their particular domestic structures. Systemic tension, for example, tends to lead to increased centralization in foreign-policy decision making in all states. The norms and laws of the international system, although perhaps not as important as other systemic characteristics, have had some restraining influence on policy, since states like to appear both moral and lawful.

The most important systemic characteristic affecting the foreign-policy behavior of the state is the distribution of power. There are arguments favoring both bipolarity and multipolarity in terms of their ability to provide systemic stability. Although there is some conflicting evidence, bipolarity seems to have resulted in less frequent but more prolonged wars. Stability appears most likely in systems in which there was a preponderance of power.

9

EXPLAINING FOREIGN POLICY

The factors that influence the foreign-policy decision-making process obviously do not operate in the simple fashion that might be implied by our treatment of each variable in a separate chapter. Rather, most of the determinants are in the background, affecting the decision makers on almost every foreign-policy choice. The particular mix of major determinants impinging on foreign policy depends on the circumstances and actors involved. At present, however, there is a paucity of empirical studies that combine several determinants of foreign policy and analyze them in terms of their interactive effects. If useful models of foreign policy making are to be developed, it will be necessary to get some notion of the relative importance of the factors that are assumed to affect foreign-policy choices. In this final chapter an effort will be made to suggest the relative importance of the determinants of foreign policy on the basis of the current state of knowledge about the subject.

But before attempting to evaluate the relative importance of such determinants, it might be well to make a few general comments about them. In the first place, whether or not a given determinant has an impact on foreign policy is dependent on perception. If the factor is ignored because of the perceptual deficiencies of the decision makers or because of communication difficulties, it obviously will not have an impact.

Second, any factor will have varying effects on different actors. Small states, for example, seem to be more affected by systemic variables than large states are; democratic states tend to march to a different drummer than dictatorships do; and economically developed states appear to react to certain variables differently from developing states, which tend to be very sensitive about issues of sovereignty because they have only recently won their independence.

Third, although we have treated each major set of determinants in a separate chapter, decision makers by no means compartmentalize them as such. When trying to make a decision they are aware of many different factors that influence their choice. The discussion of the Soviet decision to invade Afghanistan in Chapter 1 is indicative of the many factors that might help explain why the Soviet decision makers took the action they did. More research must, of necessity, be completed before one can develop complex decision-making models capable of explaining events like Afghanistan, but at least a start has been made by identifying the more important variables.

Fourth, we must remember that although the term *determinant* has been used, few of the factors discussed are fully deterministic. Individual differences still count for something. But even though they are not deterministic, a number of the factors may nevertheless limit the range of choices that can be made. If a state lacks important resources and has a low gross national product, there is no possibility that such a state can assume the role of a great power in the international system. The lack of certain economic and military sources of power clearly can constrain foreign-policy choices, but existence of abundant resources need not force the state to play an active role in foreign policy, as the behavior of the United States during the interwar period demonstrated.

In looking at the determinants discussed in the separate chapters, our analysis of psychological factors has shown that idiosyncratic psychological variables have a greater impact on foreign policy the greater the interest of a given decision maker in such matters, the higher the person is in the decision-making hierarchy, and the greater the decisional latitude allowed to decision makers in general. Conditions of uncertainty and nonroutine situations also enable psychological factors to have a greater impact. Research on psychological factors, to the extent that such factors are operative, does suggest the inappropriateness of strict adherence to the rational-actor model, since innate aggressiveness, personality aberrations, and problems of misperception dictate against rational calculation.

Some would suggest that the personality of the individual decision maker makes little difference, for each decision maker is a product of a broader society that tends to constrain the range of probable choice. According to this view, regardless of who occupies the highest foreign-policy positions, there will be little difference in foreign-policy output. Societal factors such as national character and nationalism make a difference in the way states negotiate and even in their propensity toward international conflict.

Equally constraining are the particular belief systems of a state. Such beliefs have been found to influence perceptions of the world, to define the range of choice, to facilitate the continuity of policy, and to help rationalize a foreign-policy choice once it has been made. Although the present age appears to be one of ideology, ideologies have been relatively ineffective in solidifying peoples across national boundaries. Instead, the national beliefs of individual states have generally predominated over transnational ideologies.

The structure of the decision-making process was found to have an effect on policy, suggesting that those who approach the study of foreign policy from the standpoint of bureaucratic politics or decision making have a valid position in explaining foreign policy. There is evidence that there does tend to be a difference between democratic and dictatorial foreign policy making, although perhaps more in procedure than in substance. Foreign-policy decision making appears to be more centralized than domestic decision making as parties, interest groups, and public opinion were found to have a minimal impact.

How one views the importance of economic factors in the making of foreign policy depends largely on whether one looks at the subject from a conservative or a radical viewpoint. Radical theorists generally view economic factors as highly deterministic, believing that most international conflicts can be traced back to economic origins. From this perspective, capitalism is seen as fostering imperialism and international conflict behavior. Conservative theorists, on the other hand, view such economic instruments as foreign aid, trade, and investment as benefiting the third world. There are also differences between the two theories with respect to assessments of the military–industrial complex, which radicals regard as having an exceedingly powerful effect on foreign-policy choices.

A major, if not *the* major, element affecting foreign policy is national power capabilities. Such capabilities define the range of options available and whether a state can play the role of a great power. The elusiveness of power can be seen in the changing power bases of states as economic power has gradually assumed greater importance in world politics. The fear of nuclear annihilation has almost neutralized nuclear weapons as an instrument of foreign policy, enabling other devices, such as economic power and propaganda, to play a more important role.

Finally, we should not underrate the effects of external and systemic factors in foreign policy. In a sense, without actions and pressures from outside the state, there would be no foreign policy. Action–reaction models have some predictive value in explaining arms races and conflict spirals, although some studies have found that the past behavior of a state is just as accurate a predictor of current behavior. Foreign-policy choices have been influenced not only by major adversaries but also by third parties, comprised of both states and international organizations. Systemic inputs such as norms and laws operate as yet another constraint on foreign policy and must be considered, along with the structure of the system if one is to explain foreign policy. States in a multipolar system seem to operate differently than states in a bipolar system. At the same time, expert opinion diverges on which of these two systems provides more stability and peace.

Summarizing the vast amount of research attempting to explain why states make the choices they do seems almost impossible, since so many different models and factors have been considered. Nevertheless, it would be useful to assess the relative importance of determinants in order to ascertain which might be more productive in helping us understand foreign policy. In an effort to make at least a preliminary assessment of the importance of the factors discussed in this book, the author undertook a survey of foreign-policy experts in the spring of 1965.[1] The sample consisted of 43 newspaper and radio correspondents based in Washington and New York; 39 academicians, primarily from Washington, New York, and Boston; 48 respondents from the State Department; and 41 respondents from the Department of Defense. These 171 respondents were asked whether they viewed each item on a list of possible determinants as very important, relatively important,

1. Lloyd Jensen, "Foreign Policy Calculation," in Michael Haas, ed., *International Systems* (New York: Chandler, 1974), pp. 91–92.

relatively unimportant, or unimportant with respect to the making of United States and Soviet foreign policy. The results of these estimates are summarized for the United States in Table 9-1 and for the Soviet Union in Table 9-2.

As can be seen by examining the two tables, national power capabilities were considered by the experts to be the most significant factor determining foreign policy, with 70 percent of the respondents scoring it very important for the United States, compared with 79 percent for the Soviet Union. The next highest evaluations were given to the internal economic political situation, as about half of the respondents thought these factors to be very important for each superpower. Where the two estimates differed significantly was with respect to the relative impact of ideology and the behavior of other states. Ideology was seen as a relatively insignificant factor in explaining United States foreign policy but quite important for the Soviet Union. Whether the period of detente would lead the experts to place less emphasis today

TABLE 9-1.   Perceived Determinants of American Foreign Policy

	Very Important	Relatively Important	Relatively Unimportant	Unimportant
National power capabilities	70%	25%	4%	0%
Internal economic and political situation	48	41	11	1
Behavior of other states	46	43	11	0
Personality	45	37	17	1
Ideology	22	42	31	5
Decision-making structure	18	50	26	7
Historical tradition	13	48	36	4

TABLE 9-2.   Perceived Determinants of Soviet Foreign Policy

	Very Important	Relatively Important	Relatively Unimportant	Unimportant
National power capabilities	79%	19%	1%	0%
Internal economic and political situation	57	33	10	1
Ideology	43	47	8	2
Personality	44	38	16	1
Behavior of other states	32	39	28	7
Decision-making structure	26	36	31	7
Historical tradition	10	44	34	13

on ideology as a determinant of Soviet foreign policy is uncertain, but the outcry over the Soviet incursion into Afghanistan and the rhetoric of the Reagan administration demonstrate the continuing prominence of ideological interpretations of Soviet motivation.

The other point of divergence between assessments of the determinants of foreign policy concerned the behavior of other states, which was seen as far more important to decision makers from the United States than to those from the Soviet Union. It is common for foreign-policy analysts to see other states as having less need to pay attention to the behavior of other actors in the system than is the case in their own states.

Assessments of the remaining three variables were roughly similar. Both Soviet and American foreign policy processes were viewed as considerably affected by personality factors, whereas the decision-making structure and historical tradition were viewed as somewhat less important in explaining foreign policy. In sum, what is remarkable about the expert assessments is that, except for the variables of ideology and the behavior of other states, the Soviet Union and the United States were seen as responding to the same sorts of factors in making their respective foreign policy choices.

Empirical evidence concerning the relative importance of the determinants of foreign policy has usually been anecdotal rather than systematic, and there is often a difference of opinion among experts on what determines a given state's foreign policy. For example, in evaluating British postwar foreign policy, Joseph Frankel concluded that when domestic and foreign policy conflict, priority tends to be given to domestic considerations.[2] In analyzing roughly the same period, F. S. Northedge concluded that the "internal environment of British policy is at once less complex and less significant than the external in the making of that policy."[3]

There are few quantitative studies comparing the relative potency of the determinants of foreign policy, and the results of these studies are sometimes inconsistent. Several studies appear to confirm the primacy of external variables over internal ones, as shown by East and Gregg's analysis of the conflict and cooperative behavior of eighty-two

2. Joseph Frankel, British Foreign Policy, 1945–73 (New York: Oxford University Press, 1975), p. 16.

3. F. S. Northedge, "British Foreign Policy," in F. S. Northedge, ed., The Foreign Policies of the Powers (London: Faber and Faber, 1968), p. 157.

nations during the 1950s.[4] Similar results were found in an examination of the foreign policy behavior of fifty-six nations for the period 1966–70 in which domestic factors were found to be relatively insignificant. Action–reaction phenomena appeared particularly relevant in predicting conflict behavior; the amount of variance explained by external variables increased from 1 to 50 percent when such variables were added.[5] On the other hand, James N. Rosenau and George H. Ramsey, Jr. found internal factors to be the better predictors of foreign conflict behavior in the late 1960s, but because of some concern about measurement problems, they did not regard these results as definitive.[6] Despite these conflicting results, there does appear to be some consensus that external factors are more likely to dominate over internal ones the less developed a state is and the more dependent it is on outside powers.

If the factors influencing foreign-policy choices all operated in the same direction, there would be little need to be concerned about their relative importance. The fact of the matter is that they do not. Instead, the policies dictated by each determinant may be diametrically opposed to the others. For example, decision makers might seek to understate their own military strength in order to encourage their domestic public to support higher defense spending. But by thus emphasizing their own weakness, the decision makers may encourage other nations to try to exploit the situation. Similarly, making optimistic estimates regarding the prospects of an agreement in an effort to get public support, or pressuring negotiations in order to portray oneself as a peacemaker before a domestic public and the world, can be counterproductive. For example, aspects of the SALT I agreement on offensive missiles had to be renegotiated, since the final stages of the negotiations were rushed in order to hold a summit meeting and demonstrate a diplomatic success prior to the 1972 presidential election.

Perhaps we will never be in a position to explain and understand all foreign policies. Some policies may be irrational; some may be af-

---

4. Maurice A. East and Phillip M. Gregg, "Factors Influencing Cooperation and Conflict in the International System," *International Studies Quarterly*, 11 (September 1967), 258–61.

5. Jonathan Wilkenfeld et al., *Foreign Policy Behavior* (Beverly Hills, Calif.: Sage Publications, 1980), pp. 171, 192.

6. James N. Rosenau and George H. Ramsey, Jr., "External and Internal Typologies of Foreign Policy Behavior: Testing the Stability of an Intriguing Set of Findings," in Patrick J. McGowan, ed., *Sage Foreign Policy Yearbook*, vol. 3 (Beverly Hills, Calif.: Sage Publications, 1975), pp. 245–62.

fected by so many variables that it becomes difficult, if not impossible, to separate out the impact of each factor; and some may be shrouded in considerable secrecy, making a full understanding difficult. Nevertheless, it is important that we try to understand why states act as they do, and that we look for patterns in foreign-policy behavior, for only by understanding what motivates decision makers can we know how to respond. But it is not only a question of being able to explain what motivates the decision makers of other states in order to predict their behavior; a nation must also seek a better understanding of itself. We need to recognize our own infantile or irrational responses if effective and rational foreign policy is to result.

Index